AF779503

Crime at El Escorial

The 1892 Child Murder, the Press, and the Jury

Revised Edition

D.J. Walker

University Press of America,® Inc.
Lanham • Boulder • New York • Toronto • Plymouth, UK

Copyright © 2014 by University Press of America,® Inc.
4501 Forbes Boulevard, Suite 200, Lanham, Maryland 20706
UPA Aquisitions Department (301) 459-3366

10 Thornbury Road, Plymouth PL6 7PP, United Kingdom

All rights reserved
Printed in the United States of America
British Library Cataloguing in Publication Information Available

Library of Congress Control Number: 2014934256
ISBN: 978-0-7618-6355-7 (paperback : alk. paper)—ISBN: 978-0-7618-6356-4 (electronic)

Cover artwork: "The Bogeyman" by Félix Pardo de Tavera. *La Ilustración Artística*, 1897.

∞™ The paper used in this publication meets the minimum requirements of American National Standard for Information Sciences Permanence of Paper for Printed Library Materials, ANSI/NISO Z39.48-1992.

In Memoriam

E. Cordel McDonald

For Lynette with great affection.... Win

Contents

List of Illustrations

Acknowledgments

I want to thank Pilar Varela, director, Josefina Cedillo, head of the microfilm service, and the staff of the Hemeroteca Municipal in Madrid for their efficiency and many kindnesses to me during several summers of research carried out at that institution. This book could not have been undertaken without the assistance of Connie Phelps, former interlibrary loan librarian at the University of New Orleans. I am grateful to her for her patience and persistence. I am much indebted to colleagues—especially Alain Saint-Saens, Adrian Shubert, and Noël Valis—who generously provided me with helpful insights and suggestions for improving a manuscript whose remaining flaws are solely my responsibility. Above all, I thank John T. O'Connor for his encouragement and forbearance.

Introduction

In late December of 1892, most of Madrid's high-circulation dailies carried a brief news item informing the public of the disappearance of a child at San Lorenzo de El Escorial. On Christmas day, three and one-half year-old Pedro Bravo had gone to the Royal Monastery of San Lorenzo de El Escorial to meet his brothers and sisters after mass. The children never met. Pedro was last seen shortly after noon in the Patio de los Reyes, the great interior square that lies before the church. The portal to the Patio de los Reyes is the principal point of entry into the immense rectangular enclosure that includes the palace, church, monastery, and mausoleum built by Philip II in commemoration of the 1557 battle of St. Quentin and dedicated to St. Lawrence.

No further news about the child appeared for well over a month. Then, on February 10, 1893, it was reported that his body had been found in a nearly inaccessible area of the steep terrain high above the monastery. At first, authorities speculated that the child had wandered off, and having somehow climbed up to a high place, had slipped and fallen to his death. But since it seemed unlikely that a child would have ventured up the mountainside alone in blustery winter weather, an autopsy was ordered. It revealed evidence of pederasty and death by strangulation, while the well-preserved condition of Pedro Bravo's body suggested that he had been murdered not long before the corpse was discovered. A young local man, Julián García, was soon identified as the prime suspect.

Intense press coverage of the ensuing criminal investigation led to ever-increasing publicity and encouraged a variety of participants in the promotion of the case. What began with extensive newspaper reports quickly became one of the first genuine media events in late nineteenth-century Spain. Photographers arrived from Madrid to take portraits of the accused murderer and his family, the victim's family, their respective dwellings, and the representatives of justice.[1] These photographs, as well as drawings—by Ramón Casas, along with other less well-known artists—were sold to a press avid for graphics. Figures famous for their contributions to the popular theater (*género chico*), such as José López Silva, Celso Lucio, Carlos Arniches, and Federico Chueca–the future composer of the celebrated zarzuela, *Agua, azucarrillos y aguardiente*–came in the hope of interviewing the suspects.[2]

Many ordinary people, including curious ladies from Madrid, rode bicycles or took the train to El Escorial in order to visit the alleged scene of the crime, the accused murderer in his cell, and the latter's four sisters, who had also been detained, in theirs. Reporters organized a subscription fund for the dead boy's family to which contributions flowed from all over Spain.[3] Readers wrote to the newspapers expressing their horror at the crime. On March 3, 1893 *La Correspondencia de España* reported that a woman from the province of Lugo had written requesting that the examining magistrate send her a lock of the dead boy's hair, enclosing in her letter verses she had composed in memory of his "martirio." All of Spain was obsessed with the crime. News of the case spread, as well, to the rest of Europe and to America.

SOURCES OF INFORMATION ABOUT THE CRIME

Newspaper coverage and a few references in contemporary periodical literature are the principal remaining sources for information concerning this crime. The summation (*sumario*) of the trial is not available since the archives located in the City Hall at El Escorial, where those documents were kept, were requisitioned and converted to paper pulp during the Civil War. (Summaries of the appeals made in the case to the *Tribunal Supremo* do exist and will be discussed below in reference to the crime's impact on the public's view of the jury system.) Study of the crime is thus almost entirely limited to the commercial press's representation of it. A number of newspapers in the capital, including *El Día*, *El Heraldo de Madrid*, *El Nacional*, and *El Ideal* published pieces on the story while three principal Madrid dailies—*La Correspondencia de España*, *El Imparcial*, and *El País*—sent correspondents to El Escorial from February through March of 1893. Journalists from several papers were sent to El Escorial throughout the month of May 1894, when the trial took place.

The principal socialist paper, the weekly *El Socialista* published in Madrid, did not cover the pre-trial investigation of the crime, consistent with its policy of reporting almost exclusively on offenses committed by clergy, capitalists or representatives of the law enforcement system. Nor did *El Socialista* provide coverage of the dramatic events that took place during the trial, but two days before the verdict was handed down—on May 14, 1894—the paper seized the opportunity to criticize the "bourgeois press" ("prensa burguesa") and its paid lackeys, the reporters. It faulted them for covering the Escorial crime in repugnant detail, thus satisfying the plebeian appetites of uncultivated readers—the majority—by serving them up "gross, heavy fare" ("platos fuertes") instead of educating them.

THE 1893 PRE-TRIAL INVESTIGATION

The following reconstruction of the chronology of the pre-trial investigation of the Escorial crime is based primarily on reports and dispatches filed by three correspondents: Ricardo Hernández y Bermúdez (*El Imparcial)*; Eduardo Rosón (*El País*); and Ramiro Mestre Martínez (*La Correspondencia de España*). Fite (*El Día*), and Rodrigo (*El Heraldo de Madrid*) also reported on the case, generally reworking material filed earlier by the three correspondents usually on the scene. Hernández y Bermúdez, Mestre Martínez, and Rosón appear to have stayed at El Escorial throughout most of the pre-trial investigation while the other two were based in Madrid and only occasionally travelled to El Escorial. Now and then, a Madrid paper sent a reporter to cover a particular event or to gather material on the suspects and the locale. On February 27, 1893, for example, when public interest in the prime suspect, Julián García, was at its height, *El Liberal* sent two reporters to the royal site.

The sources for the correspondents' information, according to their printed acknowledgments of gratitude, were the director and sub-director of the jail, the suspects themselves, the victim's family, and unidentified townspeople. Although the reporters denied having received information from any of the men responsible for the investigation, it is likely that the secretary (*escribano*), in particular, leaked material to them.

A guard (*guarda*) employed by the School of Forestry (*Escuela de Ingenieros de Montes*), who was out hunting and in pursuit of a hare, found Pedro Bravo's body on February 10, 1893 in a remote, steep place high above the Royal Monastery of El Escorial. The autopsy performed on February 11 and 12 indicated that the child had been brutally sodomized and strangled eight to ten days before the corpse was discovered. Pedrín, as the reporters called him, was buried on February 14. The examining magistrate then went to a house near the Puerta del Romeral inhabited by a family of three sisters and their brother, in order to resume questioning of the youngest sister. The brother, Julián García, was twenty; the next oldest, Francisca, was eighteen; Concha was sixteen; and their half-sister, Juana, was eleven years old. There was, as well, an older sister, María, whose age was not recorded. María lived a short distance away from the García family's house with her husband, twenty-three year-old Crisanto Jorge, and her two-year-old daughter.

In an earlier interview, Juana, the eleven year-old, stated that she had seen her brother, Julián, with Pedrín on December 25—the day of his disappearance—at one-thirty p.m. at the Puerta del Romeral. Because Juana changed some details of her story in the second interview, and because Francisca and Concha contradicted María's testimony as to what the family had done on December 25, 1892, the examining magistrate ordered all but María, her daughter, and husband Crisanto detained. Juana was taken to the quarters of the Civil Guard, the other two sisters to jail. Their brother, Julián, was already in jail. On February 10 he had been arrested for stealing wood on the mountainside above the monastery.

From the fourteenth until the eighteenth of February, when Juana was released from custody after denying everything she had said previously, suspicions mounted against Julián. By the sixteenth, he was the prime suspect. His half-sister, Juana, not only claimed to have seen him with Pedrín on the day of his disappearance, but she also identified a striped kerchief found near the boy's body as her brother's. Julián, an epileptic who initially seemed stupid, even imbecilic to the reporters who observed him, denied having seen, abducted or killed the child. He could not account for his whereabouts on December 25, however, nor were there any witnesses who recalled seeing him on that date. Despite his half-sister's testimony and his own failure to come up with a plausible alibi, several reporters noted on February 19 that the case against Julián was inconclusive, depending as it did, on a child's allegations, unproven suspicions, and coincidence—such as the proximity of Julián's house to the Puerta del Romeral where several other children now claimed to have seen the child on the day of his disappearance.

On February 20, a dramatic development revived the case against Julián. His brother-in-law, Crisanto Jorge, after having been closeted with a member of the Civil Guard for some time, asked to make a statement to the examining magistrate. He declared that on January 25, 1893, Julián had approached him on the street and solicited his help in disposing of the body of the quarry worker's son whom he had killed and whose body was in the loft (*desván*) of his house. For two days Crisanto's wife, María, together with Francisca and Concha, denied any knowledge of the crime alleged by Crisanto to have taken place in their house. But on February 22, Francisca declared that Julián had kidnapped Pedrín, that she, Concha, and Juana saw the child in the *desván* on December 26, and that a friend of Julián, Isidoro Muñoz, helped their brother remove the corpse on or about January 25. Another friend was also implicated by the sisters, but after questioning he was released. María, the eldest sister, then declared that she also knew the child was being held by Julián.

From February 22 until the pre-trial investigation reached near completion in the first week of March, the sisters and Crisanto contradicted themselves and each other repeatedly. There were more contradictions during the frequent face-offs (*careos*) with Julián and with the many witnesses called in for depositions.

In addition to the striped kerchief, the evidence included a boot lace, also found near the boy's body, said to be like those Isidoro Muñoz used, mats (*esteras*) with stains taken from the *desván*, two blonde hairs (Pedrín was blonde), and a sack containing a few straws and some pine nut shells. Since Pedrin had half a pine nut shell in his pocket when his corpse was found, the assumption was quickly made that his body had been transported in that very sack.

The evidence was first examined at El Escorial. A village shoemaker testified that the boot lace was exactly like those worn by Isidoro. The two hairs were examined under a microscope at the School of Forestry, but identification was deferred until a chemical examination could be made. A report submitted by local doctors, however, declared the hairs to be identical to those of the dead child. Finally, a baker testified that the bread crumbs found in Pedrín's pocket were from bread baked in his bakery.

When the summation was completed on April 14, 1893 it consisted of 700 folios and 14 pieces of evidence. Over 90 people had given depositions. This material was first handed over to the court (*Audiencia*) in Madrid. It was then passed on to the seven lawyers who would figure in the trial. They did not finish their review until February 1894.

In the meantime, on September 25, 1893 Julián García appeared before the *Audiencia* in Madrid to be tried for stealing wood in February of that year. The reporter for *El Día* described the large crowd that went to see him. It filled the courtroom, he wrote, spilling over into the hallways. Julián was found guilty and sent to the *Cárcel-Modelo* in Madrid to serve his sentence. On October 12, the director of the jail requested that the prisoner complete the remainder of his term at El Escorial since his frequent epileptic seizures posed a threat to his life. As *El Día* reported on that date, it was thought that the regimen of the jail at El Escorial might alleviate his condition.

THE 1894 TRIAL AT EL ESCORIAL

Reporters and public alike had originally assumed that the trial would be open to the public and would take place in Madrid. In accord with Spanish judicial procedure, suspected criminal acts were first investigated by an examining magistrate (*juez de instrucción*). His pre-trial investigation and report constituted the summation (*sumario*). The summation was examined in the provincial court (*Audiencia*) where the state prosecutor determined whether there was a case, and if so, the summation was then made available for their perusal to the lawyers concerned. The ensuing trial normally took place at the *Audiencia* of the province in which the alleged criminal act had been committed. But circumstances might warrant convening one of the *Audiencia's* courts in a designated judicial district seat. El Escorial had been granted the status of municipality (*municipio*) and head of a judicial district (*cabeza de partido judicial*) in 1887.[4] Although the defense lawyers opposed the decision, a ruling came down from the Madrid *Audiencia* authorizing the removal of the fourth criminal court to El Escorial on the grounds that its presence there would facilitate examination of the García house—where Pedrín had allegedly been sequestered and then murdered—and because it would accommodate jurors and witnesses, nearly all of whom were from the vicinity of El Escorial, two hours distant from Madrid by rail. Thus was the trial of the murderer of the Child from El Escorial (*El niño de El Escorial*) scheduled to be held in the City Hall (*Ayuntamiento*) at El Escorial.

The Jury Law (*Ley del Jurado*) of 1888, which reinstituted the jury in Spain after a hiatus of thirteen years, established a two-step procedure for the selection of a jury pool in each judicial district. Formation of the primary lists was entrusted to a council or junta in each municipality composed of the municipal judge and prosecutor, the mayor, and four major tax-payers. From that list jurors were selected by lot in the provincial *Audiencia*. The role of the jurors was to declare the culpability or non-culpability of the accused with respect to the evidence presented for their consideration. The jury also declared whether circumstances that might limit responsibility were present. An absolute majority of jury votes determined the verdict. A tie led to a verdict of not guilty.

The representatives of justice presiding at the 1894 Escorial trial consisted of the court of fact (*jurado de hecho*)—the twelve jurors and two alternates; and the court of law (*jurado de derecho*)—the four magistrates consisting of the state's attorney or prosecutor (*fiscal)* and three attorneys. One of the latter served as president of the court. The magistrates comprising the court of law made juridical decisions based on the facts considered proven and applied penalties in accord with the Penal Code of 1870. Appeals could be made to the Supreme Court (*Tribunal Supremo*). In addition to the government prosecutor and magistrates, and the lawyers for the defense and prosecution, the Code of Criminal Procedure of 1882 gave the victim's family the right to courtroom representation by private counsel. By late February 1893 a lawyer, Manuel Pico Martínez, and a solicitor (*procurador*), Rufino García, offered to represent the Bravo family, free of charge. The defense in the Escorial case all volunteered their services.

There was great disappointment when the much-anticipated trial was not held at the Madrid *Audiencia*. That disappointment was compounded when it was reported on April 20, 1894 in *El Día* that the state's attorney, Gonzalo de Córdoba, had successfully requested that the trial be held behind closed doors because of the sexual nature of the crime. A public trial would undoubtedly have turned into one of the most publicized spectator events in the

Madrid of the nineties. Spain had not had a public trial comparable to that of Jean-Baptiste Troppmann's 1869 trial in Paris in which over the course of a month's time thousands of people witnessed the sight of the full weight of the French judicial system bearing down upon the twenty-year-old murderer of an entire family.[5] The public prosecution of Julián García would also unquestionably have drawn great crowds, prepared by the press to expect sensational revelations of evil. In the event, the trial held in the *Ayuntamiento* at El Escorial took place in a chamber fitted out with the essential trappings of justice, but empty of spectators, including reporters. As was the case during the pre-trial investigation, reporters depended upon second-hand information except for their personal interviews with the accused and others involved in the trial. The public's role was limited to looking at the defendants as they were conducted through the streets from the jail to the City Hall and back again.

It is possible that a public trial might have affected the outcome. The sight of the members of the García family in the flesh and the opportunity to listen to their testimony would have offered a strong contrast to the press's representation of the defendants, which may fairly be described as demonized. An urban trial-going public might also have reacted quite differently than the rural jurors to the presentations of the lawyers—whether prosecution or defense. Jurors who believed in good conscience that they were charged with representing public opinion might, in turn, have modified their opinions regarding the culpability of the accused if they had seen that the public was altering its views.

After several postponements the trial was scheduled to begin on May 7, 1894 in El Escorial. Ten to twelve reporters were present, according to Domingo Blanco who replaced Hernández y Bermúdez for *El Imparcial*. A Hugues machine provided the most up-to-date technology.[6] It promptly began transmitting thousands of words relating information and impressions of the setting (the town and the steep terrain above it where the child's body had been found) and developments at the trial.

On the first day, the secretary summed up the case before the four presiding magistrates (the prosecutor and three attorneys), the seven lawyers, four solicitors, twelve jurors, and the accused. The prosecutor charged Julián García with abduction of a minor, sexual abuse (*abusos deshonestos*), and murder. He asked for the death penalty for Julián, nine years for Crisanto Jorge as an accomplice in the abduction, nine years for María and Francisca, three years for Concha, and three months of detention for Juana. He asked for seven years for Isidoro Muñoz for having concealed the murder, that is, for having acted in such a way as to cover up the crime (*encubridor*). The lawyers for the defense contested the version of events presented by the prosecutor and asked that all charges against their clients be dropped.

Several hours into the trial, Crisanto Jorge declared that his accusation against Julián García had been coerced by two members of the Civil Guard. Julián's sisters then proclaimed that the examining magistrate had threatened them, forcing them to provide corroborating testimony to support Crisanto's account. Isidoro Muñoz, who had always denied any role in the crime, again avowed his innocence. Following this dramatic turn of events, the trial, like the preliminary investigation, was marked by still more abrupt changes in testimony, by emotional outbursts, and by Julián García's epileptic seizures.

The trial continued from May 7 to May 13 without interruption except for a suspended session on May 10 due to the illness of María García. She had given birth to a daughter while in jail and, having lost her appetite, was having difficulty nursing. Lack of nourishment made her too weak to appear on the bench.

The entire court walked to Julián's house on the first day to examine the storage loft where Pedrín had allegedly been kept bound hand and foot in temperatures plunging at times to four degrees below zero centigrade. The dead boy's mother came before the court but, overwhelmed with weeping, could not testify. His father, aunts and uncles not only testified but also confronted Julián García. Witnesses, who had testified earlier, testified again. Some new information came to light: the hairs that the local barbers believed were identical to Pedrín's were declared by a professor from the School of Forestry to be from a cat; the sexual attack Julián allegedly made against a young boy in 1884 was denied by the boy himself and by his father. A series of irregularities in the pre-trial investigation were entered into the record at the request of the lawyer defending Julián.

The concluding arguments against the accused recapitulated the opening charges except for an added charge of homicide against Crisanto Jorge. The defense pointed to the lack of proof, the accumulation of circumstantial evidence (Rosón in May 13 in *El País* referred to "la fatalidad de las circunstancias"), and the failure from the outset to pursue other leads. The verdict was delivered on May 14, 1894. Julián García was found guilty of abduction, sexual abuse, and homicide. Crisanto Jorge was found guilty of abduction and homicide. The sisters were found guilty of concealing the crime. Isidoro Muñoz was declared innocent of having acted as an accomplice in the removal of the child's body. Julián was sentenced to thirty-six years in prison; fifteen for abduction, seventeen for homicide, and four for sexual abuse (*abusos deshonestos*). Crisanto, who had a prior conviction for assault with a weapon, got eighteen years for the homicide and eight years for the abduction—a total of twenty-six years. The two older sisters got eight years, Concha three, and Juana three months.

The public was stunned. It had expected that Julián García would be found guilty of murder in the first degree (*asesinato*) and sentenced to death. In particular, the jury's response to question number twenty was incomprehensible to the nation: Regarding the fact of having caused the death of the child, Pedro Bravo, did the circumstance obtain that because of the latter's age, his lack of nourishment in the days preceding the deed, and the injuries he suffered to his eyes, the act was executed without risk to the aggressor or aggressors which could have resulted from acts of self-defense which the aforementioned child might have "mounted?"[7] The jury's response was "No." When asked whether Pedrín's murder was premeditated, the jury also responded in the negative. These answers denied the aggravating circumstances which would have made the crime murder in the first degree rather than homicide.

Public incredulity in view of what seemed to have been an inexplicable miscarriage of justice led commentators in the press immediately to set about addressing the issues raised by the jury's replies to the questions put to them by the president of the court of law. Appeals were filed with the Supreme Court. For another two years developments in the prosecution of the Escorial case continued to appear in the press.

What follows is a study of the Spanish press's representation of the notorious crime at El Escorial and of the ensuing debate over the jury system. The effective demise of the jury system in 1923 signaled the defeat of one of the most cherished objectives of the revolutionaries who overthrew Isabel II in 1868. The years between those two dates witnessed much elite discussion of education for the masses. By the 1890s such discussion had already produced the coherent definition of mass taste and of mass readers that was shared by virtually all Spanish intellectuals and publicists. The first part of this book establishes a context for the study of the Escorial crime and the controversy over the jury by adducing attitudes and ideas expressed by the elite in their commentaries on crime reporting and their critiques of the mass readership it catered to. Elite analyses of mass phenomena—the more persuasive because of the scarcity of authoritative opposing views—ultimately shaped the direction taken by the public debate on the jury in the 1890s. Reiteration of such views, especially those printed in newspapers, helped to persuade the public that the masses were deficient and, by extension, that the ordinary, uncultivated man's incapacity to serve as juror was an undeniable, and perhaps an inalterable, reality.

Sensationalized press coverage of the abduction, brutal sexual abuse, and murder of the blonde, blue-eyed, three-year-old Pedro Bravo sustained public interest which might otherwise have waned. While themes and techniques appropriated from terrorific fiction—Gothic and vampire tales, in particular—were commonly used in crime reporting at the time, they proved especially well-suited to the circumstances of this story. The use of fictional techniques familiar to newly-literate readers of newspapers through their acquaintance with popular literature and oral tradition ensured widespread interest in the case. Press accounts of the Escorial crime thus provide an unusually rich and problematic example of the journalistic conflation of fact and fiction. Newspapers enjoyed increased circulation while the themes and devices of terrorific fiction and melodrama enlisted in this instance served to reinforce conservative values. Whether out of conscious intention or not, reporters effortlessly imposed the polarizations characteristic of the melodramatic mode upon their narratives. By doing so, they effectively advanced particular aspects of Restoration social and political agendas. Most notably, reporters opposed the murdered child's poor but hard-working family to the "degenerate" unindustrious members of the accused murderer's family; the authority exercised by the male head of household in the child's family to the accused murderer's failure to exert authority in his; the legitimate fecundity of the dead child's parents to the unmarried, childless, purportedly licentious way of life of members of the alleged murderer's household; and, above all, the essential feminine figure of the child's grieving mother to the "unnatural," defeminized sisters of the accused man.

Press coverage of the Escorial crime offers considerable information about the daily lives of the poor, illiterate individuals involved. I have treated this material gingerly, supplementing it with other historical documents, first, in order to provide a reliable background to offset the occasional inventions of some of the reporters on the case, and second, to afford a broader perspective on the lives of a segment of the population about whom relatively little is known—the small-town inhabitants of rural Spain in the 1890s.

Newspaper coverage and public reaction to the Escorial crime offer an instructive contrast to the treatment and reception of similar crimes in other countries. Several cases in the 1890s involving child abuse in England, France, and the United States led to press campaigns advocating the reform of child protection legislation. In view of the intense interest and concern the Escorial murder trial created throughout the country, the failure of the Spanish press—both commercial and non-commercial—to launch such a campaign is striking and significant. As the press itself accurately reported, the focus of popular interest in the case's aftermath did not center on inadequate laws, on penalties in need of revision, or on questions of criminal responsibility, but rather on the perceived deficiencies of the recently reinstituted jury. And reporters themselves made no attempt to shift public attention to other pertinent legal issues. In Chapter 5, I discuss possible explanations for this aspect of the press's handling of the Escorial case.

NOTES

1. *La Correspondencia de España*, 2 March 1894, noted that Sr. Herrero and Sr. Oliva "are preparing a magisterial collection of photographs depicting the persons and sites which have acquired a most unfortunate celebrity in this trial, and which will strongly attract the public's attention when they appear ("preparan una magistral colección de vistas fotográficas con los personajes y los sitios que han adquirido más triste celebridad en este proceso, y que han de

llamar poderosamente la atención cuando salgan al public"). The two photographers sold several of their photos to the press. Throughout this book the translations from French and Spanish are my own.

2. José López Silva (1861-1925), Celso Lucio y López (1865-1915), and Carlos Arniches (1866-1943), all sometime artistic collaborators of Chueca, accompanied the latter and an impresario, a Sr. Aragués, to El Escorial on February 27, 1893 where "they visited the accused and gave them aid" ("visitaron a los procesados, socorriéndolos") (*La Correspondencia de España*, 28 February 1893).

3. *El Imparcial*, 2 March 1893, reported having received 100 ptas. to date from other newspapers and from individuals. The School of Forestry in El Escorial had already set up a subscription to help Pedrín's family and by February 26, 1893, had collected 200 ptas. *La Correspondencia de España* collected over 400 ptas. by March 3, 1893. According to this paper (28 March, 1893), the Augustinian friars at the Escorial monastery had also set up a subscription. I do not know how much money was finally handed over to the Bravo family. For the sake of comparison, in 1893 an American dollar equalled 5 ptas. In 1894, a liter of milk at El Escorial cost 80 céntimos. The price of a month's subscription to *El Nacional* was 1 pta. A pair of men's woolen trousers cost from 6-25 ptas., and Pedrín's coffin cost 15 ptas.

4. José María Quadrado, and Vicente de la Fuente, "Castilla la Nueva," Vol. 1, *España. Sus monumentos y artes-Su naturaleza e historia* (Barcelona: Daniel Cortezo y Cía., 1885), 918.

5. Pages 3-60 of Katherine Fischer Taylor's *In the Theater of Criminal Justice. The Palais de Justice in Second Empire Paris* (Princeton, N.J.: Princeton University Press, 1993), contain a vivid account of the impact of the Troppmann trial on the enormous public it attracted. The author analyzes how the architecture, iconography, placement of the representatives of justice, of the accused, and of the public (along with other elements) contributed to that impact.

6. The Hughes machine, a type-printing telegraph instrument, was the invention of David Edward Hughes (1831-1900), an Anglo-American electrician. Hughes patented the machine in the United States in 1855. By 1860 it was widely used in Europe. *Encyclopaedia Britannica*, 11th ed., s.v. "David Edward Hughes."

7. Question twenty was couched in language that drew criticism from legal scholars, as *El País*, 18 June 1894, noted in its editorial: "We are not going to enter into a discussion of the verdict nor shall we elucidate the extent to which the Court of law can be accused of incongruity and poor syntax in the questions presented to the jury, which in the opinion of jurists, led to the verdict the jury delivered. We assume that the magistrates will be the first to lament their error, and if this assumption is accurate, it would be inappropriate to accuse them of malice" ("No hemos de entrar en el examen del veredicto ni dilucidar hasta qué punto el Tribunal de derecho puede ser acusada de la incongruencia y falta de sintaxis en las preguntas formuladas al Jurado, que en opinión de los juristas han dado motivo al fallo pronunciado. Suponemos que los magistrados serán los primeros en lamentar su error, y en esta hipótesis no cabe atribuirles malicia").

Chapter One

Mass Taste and Crime Reporting in the Spanish Press of the 1890s

On May 7, 1894 the high-circulation Madrid daily, *La Correspondencia de España*, published a cartoon whose left-hand panel depicts a newsboy announcing excerpts from the most recent writings of Castelar, Galdós, Echegaray, Salmerón, and Núñez de Arce. No one is buying. The result, according to a legend placed below the panel, is "A Void" ("El vacío"). In the panel on the right, the boy is mobbed by men clamoring for copies when he shouts out that the issue also includes the latest on the crime at El Escorial. The result: "Delirium!!" (¡¡El delirio!!").

The cartoon's title, "Cultivated People" ("Los Pueblos Cultos"), poked fun at readers whose cultivation was unmistakably confirmed by the bowlers and top hats they wore on their heads, but who were nonetheless indifferent to the information and uplift proffered them by Spain's most eminent literati. They chose instead the sensation and smut available in crime reports. By identifying the buyers as middle and upper-class men, the cartoon punctured the pretensions to superiority of this segment of the reading public, lumping them together with the growing body of newspaper readers routinely characterized by their execrable taste in Spain as elsewhere in Europe, Britain, and America in the 1890s.[1] Such readers were more typically represented in Spain as part of an undifferentiated herd: "la masa," "el público," "el pueblo," "las multitudes."

The cartoon's irony depends upon the perception that the Escorial case interested the cultivated and the uncultivated alike, that the attraction of sensationalized crime reports was too great to be resisted regardless of class or culture. Many observers besides cartoonists noted the intense interest and enjoyment taken in newspaper crime narratives by all classes, often in preference to material considered serious or of indisputable artistic value. Much adverse criticism of the press during the 1890s focused on its failure to elevate the taste and stimulate the critical judgment of the masses. More tellingly, there was evident dismay at the press's leveling effect—the downward pull newspapers exerted on educated Spaniards. This dismay was seldom articulated except when—as in the cartoon—it surfaced in the guise of humor or satire.

In their commentaries on the press, representatives of the intellectual elite such as Leopoldo Alas, Azorín, Pompeyo Gener, Dorado Montero, and Joaquín Costa specifically alluded to the public's preference for newspaper crime reports. Their comments appear in the context of general remarks on the state of mass culture and on the press's responsibility to improve it. The following review of criticism of crime reporting in the Spanish press of the nineties may thus provide insights into how those journalists, artists, literati, social scientists, and scientists viewed certain significant national issues, including the current cultural status of the majority of the population and the effective promotion of literacy and education for the masses during the years just before the crisis of 1898 and immediately afterward—a period when the elite was becoming increasingly aware of itself as a group separate from the political establishment and from the wider public.

Raising the newspaper-reading masses—including those who were newly-literate—to higher levels of esthetic and critical awareness, first of all, required the identification and characterization of the readers who were to be changed. Critics could then prescribe remedies whose effects would place themselves and readers more nearly on the same cultural level. In addition to revealing what intellectuals took to be the masses' deficiencies, these public discussions also furnish clues as to how the elite perceived or failed to perceive the difficulties implicit in the transition of newly-literate Spaniards from an oral to a written culture, and how the elite defined itself and its role as advocate of the cultural enrichment of the people.

What did the elite mean by "culture"? What did the masses have to gain by approaching the cultural level of the elite? How would the elite benefit? The meaning of the term "culture" must be teased out in context: the benefits of acquiring it were rarely spelled out, presumably because they were thought to be self-evident. Some plausible answers to the first question emerge in the process of contextualizing the press's presentation of the Escorial crime: notions about what culture meant to the elite may be inferred, to an extent, from their statements in the press declaring what it was not. Answers to the questions concerning the benefits of cultural approximation, both to the elite and to the masses, are more elusive. Indications of how the elite saw itself, how it defined and set itself apart from the masses are relatively plentiful. But, for the most part, the public lacked a voice or spokesmen to express its views on matters such as education or culture, how to acquire it, and what benefits it might bring.

Recent studies of formal educational projects undertaken by the elite on behalf of the newly-literate masses contend that the social, economic and political conditions of the Restoration regime led in the end to the imposition of the customary aim of education—control. Antonio Viñao Frago has described the "cultivated" and "urbane" bourgeoisie who initiated the program of acculturation of the people (*pueblo*) through the peoples' libraries (*bibliotecas populares*) along with the aims of those who in 1885 established the Library for the Promotion of the Arts (*Biblioteca del Fomento de las Artes*). As for the results of their efforts, Viñao Frago concludes:

> It does not seem reckless to affirm that even if the initial practices and principles had remained intact, the outcome—although arrived at differently—would still have been their stagnation and inefficacy. Without public financial support and with minimal funds, without connections to other measures for social reform in which reading would constitute an additional element or consequence, and with such high doses of paternalism or control in the choice of suitable or unsuitable texts, the experiment was headed either toward self-correction or failure.[2]

In the last decade of the nineteenth century, the University Extension movement in Oviedo exemplified one of the few concerted efforts on the part of intellectuals—including the historian, Rafael Altamira, the writer and law professor, Leopoldo Alas, the educator, Adolfo A. Buylla, and the sociologist, Adolfo Posada—to impart education to workers. What would that education accomplish? Such efforts, in José A. Piqueras Arenas' view, essentially aimed at establishing a more judicially equitable *status quo*:

> From 1875 on, attempts at educational renovation were mixed up with *regenerationism*. But the regenerationists were to turn-of-the-century Spanish capitalist reality what enlightened thinkers were to the feudal reality of two centuries earlier: they in no way questioned the established economic order and at most aspired to correct the judicial order. For both groups education resolved social problems and corrected inequities. Meanwhile, official bodies made it clear by their actions that they had opted once again to consider measures of control rather than those which might promote upward movement. A subtle difference.[3]

The results of an inquiry into the education and culture of the working classes were released between 1889 and 1893. The report, initiated by the Commission for Social Reform (*Comisión de Reformas Sociales*) established in 1883, constituted the first official publication issued during the Restoration in which the voices of workers were heard. Working people also set out their own educational objectives and the benefits they hoped to achieve in the statutes and rules which governed numerous workers' associations.[4] The dissemination of workers' views about their present state and future aspirations was, however, minimal compared to the wide-spread currency—made possible especially through the press—of elite formulations of the cultural state and capacities of the newly-literate masses.

A CAPRICIOUS PUBLIC AND A VENAL PRESS

A commonly-held view of the public in the 1890s reflected attitudes often articulated during the seventeenth century concerning the nature and demands of the people who thronged Madrid theaters during that period. In an 1893 essay entitled "The Press" ("La Prensa periódica"), F.F. Villegas recalled Lope de Vega's well-known precept that it is impossible to live off the public and, at the same time, to go against its tastes and capricious desires. Contemporary newspaper readers, wrote Villegas, are no less tyrannical while their particular taste for the horrifying requires that they regularly be served up a highly-seasoned crime of the day. And, he added, if this does not seem to be in the public's best interest, "What does it matter? Business has no conscience."[5]

These two ideas were echoed repeatedly during the 1890s: first, that the public's taste is not only capricious but debased, and that it is tyrannical in its demands for the satisfaction of those tastes; second, that the commercial nature of the mainstream press requires it to pander to public demand. Consumers and producers, in this view, were seen as complicit, locked into the relationship Lope had described as inevitable if consumers were to be satisfied and producers were to survive. The elite who wrote for newspapers (not those relatively few who were exclusively journalists by profession) occupied a unique position in this model: ostensible advocates of the masses' best interests, they were nonetheless associated with the class interests of the producers, the owners of the papers. While the intellectual elite leveled criticism at producers and consumers from vantage points which were somewhat ambiguously both inside and outside the process, producers and readers persisted in their complicitous daily production and consumption of copy whose inferior nature darkened elitist hopes of securing a higher level of culture for the masses. The popularity of crime reports was singled out in Spain, as elsewhere, as the clearest evidence of the public's debased cravings.

One of the principal organs of Marxist thought and opinion in the 1890s was the Madrid weekly newspaper, *El Socialista*. On May 11, 1894, the paper responded to a question posed by a reporter for *El Heraldo de Madrid*: was the public or the press responsible for the detailed, nauseating descriptions of the crime committed at *El Escorial*? The answer *El Socialista* provided was that in absolute terms neither public nor press was responsible:

> The uncultivated public, which constitutes the majority, wants to satisfy its unhealthy curiosity, and the press, more interested in business than in the

> education of the people, satisfies its gross appetites by providing it with spiced-up fare.
> Business interests oblige newspapers to cater to the public rather than to educate it; similarly, they oblige the reporter—who has to participate in a factory-like regimen—to employ his mental energy in the confection of dishes which revolt his stomach and his conscience alike.

But, regarding the purportedly inferior moral condition of the uncultivated public, *El Socialista*, in the same article, argued that the peoples' morality was no worse than that of the more privileged members of society:

> It would be notoriously unjust to cast aspersions on the unlettered masses.
>
> In the same number in which *El Heraldo* expresses its well-founded scruples for having to cover repugnant stories such as the crime at El Escorial, it also reports on the complaint filed in court against a Jesuit instructor at a boys' school who has been accused of the same disgusting crime that has put the *Chato* in jail. [*El Chato* was the nickname of Julián García, the man accused of the abduction, sexual abuse, and murder of three-year-old Pedro Bravo.]
>
> The *Heraldo* should compare these two phenomena, and it will see that if a sense of morality has been lost in the lower classes of society, it would be pointless to seek it in those who by virtue of their learning were most obliged to give evidence of it.[6]

A few years later, on December 31, 1897, the paper printed without comment a passage from Renan's *L'Avenir de la science* whose argument was that demand on the part of the rich determined supply:

> Express or implied demand determines production in the realm of the mind as in all else, and it is in the nature of things that wealth should create demand. Whoever intends, then, to live from the products of his intellect must, above all, try to divine what it is that the rich want in order to conform to their wishes.

Complicity among producers and consumers in this model may have appeared to be more acceptably Marxist since it left the new reading masses out of the equation except as passive recipients. In any case, the nature of the products in demand was equally inferior and merited the Frenchman's scorn:

> Now then: what do the rich want in the way of intellectual products? Serious literature? Philosophy, or—regarding pure and severe productions—exalted works of morality? Not at all. They want diverting literature, *feuilletons*, stories [...]. This explains why it is that someone who grinds out *feuilleton* novels can make a brilliant fortune and attain to what is called a position in the world, whereas a serious savant—even if his accomplishments equal those of men like Bopp or Lassen—would never be able to live off the material returns from his works.[7]

The position on supply and demand taken by the Catholic press, according to Francisco J. Díaz de Castro and Isabel Moll Blanes, was similar to that of the Marxists: it viewed the liberal press as the "indoctrinators of the great masses in behalf of the economic interests of the powerful."[8] The masses' role, in this view, again emerges as one of passive reception.

The conservative version, in which the uncultivated masses bore a large part of the responsibility for products offensive and unacceptable to the elite, was most widespread among intellectuals writing in the 1890s.[9] In article after article, members of the elite condemned the press's willingness to satisfy public demand, but they nonetheless identified the public as the worst culprit. Critics claimed that its insatiable curiosity led, among other things, to appalling invasions of privacy. An anonymous contributor to *El Imparcial* on January 31, 1893, referred to that troubling aspect of contemporary reporting when he wrote that it was impossible to continue down that road even if it did please the public which was primarily to blame.

Inexperience, even the childish nature so often ascribed to the masses, could not wholly diminish their accountability in the eyes of the elite. The press's partial responsibility for the sorry state of mass culture was acknowledged, but it was excused, if not justified, on the grounds of financial necessity. It was tacitly granted that the Spanish press could not resist the increasing pressure felt by newspapers everywhere to provide fare appealing, above all, to popular taste. And newspapers which depended on sales and advertising for revenue could not forego the boost in circulation which crime reporting, in particular, ensured.[10] The independently-funded religious and political press, in contrast, either ignored it or dealt with crime reporting as suited the aims of each individual paper and its director. Pi y Margall's republican federalist paper, *El Nuevo Regimen*, for example, seldom printed information about crime. *El Socialista* seemed to view reading about criminal acts in newspapers as equivalent to wishing to commit them—a view which was widely-accepted at the time—or at least, wanting to experience them vicariously. While it did not print extended reports on crime, it did underscore its positions on the corruption of the Church, the exploitation of the working class, and the failures of the criminal justice system by occasional, selective reporting of crimes—typically choosing to provide brief notices on those committed by the clergy, by capitalists, or by representatives of law enforcement.[11]

NEWSPAPERS AND THEIR READERS: LITERACY IN THE 1890s

In the early 1890s Madrid had three newspapers which were reliable sources of crime reports; *El Resumen*, *Las Ocurrencias*, and *Los Sucesos*. The latter had a regular feature entitled "Crímenes y Misterios." In addition to brief reports presented under the rubric "Tribunales," more extensive, long-running accounts of crimes—of which the Escorial case is representative—allowed the reporter to set the scene, examine motivation, provide telling details, and speculate on the outcome. Such accounts appeared in major papers such as *El Liberal*, *El Imparcial*, *El País*, *El Día*, *La Correspondencia de España*, and other Madrid dailies.[12] Under the title, "An Unnatural Mother," ("Una madre infame"), the following short report of March 9, 1895, in the monarchist paper, *El Correo*, exemplifies the moralistic spin often given to copy which critics thought little more than a pretext for sensation and titillation:

> People passing through Santiago plaza in Linares yesterday morning witnessed the astonishing sight of a dog carrying a new-born infant in its mouth. The tender creature, which was still alive, was half-devoured.
>
> A man who tried to get the dog to release the infant had to desist because of the ferocity with which the animal defended its prey.
>
> A few more men together managed to get the infant away from the dog, but all that remained was the head, the thorax and the lungs.
>
> Presumably, the infant was abandoned in the countryside where the dogs began to eat it.
>
> The Civil Guard and the Municipal police are searching tirelessly for the unnatural mother who so cruelly abandoned her offspring.[13]

Crime reports which were largely dependent on sensational effects disturbed cultural critics such as the author of *La Regenta*, Leopoldo Alas. In *El Globo* on February 10, 1894, the year after Villegas published his remarks on readers' tastes, the novelist and critic wrote that the public which was beginning to read by reading newspapers, gravitated toward "inferior" material. He continued: "When, a few weeks ago, everything seemed to consist of crimes and recriminations, catastrophes, both deliberate and accidental, unhealthy excitations, precipitate judgments and a craving for strong sensations, it seemed that the intellectual sphere, tranquil literature, above all, did not in the least matter to the public, and that the times predicted by Max Nordau in his recent book, *Degeneration*, had arrived for Spain—a time in which literature would be scorned as something sickly, atavistic and useless."[14] He found grounds for hope in the offerings of some papers, notably *El Imparcial*, *El Liberal*, *El Globo*, *La Justicia*, *El Día*, and *El Heraldo de Madrid*. He also noted that editions of *Los Lunes de El Imparcial*, whose content was literary and artistic, typically sold 100,000 copies, and "that were were no crimes there, but rather articles by Balart [an art critic, primarily]" ("allí no hay crímenes; hay artículos de Balart"). In fact, three months later to the day, *Los Lunes de El Imparcial* featured a story on "El Crimen de El Escorial." It appeared on the first page, complete with drawings and reproductions of photographs showing the site of the murder, the victim, and the alleged killer.

Nonetheless, Leopoldo Alas later reiterated his confidence in the press's ability to mold and direct the misguided though malleable masses. Readers, he wrote in *El Imparcial* of May 8, 1895, were still uninterested in "literary" offerings in newspapers, but Alas again attributed this to inexperience, to the fact that "the masses are now beginning to spell out words and newspapers are their primary texts" ("el pueblo en masa ahora empieza a deletrear y tiene por silibario los periódicos"). He thought it unlikely that such readers would turn to books in the near future. The press therefore, had to assume responsibility for educating and raising the cultural level of its readers. How it was to do so without sacrificing its economic interests was a problem neither Alas nor other like-minded advocates of a didactic press normally broached. Critics invoked the financial realities of producing newspapers in this context only to decry and lament them. Often they were not mentioned at all. On August 23, 1893, for example, F. Pi y Arsuaga wrote an article for *El Nuevo Régimen* entitled "The Press of the Future" ("La prensa del porvenir"). He observed first that it would be more fitting to say that Spain's press, rather than the novelist, Fernández y González had "set half of Spain to reading" ("soltado a leer a media España"). The greater the paper's circulation, he wrote, the greater the obligation of reporters to guide the public's conscience and raise the level of culture. How the paper had earned its high circulation was not a question Pi y Arsuaga dealt with in his article.

Few assessments of Spanish newspapers and, especially, of their readers in the 1890s differ substantially from those of Villegas, Leopoldo Alas, Pi y Arsuaga, and many other intellectuals of the period. In 1894, Juan Valero de Tornos edited a volume, *España de Fin de Siglo*, in which a divergent view—noteworthy for its optimism—provides an opportune introduction to the question of literacy in Spain. The editorial staff authored a section claiming that Spanish dailies, which were said to treat all material with great measure and circumspection, together with weeklies "containing artistic and literary wonders" ("conteniendo primores artísticos y literarios") had built a large readership. They had done so, "by making reading attractive to that immense anonymous mass which constitutes a tribunal of opinion without appeal—a tribunal of opinion which is always hasty and impressionable, and often unjust." Those readers were said to have raised their level of culture to the point where all classes, even the least cultivated, could follow the current of public affairs.[15]

The number of literate Spaniards was low, in fact, compared to other European countries. Literacy figures based on the census of 1889, compiled by the Institute of Geography and Statistics in 1893, were, in fact, described as "frightening" ("aterradores"), by *El Día* on June 12 of that year: "Data referring to the Spanish population's level of instruction are genuinely frightening. Those who know how to read only: Men–221,613. Women—380,392. Total: 602,005. Those who can write: Men—3,317,855. Women—

1,686,615. Total: 5,004,470. Those who do not know how to read: Men—5,067,098. Women—6,878,773. Total: 11,945,871."[16] The total population in 1889 was approximately 17,550,000.

In 1987, José Piqueras Arenas noted that information on literacy had formerly been derived from census-based statistics which included children under seven years of age, and that this procedure was contrary to that followed elsewhere in computing similar data. Piqueras Arenas showed that once the figures were adjusted by discounting those under seven, Spain had approximately the same level of literacy in the last decade of the century as Italy. By 1900 45.7 percent of Spanish men and 66.0 percent of women over the age of ten were literate, i.e., 56.2 percent of the total population of 18.6 million. Even so, only Portugal in the rest of Western Europe had a higher rate of illiteracy.[17]

General characterizations of Spanish readers in the second half of the nineteenth century emphasize their youth, their location in primarily urban areas, and the fact that they were predominantly female. In 1976 Romero Tobar summarized the current state of knowledge about late nineteenth-century readers, a summary which remains applicable despite later refinements. Noting first that the majority of Spaniards did not read, he added: "groups of readers were concentrated in urban nuclei and belonged to the bourgeoisie—from its most brilliant to its lowest levels—or they consisted of smaller groupings composed of artisans and proletarians." In his discussion of readers of *feuilleton* novels, Romero Tobar referred to the continuity of popular tradition and oral communication: "We must also realize that interpersonal communication or communication among small groups—telling stories, reading aloud—so characteristic as a means of propagating traditional, popular literature, had to play an important role in the transmission of the information and content of the *feuilleton*. And that means of communication is difficult to measure."[18]

POPULAR ORAL TRADITION AND THE PRESS

The oral propagation of popular literature suggests similar difficulties in measuring the distribution of newspapers since, in many instances, newspapers were read aloud to illiterate listeners. The transition from typical themes and techniques found in popular oral tradition (broadsheets; blind men's ballads, ballads and related material) (*literatura de cordel; coplas de ciegos, romances*) to newspaper crime accounts raises a different question. Did the intellectuals writing in the press who wanted to raise the level of the people's culture acknowledge the continued attraction of that body of oral crime narrative? A rare reference to the persisting older tradition occurs in an 1893 article written by the journalist and deputy to parliament, Kasabal (José

Gutiérrez Abascal). He wrote that it was necessary to educate the public which flocked to public markets to hear the stories of horrible crimes sung by blind men: “Each one of these gatherings is a platform from which taste is corrupted and evil passions fed, and it is necessary to break them up as foci of the most destructive immorality.”[19] Kasabal believed that better journalism was essential to educate the people, but he did not discuss what might replace crime-reporting as currently practiced, nor did he specify how newspaper reporters were to capture the people’s interest. Once again, a call for change by a representative of the elite omits any proposal for a program or specific suggestions to effect change. Kasabal, like most of his colleagues, also left unexamined the assumption that crime reports spread a kind of contagion harmful to morality.

The late nineteenth-century public for broadsheets (“littérature de colportage”) gradually diminished. As late as the Restoration, according to J.-F. Botrel, private reading finally began to take precedence over listening to someone else read as part of a group.[20] Private reading (all reading in fact) prevailed on an admittedly limited scale with newspapers doing their part to facilitate a transition between a lingering persistent oral tradition and a written one. But which written one? David Vincent touches on this problem in his detailed discussion of the reading choices open to the newly-literate in late nineteenth-century Britain. He refers to the schools’ attempts to promote “‘the mental culture of youth’” through the “‘formation of a purely literary taste’” which had no relationship to the oral tradition or to street literature.[21]

For Spaniards vocal on this question in the press, being cultivated similarly implied a taste for, and a reasonably sophisticated appreciation of “good” literature. Journalists and editors during this period were often creative writers themselves. Furthermore, the role of imaginative literature in entertaining and motivating newly-literate readers was as unquestioningly accepted as was the role of the intellectual elite in determining what literature was appropriate for the masses who were learning to read. Accordingly, raising the level of culture of the newly-literate who read newspapers generally implied inserting prose fiction into those papers. (The left-wing press routinely used monologues, short dramas, stories and verse to convey its ideological messages.)

Restoration newspapers often printed chapters from forthcoming novels. In 1891 alone, *El Liberal* published a chapter from Leopoldo Alas’s *Su único hijo*, while *El Imparcial* printed a selection from the second part of Benito Pérez Galdós’ *Angel Guerra*, as well as a part of Jacinto Octavio Picón’s *Dulce y sabrosa*.[22] Literary sketches and short stories also appeared frequently in the press.

Some newspapers made occasional attempts to improve the quality of the *folletines* they printed. In 1891, for example, *El Globo* serialized Charles Dickens’ *Martin Chuzzlewit*, and in April of 1894, it began Émile Zola’s

Lourdes. Not all such attempts to provide the public with "good" literature were successful; for example, reader reaction in 1895, when *El Imparcial* serialized Juan Valera's *Juanita la larga*, was not promising. Nor did other efforts in that paper aimed at presenting "good" literature—H.G. Wells's *War of the Worlds* and *The Invisible Man*—engage readers.[23] Nonetheless, the level of *folletín* offerings during these years was occasionally "elevated": Leopoldo Alas's *La Regenta* began to appear in the *folletín* of *La Publicidad* (Barcelona) in January 1894; Blasco Ibáñez published *Arroz y Tartana* in 1894, *Flor de mayo* in 1895, *El despertar de Budha* in 1897, and *La barraca* in 1898 as *folletines* in his daily, *El Pueblo*.[24]

Meanwhile, in 1894, the year in which *El Imparcial* covered the trial of the accused murderer at El Escorial, the paper had its greatest *folletín* success to date with the publication of the first part of Ponson du Terrail's Rocambole series, *L'Héritage mystérieux*. The novel was so popular that failure to publish a segment of it for even one day brought on "an avalanche of insulting and threatening mail."[25]

Belles lettres and popular fiction were both on offer in high-circulation newspapers, but it is difficult to assess how readers availed themselves of that offer. Undoubtedly, many people read both. Padre Blanco urged the adolescent Manuel Azaña, a student from 1893 to 1897 at the *Real Colegio de Estudios Superiores*, the Augustinian university at El Escorial, to raise the level of his reading material: "He wanted to improve my taste so he gave me Pereda to read. That was legitimate reading and we used to alternate it with installments of Rocambole delivered on the sly. Later he gave me *Pepita Jiménez*. It bored me."[26]

Critics who concerned themselves with cultural developments were generally not impressed by the press's attempts to make "literary" titles available to the public, nor were they convinced of their effectiveness. They continued to deplore the commercialism of most Spanish papers as well as the backwardness of readers whose inclinations, in the opinion of José Martínez Ruiz (Azorín), led them to prefer "interminable accounts of crimes and trials" ("las reseñas interminables de crímenes y procesos"). And—it might be added—serialized adventure stories. Mass reading taste was significant: "Nothing," the same critic wrote, "is a better indicator of the condition of a people than its press."[27]

Although Azorín's remarks were published in 1895, long before he had metamorphosed into a conservative, his analysis accords with the views of most conservative critics for whom the masses were as much, if not more, at fault as capitalists for the degraded state of the commercial press.

CONCEPTUALIZATION OF THE MASSES AT THE TURN OF THE CENTURY

Toward the end of the nineties assessments of readers became increasingly pessimistic and strictures against the press harsher. Currently fashionable notions of decadence and degeneration along with the old charge of widespread barbarism strengthened explanations put forward for a variety of ills, including the inadequacies of the press and reader preferences. In 1896 Pompeyo Gener, who considered such preferences symptomatic of national decline, wrote: "Blood-soaked novels and hair-raising dramas, just like the blind men's ballads that tell of countless crimes, are still the most popular. At bottom, the people always ask for `more horses!' [to replace those gored by the bull]. Blood satisfies and intoxicates them."[28]

In Joaquín Costa's 1902 summing up of the psychological and institutional defects that characterized Spain and Spaniards at the turn of the century, a premature and irresponsible press, along with the unprepared masses it catered to, came in for severest criticism:

> The introduction of newspapers into a nation that had been taught how to think would have been very useful; but to introduce them suddenly, mechanically, and inorganically into a semi-African nation, 400 years behind the rest, had to be harmful for the same reasons that the introduction of parliament has been harmful. Those who learned to read had soft, lazy, weak brains lacking discipline. Of course they read what was put before them every day and what spoke to them of their personal interests, of political crises and battles, bullfights, sensational crimes, the national lottery, scandals and gossip in and out of the country—in short, the newspaper. It did not take long for them to surrender to it passively, abandoning their capacity to think. They grew accustomed to living on manufactured thought.[29]

For well over a decade the Spanish elite had observed and commented on the deficiencies of the press and the newspaper reading public. Yet Costa's remarks in 1902 provide little evidence that he had given serious thought to the kind of education needed by the masses if they were to redirect their interests and curiosity to higher ends. Similarly, he included no discussion as to how a commercial press could guarantee quality. Instead, Costa invoked a number of characteristics which had been attributed to the masses throughout the preceding decade: unhealthy curiosity and an insatiable hunger for novelty; weak and undisciplined habits of thought; passivity. Once again the people bear the brunt of the blame: they take what is put before them by newspapers which cater to their inferior tastes, and they become accustomed to letting others think for them. Like most commentators on mass taste, Costa condemned it, without attempting to analyze it.

Not long after Costa's presentation at the Ateneo, an article from the *Diario Mercantil* entitled "Leafing through the Press" ("Hojeando la prensa") was quoted in *La Vanguardia* of December 1, 1903. The anonymous author framed his complaints about the press's coverage of crime, its choice of *folletines*, and not least, the debased popular taste it catered to, from a different vantage point. He began by emphasizing the press's moral obligation, imposed by the disaster of 1898, to enliven and uplift the spirit of the people: "The minute recounting of trials and the publicity given to the most horrendous crimes may appease the morbid curiosity of a sick society, but it does not invigorate the spirit or raise up hopes to the contemplation of more generous and patriotic ideals." But, having indicted the press and the morbid curiosity of a "sick society"—which presumably included all Spaniards—the author proceeded to zero in on the deficient tastes of the masses in particular. With the high-circulation papers' offerings of *folletines* "'past errors are not remedied nor is a great and vigorous country forged; the masses are amused and distracted, and the terrain prepared for a national neurosis to take root and flourish.'"[30] The author's reference to the press as short-sighted panderer to readers' unhealthy demands is commonplace, but the image of the masses as willingly but inappropriately fertilized soil made it possible to conceptualize the role of the masses in national life in a different way. Likening the masses to an underlying foundation made it plausible to hold them responsible not only for their own condition, but also for the condition of the nation as a whole.

This way of viewing the masses is touched on in a 1986 essay by Serge Salaün dealing with late nineteenth-century Spain and entitled "The Problematic of the Infra-Culture" ("Problématique de l'infra-culture"). In his exposition, he included a 1933 comment of Antonio Gramschi on the significance of the success *feuilletons* enjoyed among the masses: "'It is this question, moreover, that constitutes the major part of the problem confronting a new literature expressive of an intellectual and moral renewal; for it is only by starting with readers of *feuilleton* novels that one can select a large enough reading public to serve as the cultural base of a new literature.'"[31] These remarks resemble those of the anonymous writer for the *Diario Mercantil* insofar as the masses are envisioned as constituting the essential ground upon which self-conscious agents construct a culture—for good or ill. The difference lies in the Spaniard's apparent sense that the current passive condition of the masses would not change nor could it be changed for the better in the near future.

Most of the intellectuals cited so far, viewed the public as different and deficient. They pointed out the deficiencies and advocated reform, yet there is little indication that the state of mass culture was considered a pressing, crucial one for the nation. A few voices—Unamuno, the writer for the *Diario Mercantil* quoted above—suggest that new attitudes toward the masses were taking shape. The masses were coming to be seen as a fundamentally unknown entity—the unexplored foundation, subsoil, or subterranean waters—which could either nourish and support, or undermine national health and survival.

In 1895 Unamuno clearly linked receptivity to contemporary European thought, together with knowledge of, and then activation of the *pueblo* to the fate of all Spaniards. Yet, he believed that the elite was largely ignorant of plebeian literature; that is, of the "blind men's ballads [...] broadsheets and half-penny novels which are the usual fare for those who do not know how to read and who must be read to [...]" ("coplas de ciegos [...] los pliegos de cordel y [...] los novelones de a cuartillo de real la entrega que sirven de pasto aun a los que no saben leer y los oyen [...]").[32] Unamuno's belief that the elite was unfamiliar with the culture of the *pueblo* made the task formidable. No one, Unamuno wrote, asks what books are gathering soot next to the cooking fires of poor farmers, nor does anyone ask which books are being spelled out by groups of workers. Those in search of this kind of knowledge—essential if the *pueblo* is to be understood and mobilized—must immerse themselves in the people. The *pueblo* in Unamuno's imagery is like a deep, river whose quiet surface, ruffled by winds blowing in from Europe, could presage an awakening of great power, at present wholly concealed from sight.

In the aftermath of the Cuban War intellectuals paid renewed attention to the need to do something about the perceived deficient cultural condition of the masses. For Emilia Pardo Bazán, Spain's backwardness was not due to the supposed failure of the intellectual elite to participate in the nation's governance: "We must search elsewhere for the cause of our backwardness—in the intellectual condition of the masses. The people are in their infancy; they are simple or they are wild, never are they enlightened and self-conscious." Everyone, she says, recognizes the need to educate the masses, but the will to do so is lacking. Meanwhile, the masses drag down the entire country: "With souls atremble, with minds athirst for culture and greatness, we lie bound to our rock, dreaming that the Spanish people will awaken in the end and—forgetting all causes for division—will get on with the great but relatively easy task of instituting the Fatherland."[33] The self-dramatizing image Pardo Bazán conjured up in the last sentence vividly portrays a martyred intellectual's sensibility. It also registers the apathy which she (and others) observed around her and which she believed had to be overcome if the elite and the masses were to draw together.

The hope that Unamuno and other like-minded intellectuals held toward the beginning of the Cuban insurrection for bringing elite and masses together in order to harness the energies of the latter evidently flagged in the years following the Spanish defeat. Anarchist and socialist activism generated class distrust and fear in the final decade of the century. More specifically, apa[illegible] ...ng cultural rapprochement of the classes may [illegible] given the stark and unresolved polarization that result[illegible] ...nment's recruitment policy during the war. The well-off pu[illegible] ...mption from military service while the poor, the *pueblo*, who co[illegible] not put up 1,500 ptas. were conscripted to serve in Cuba. The wedge driven between the classes by the widely-perceived injustice of that policy could not be ignored or easily glossed over.

CRIME REPORTS AS SOURCES OF INFORMATION AND ETHICAL DEBATE

Throughout most of the 1890s commentators expressed concern, but not alarm about the press's failure to educate its deficient readers. Meanwhile, there was no doubt that newspapers did indeed constitute the primary source of the reading matter of the masses. Recent research concerning the press and publishing history, workers' associations, libraries and popular education in general in the nineteenth century, has singled out certain social and political developments for discussion, indicating how they affected the reading habits of the newly-literate by the 1890s. Viñao Frago notes "the spread of the libraries and reading rooms of various sorts of clubs, literary and scientific associations, public lecture societies, schools, and recreational cultural organizations of Catholic, bourgeois-reformist, or working-class orientation [...]," and remarks that in those settings, "The periodical press was the reading matter emphasized."[34]

What the public wanted to read is less easily verified than the fact that the newly-literate nineteenth-century reader was greatly dependent on the press for reading matter. Contemporary observers who discussed readers' tastes and competence seldom pointed out the connection between newspaper crime reports and the coverage they contained of otherwise largely inaccessible scientific, legal and sociological information. Yet newspapers—often as underpinning to crime reports—offered news about current speculation in related areas of investigation in a way comprehensible to laymen, thereby satisfying a legitimate need to keep abreast of modern developments. *El Globo* of March 8, 1894, for example, ran an article entitled "Measuring Man" ("Antropometría") with drawings of heads, arms, hands, and ears being measured in accord with the method developed by Alphonse Bertillon for the identification of recidivist criminals—a method which was cheaper and more accurate than photographs. Crime stories provided the real life, complex material in relation to which new findings and even theories could be explicated. Scientific assessments of criminal responsibility in connection with maladies such as epilepsy, for example, appeared in newspapers as subjects for debate.

In a long article on crime reporting in *La Ilustración Ibérica* on February 11, 1893, Kasabal observed that: "Recent crimes have highlighted grave defects found in the Madrid housing rented by the lower classes. Greedy landlords diligently exploit their properties to the detriment of sanitation and morality" ("Los crímenes recientes han puesto también de relieve defectos gravísimos de las viviendas madrileñas que alquila la gente del pueblo y donde la codicia de los propietarios aprovecha afanosamente el terreno con perjuicio de la higiene y de la moral"). The occasional vivid descriptions in the press of the living conditions of the urban poor do, in fact, emerge as background for stories on rings of beggar children, accounts of abused children, murders, and other crimes. Those descriptions, in Kasabal's view, properly raised issues that cried out for reform.

Kasabal's essay began with discussion of the ethical questions often posed by crime reporting. One of the most serious, the press's invasion of privacy, had long been recognized as problematical. By 1888, coverage of the "Crimen de la calle de Fuencarral" clearly indicated that no details were too intimate for reporters to root out and display to their readers. In the same year, Armando Palacio Valdés made use of the topic in his novel, *El cuarto poder*. In this work, an anonymous newspaper item refers to a wife's adultery. The parties involved in the affair, though not identified by name, are clearly recognizable. As a result of this publicity, the husband feels compelled to act in defense of his honor, thus precipitating a violent ending. By 1893 F.F. Villegas was able to claim that: "There is no door impenetrable to the reporter's searching gaze, no grief he does not profane, nor anything public or private which he does not recount to the indifferent and not very pious multitude. It is a sad thing to think that our reputations, our standing, our misfortunes can be sold for a few pennies in the public square!"[35]

In his 1895 novel, *Halma*, Benito Pérez Galdós included a dialogue in which two reporters defend their intrusions into the private lives of two characters—Nazarín and Andara—who are involved in a scandalous trial. Don Manuel, the priest who is ministering to the accused, disapproves of the publicity:

> "What's to be done, don Manuel? The beast demands more flesh, more news, and there's nothing for it but to give it to him," said the first of the two men, a lively and attractive fellow.
>
> "We've exhausted the vein," said the second, "but seeing as how it's necessary to serve the public something every day, yesterday I gave it an exact account of what Nazarín eats, and an interesting review of his mother's difficult births."
>
> "But, my dear fellows," said the priest, with more kindness than annoyance, "your reports are going to drive us all crazy. You have written a number of things that shouldn't have been revealed, others that don't matter to anyone [...]."

> "We serve the public."
>
> "But wouldn't it be better served if you were to guide it rather than letting yourselves be dragged down by its capricious and unhealthy desire for novelty?"
>
> "It's not us poor wretches of reporters who light the bonfires. They order us to pile on whatever burns—dry wood, if there is any; if not, new wood for sparks, and even straw if we can't find anything else."[36]

It is worth noting that the reporters' characterization of the masses as a wild beast clamoring for flesh is a variation on an image found repeatedly in the nineties. Insatiable hunger was one of the principal traits the elite attributed to the masses; indeed, ingestion seems to have been thought of as essentially vulgar—at least when the lower classes engaged in it. Galdós and others satirized reporters who printed menus of jail meals. Such reports, common during the nineties, aimed to satisfy the public's purported curiosity about food eaten by criminal suspects from José Vázquez Varela—one of the accused in the Fuencarral case—to Julián García, the principal indicted in the Escorial abduction and murder.[37] Easily mocked as this kind of information was, it could, of course, do more than satisfy idle, misdirected curiosity. Descriptions of the elegant and plentiful meals Vázquez Varela enjoyed in jail, undoubtedly fueled class antagonism in some readers. Varela had long been the object of public opprobrium because of his alleged self-indulgence and immoral conduct. As for Julián García, his appetite for great amounts of plebeian fare such as stews made of garbanzos, fatback and greens (*cocido*) signified his coarse, brutish nature to better-off, urban readers.

Critics of crime reporting viewed revelations about what people ate as distasteful, meaningful primarily because they exposed the inferior quality of the curiosity demonstrated by mass readers. Serious invasions of privacy occurred when the press named victims and suspects in criminal cases. Anonymity in the mainstream press was, in fact, granted haphazardly to those involved in sexual crimes (whether perpetrators or victims) regardless, it seems, of class, status, or wealth. The names of pre-pubescent girls and boys who had been sexually abused were sometimes published in the press along with the names of their abusers.[38] On occasion, as in Palacio Valdés's novel, the individuals involved were not named, although they could be identified by references to the site of the crime provided in the report.[39]

A particularly egregious example of the press's apparently unlimited license to invade privacy was the practice of publishing results of gynecological examinations performed on female victims of alleged rape and on female murder victims; and even, in the Escorial case, on females under suspicion of being implicated in a crime. The examining physician's opinions or conclusions as to whether the victim was "intact" were made public, thereby providing information often upsetting to the family and friends of the victim, to readers, and occasionally to reporters. Kasabal (in the essay referred to above) cited a case in which the press revealed that a young woman killed by her fiancé did not die a virgin—a revelation that caused much additional grief to her mother.

Another incident described in Kasabal's essay further underscored the gratuitous damage that the press's invasion of privacy could inflict. In the investigation of a street assault, the true paternity of a child, previously unknown to the putative father, was brought to light. Kasabal wrote:

> I confess that I could not help being profoundly moved when I read what the husband of a woman wounded on San José street told one of my colleagues. Asked what he would do if his wife survived the attack, the unfortunate fellow replied, "Maybe I would have pardoned her because I loved her a lot. But considering what the papers have said, it's impossible now for me to go back to her."[40]

In view of the prevalent public opinion, Kasabal showed considerable independence of judgment, when he argued that the accused in the Escorial case had a right to privacy: "There can be no question of feeling compassion for the author of the crime or for his family, none of whom inspire the least sympathy. But I do not believe that anyone has the right to torment a man who has fallen afoul of a system of justice which will see to it that he expiates his horrible crime in accord with the law."[41] At this point in the investigation, Kasabal objected to the reporters who were besieging the suspects with questions in their cells at the Escorial. Before long, readers of the papers would be apprised of many intimate details concerning "*El Chato*" (Julián García) and his family. They would read about the accused man's epilepsy, his alleged longstanding practice of masturbation and its supposed effects on his memory, and his purported homosexuality. They would also learn whether his sisters—suspected of being accomplices in the crime—were virgins.[42]

The kinds of stories Kasabal referred to in order to illustrate press invasion of privacy were not what most parents—newly-literate or not—wanted their young daughters to peruse. If for no other reason, this consideration ensured that newspaper coverage of crime would pose ethical questions for many readers—and not just the bourgeoisie, but also working-class socialists and anarchists who often stated their severe stance on sexual morality in their writings.[43] Young girls themselves, however, as contemporaries recognized, profited from newspapers, taking what they wanted from them just as other readers did. In *New Grub Street* (1891), George Gissing referred to Amy's liking of "solid periodicals." She did not read Darwin but knew about his ideas: "She was becoming a typical woman of the new time, the woman who has developed concurrently with journalistic enterprise."[44] In Mary S. Hartman's study, *Victorian Murderesses*, a French observer is quoted as saying that "at age seventeen the French girl was plunged into hopeless ignorance 'unless she had borrowed some novels from her mother's maid.' And there were other means of access as well, such as the daily papers which contained serialized romances."[45] Perhaps not all female readers were as high-minded as Amy, yet conventional contemporary perceptions of ordinary newspaper readers—male or female—as primarily motivated to satisfy idle, misdirected, or merely prurient curiosity about other peoples' lives were unjust. They downplayed or altogether ignored aspirations for acquiring information and opportunities for exercising judgment to be met, in some measure, through exposure to the press.

DELETERIOUS CONSEQUENCES OF CRIME REPORTING

Everyone agreed that one of the gravest ethical problems raised by press coverage of crime lay in the universally accepted "fact" that crime stories led some susceptible readers to commit crimes themselves. "It is proven," wrote Kasabal in 1893, "that publicizing crimes in full detail incites others who are predisposed to commit crimes. That is why a famous crime which has interested and upset the public is so often followed by others which resemble it."[46] In the 1893 essay on the press cited earlier, F.F. Villegas agreed with Kasabal: "It is certain that such reports [of crimes] can twist the judgment of the impressionable multitudes, perhaps placing the freedom, honor, and even the lives of innocent people in jeopardy" ("Cierto que tales relatos pueden extraviar el juicio de las impresionables multitudes, quizá se comprometa la libertad, la honra, la vida, acaso de algún inocente"). In 1895, Baldomero Lois speculated that a predisposition to crime was not necessary. It was possible to commit a criminal act simply as a result of falling under the influence of a crime report in the newspaper. Persons quite innocent of criminal inclinations could thus be influenced by the press: "Excessive publicity," he wrote, "is the primordial cause of a multitude of misdemeanors and even crimes."[47]

Pedro Dorado Montero, the distinguished jurist and penologist, a professor of law at Salamanca at the turn of the century, agreed that the immense suggestive power of newspapers affected readers: "We are all susceptible in differing degrees to the power of the written word, and we are all given to imitation; but those who are most inclined to the latter, and those who most intensely experience the former are the inferior members of society, those whose personalities are less well-defined, those with least self-control and the greatest propensity to execute certain kinds of acts."[48] Some of these individuals required only the slightest of suggestions in order to act: "And that suggestion is often found in newspaper accounts and descriptions. How much blame—even if it was not incurred intentionally—must be ascribed to such reports whenever we find ourselves in the midst of a strange and alarming crime wave, such as these crimes of jealousy, murders committed by rejected lovers, or double suicides!"

As a follower of Darwin, Dorado believed that our animal origins, buried deep below more recent layers of civilized thoughts and feelings, cause us to respond sympathetically to descriptions of brutality: "When we least expect it, the man-beast rises up in each one of us, and we bow down before his bestial acts" ("Cuando menos lo pensamos resurge en cada uno de nosotros el hombre bestia, y a sus actos bestiales rendimos culto"). Newspapers awaken the beast within us, "By converting those criminal acts which lend themselves to it into material for a *feuilleton* novel of the type the public devours with feverish avidity [newspapers] contribute mightily to stoking the fires of our savage passions."[48] Dorado also concurred with other commentators who believed that some individuals wishing to stand out from the crowd committed crimes in order to figure in newspaper crime reports.

The Escorial case presented critics of detailed, dramatized crime reports with an instance of a further deplorable effect on readers. Dorado may not have known that at least one parent lost her reason as a result of reading about the child murdered at the Escorial: "An unfortunate mother of two small children, overly excited by the minute details in the papers concerning the terrible death of the child at El Escorial, has lost her mind. Terrified at the idea that her beloved children might suffer a fate like that of poor Pedrín, her mania consists in seeing El Chato in everyone who approaches her children and in crying out that he means to kill them."[49] In view of the pernicious effects of newspaper crime reports which he did know about, Dorado called upon the *Asociación de la Prensa* to recommend self-censorship and, if necessary, to stop the printing of dramatic, circumstantial accounts of crimes such as the one committed at the Escorial.

To an extent, some commercial papers and the reporters who worked for them did impose self-censorship even before Pedro Dorado proposed it as a solution to what he and other critics saw as the unacceptable consequences of crime reporting: intrusions into privacy; unrestricted access to sexual and other information; and the provision of models for potential criminals to imitate. Self-censorship, on this view, was justified since it aimed to shield the public and protect it from its own worst instincts and inclinations. Few commentators seem to have credited the public with other than primitive, immature responses to crime reporting. Kasabal was one of the few to point out that crime reports increased the public's awareness of social problems (inadequate housing, extreme poverty, child mendicancy and prostitution, etc.) and encouraged reflection on the criminal justice system. Salvador Canals, responding in *El Nacional* on 17 November, 1895 to the decision made by the *Tribunal Supremo* on the Escorial case, apparently agreed with that minority opinion. He observed that questions of justice were not represented nearly as forcefully and effectively in contemporary dramas, such as José

Echegaray's *El estigma*, as in real cases—presumably as reported by the press.

Certainly, many verdicts handed down in criminal trials in the 1890s furnished occasions for discussing specific problems of justice, the failings or successes of jurors and magistrates, and related matters. Public opinion, outraged by the verdict in the Escorial case, was especially vocal and widely commented on. Kasabal wrote in *La Ilustración Ibérica* (26 May, 1894) that, "Mothers, fathers, all honorable people have protested the jury's verdict, and for many days the inadequacy of the penalty in comparison to the enormity of the crime has been the sole subject of discussion in the bosom of the family as well as in places of public resort" ("Las madres, los padres, todas las personas honradas han protestado contra el veredicto del jurado, y durante muchos días no se ha hablado en el seno de las familias, ni en los sitios públicos, de otra cosa que de lo insignificante de la pena comparada con la enormidad del delito").

In addition to controversial actions taken by those within the justice system, from the outside, anarchist terrorism and changing social mores put that system to the test, and the results frequently divided public opinion. The following article illustrates the pressures put on the jury—a recently reinstituted part of the criminal justice system. In this case, a jury firmly ensconced in a rural, patriarchal society proved incapable of judging acts formerly acceptable in that society with different, modern criteria. The article, significantly entitled "A Very Benevolent Jury" ("Un jurado muy benévolo"), appeared in *La Época* on February 24, 1894:

> The trial for parricide brought against Fernando Segura of Valcarlos (Navarra) was held at the Court of Assizes of the Bajos Pirineos.
>
> On September 27, a boy found the body of Catalina Segura, oldest daughter of the accused, half buried in nearby uncultivated terrain. She had three serious wounds in the head produced by a heavy instrument.
>
> Catalina's father was the killer: the motive for the crime was the daughter's dishonor. She had given birth once before and found herself pregnant again.
>
> Fernando Segura declared before the court that he had intended to punish, not to kill her; that if he buried her body afterwards, it was to conceal her dishonor and his crime. he said that his wife was the one who helped him move their daughter's body.
>
> The jury found him not guilty, and the judge absolved Segura who was immediately set free.[50]

Reports of this kind raised grave doubts about jurors'—especially rural jurors'—willingness to bring in a guilty verdict for murder and thus had considerable impact on the public's view of the kind of justice meted out by the jury.

SCIENCE AND ANALYTIC THOUGHT IN THE PRESS

Readers drawn primarily to crime reports in newspapers undoubtedly glanced at other items just as readers interested above all in political and cultural news read accounts of the Escorial crime. Would an initial interest in crime stories have led the newly-literate to read on, thus expanding their mental horizons beyond the examples already touched on? And, if crime reports served as a hook to entice readers into reading material they would not otherwise have attempted, what did newspapers offer them? Writing in reference to mid-nineteenth-century Britain, Thomas Boyle claims that, "The news media began to occupy a more significant place in the spirit of the times. This 'low culture' of popular journalism began to bring to bear a radical intelligence on the same concerns which obsessed the 'high' culture of poetry, criticism, and science. Indeed, it is arguable that the newspapers provided much of the inspiration and subject matter for many of these more eminently `respectable' intellectual endeavors."[51] If it were a question of "inspiration" and "subject matter" alone, the same argument could be made for the Spanish press in the last decade of the nineteenth century, and the prospects for readers willing to be raised to a higher cultural level would appear to have been good. Nonetheless, contemporary foreign observers faulted Spanish journalists on two counts—their generally inadequate information and their lack of analysis.

Modern students of the socialist press, in particular, point to its failure to bring a "radical intelligence" to bear on the subject matter, i.e., to promote the powers of conceptualization in readers. All agree that throughout the 1890s the press and the editorial house controlled by the Socialist Party were unable to provide an effective forum for the dissemination of information and its analysis. Marie-Madeleine Compère summarizes some recent findings in this way:

> The party's active promotion of intellectual analysis amounted to little. A collection, begun in 1895, offered works of Marx and Engels in translation. The socialist papers provided little nourishment under the rubric of literary, scientific and cultural fare. The special annual number of the magazine *El Socialista,* which commenced publication in 1893 on the occasion of the May Day celebration, was exclusively devoted to cultural problems.[52]

El Pueblo, founded by Blasco Ibáñez in 1894, and intended to serve as a vehicle for his republican ideas, had two regular features: a commentary on current political developments, and a section on literature. The literary orientation he gave to his paper scanted his readers' scientific and intellectual education, although it may well have raised their cultural level—in the predominantly literary sense accorded the term "culture" at that time.[53] As for other republican papers in the nineties (*El País* and its rival, *El Ideal, El*

Progreso, *La Publicidad*, the weekly *Progreso*), José Álvarez Junco writes: "One has the impression that the real communication of knowledge and of the scientific mentality interested them less than the global reference to the world of science as guarantor of their political projects."[54] He also notes that *El País* began a section on "Ciencia moderna" in 1889 which did not appear regularly, while long articles on science were rare in that paper. The science section in *El Progreso* also appeared irregularly, and *La Publicidad* lacked such a section altogether. The weekly, *Progreso*, did have a more regular "Crónica científica."

If the socialist and republican press—at least in the cases cited—was relatively ineffective, the right was accused of actively discouraging the spread of scientific information, to judge from F.S.P.'s review of Flammarion's *What is the Sky*? (*¿Qué es el cielo*?), in *El Globo* of October 15, 1896. He praised the popularizers of science, while charging that partisans of reaction aimed to keep the masses ignorant. Wanting scientific knowledge to be the privilege of the few they managed to concentrate it, he wrote, in brightly illuminated foci of activity which stand out vividly against the background of dense clouds in which the rest of the nation lay submerged. The column entitled "Wanderer" in *El Imparcial*, was one of the few in the high-circulation press of the nineties to inform the newspaper-reading public of important scientific discoveries. But the information it dispersed often required correction. At one point the columnist, having recently learned that there were spots on the sun, concluded that it was sick and dying, and that the earth was in danger of falling ill with the same malady.[55]

Miguel de Unamuno used Wanderer as an emblem of the low level of general scientific culture in Spain: "It seems that the malady is getting worse and spreading. Every day, ignorance is more widespread and it is the worst of all kinds of ignorance—the kind that doesn't recognize itself for what it is, that of a presumptuous semi-science. And in the midst of all this, much denigration of French frivolity and negative criticism of the highly successful Larousse—almost the sole source of information some of our illustrious men possess. But what can we expect when those who criticize and find fault haven't gotten beyond Wanderer."[56] If the press generally provided inadequate scientific information and analysis to readers, evidence such as the remarks of Unamuno or those of the reviewer for *El Globo* indicates that it may not have been altogether due to lack of interest on the part of those readers.

NEWSPAPERS AND NOVELS

Many commentators believed that easily accessible newspaper crime narratives were supplanting novels to some extent in the nineties. Such a claim is difficult to document in relation to middle-class readers such as those spoofed in the cartoon described at the beginning of this chapter. José de Siles, for example, in an article called "Current News. A New Literary Genre" ("Actualidad. Un nuevo género literario"), was clearly referring to middle-class readers when he wrote that "If a book is well-edited with clearly readable print, smooth paper and good illustrations, it is acquired at best as if it were a piece of furniture, as if it were a precious object, a *bibelot* which may be set out to adorn a table or an *étagère*. It is bought like any other costly knick-knack. It is opened at odd moments, leafed through quickly and then closed without being read." It is difficult to gauge to what extent such remarks were motivated by the moralist's wish to castigate contemporary readers: "Nowadays the timely article, the humorous piece, is the literary work which is notably popular. There are many people who remember all of Taboada's articles, and yet, do not know so much as the titles of any of Galdós' novels."[57]

In 1894, journalists related the public's unchanged reading habits to the poor sales of Galdós's most recent novel. On January 15, 1894, Kasabal wrote in *La Época* that the "pueblo culto" was turning away from so-called "higher" literature. After consulting with representatives of two publishing houses, Guttenberg and Fe, he had to conclude that books were not being published, nor were those already published being sold. *Torquemada en la cruz*, the latest novel by Pérez Galdós'—one of the public's favorite authors—was, he wrote, piling up in stacks at bookstores for lack of purchasers. On January 30, 1894, Aurelio Ribalta wrote in *El Globo* that not only science, but also *belles lettres* were languishing in Spain for lack of public support: "Galdós, for example, has just published a novel which might as well have been thrown into a well since no one discusses or reads it. If this happens to Galdós, what will happen to the others?" ("Galdós, por ejemplo, acaba de publicar una novela, y cae en el público como en un pozo, sin ser discutida ni leída apenas; si a Galdós le pasa esto ¿qué les sucederá a los demás?"). In a review (*La Época* 9 March, 1895) of Emilia Pardo Bazán's recent articles on current literature in Spain, E. Gómez Baquero agreed with her claim that the novel had succumbed to the greater attraction of the press. And, in a frequently quoted passage from his response to Isidro Fernández Flórez' reception address at the *Real Academia Española* in 1898, Juan Valera claimed that in time newspapers might well stimulate an appetite for reading books, thus indicating that the primary reading matter for most people was still the press.[58] This remark may, of course, have been partially motivated by a desire to please the new member, who was a journalist. Four years later the possibility that newspapers were gaining on novels remained open: a survey conducted by *Nuestro Tiempo* inquired about the prospects for the novel's survival. The Spanish literati who responded (Unamuno and Pío Baroja, among others) did not agree with Jules Verne's prediction that the novel would eventually be supplanted by the newspaper—a prediction that had prompted the survey in the first place.[59]

Anecdotal information of the type provided above, even if it were supplemented by newspaper circulation figures and data on book sales, could not finally resolve questions about readership, respectively, of novels and newspapers. Books were often passed around to several readers while clubs and associations subscribed to newspapers which were also shared by a number of people.

What is clear is that newspaper readers then as now, in addition to more socially acceptable tastes and interests, also liked sensational copy, especially in the form of crime stories, and the press—for the usual commercial considerations—aimed to satisfy that preference. As Alfonso Pérez Nieva wrote in 1894, commenting on a proposal in Switzerland to limit crime reports to brief summaries: "The great press, as the high-circulation press is called in the jargon of the profession, is not about to sacrifice what guarantees sure results and the retention of thousands of readers, namely; satisfying the public's voracious appetite for puffed-up, hyperbolic and lugubrious reports."[60] Two years later, a reporter for *El Globo* (22 April, 1896) noted that educated people were fascinated by newspaper crime stories.[61] Even cultivated people, he wrote, preserve a childlike capacity to experience pleasure deliciously mixed with fear as they absorb every detail of a story about some horrible crime. Such views seem to acknowledge universal tastes that reach back into childhood and pre-literate times and, at the same time, to bemoan a drift toward a culture dominated by what was coming to be characterized as mass taste.

THE APPEAL OF CRIME NARRATIVES

How did contemporaries account for readers' perceived preference for newspaper crime narratives over "good" literature—a preference nearly everyone took for granted? In one way or another, many of the explanations offered speak of the desire for access to relatively unmediated reality. This desire was not limited to the masses nor was it satisfied strictly by crime reports. Toward the beginning of the century, in the "General Preface" to *Waverley*, Sir Walter Scott wrote that following a period of illness in early youth during which he had read fiction voraciously, he had turned away from it: "Familiar acquaintance with the specious miracles of fiction brought with it some degree of satiety, and I began, by degrees, to seek in histories, memoirs, voyages and travels, and the like, events nearly as wonderful as those which were the work of imagination, with the additional advantage that they were at least in a great measure true."[62] A few years later, the youthful Henri Frédéric Amiel, reflecting on the nature of newspapers, remarked on the advantage of unmediated representation which they offered: "*A newspaper is the drug-store of the soul*, it contains at one and the same time, drugs to calm us, tonics and stimulants. Another advantage: it leads us to what is natural, to the simple truth; for fidelity to the immediate impression is its first, its only rule."[63] Nearly half a century later, in response to Jules Huret's *Inquiry into Literary Evolution* (*Enquête sur l'évolution littéraire*), Joseph Carguel wrote: "We are, I think, on the eve of studying creatures and things directly, without transpositions of any kind. Memoirs will be the literature of the future."[64] And in Spain, J. Ortega Munilla in *Los Lunes de El Imparcial* (7 February 1892), discussed the abiding popularity of one of Spain's best-selling books in the nineteenth century, Pedro Antonio de Alarcón's 1860 *Diary of a Witness of the African War* (*Diario de un testigo de la guerra de Africa*). Ortega Munilla attributed the work's success to its seldom-achieved combination of good writing with first-hand observation of reality.

Many members of the general public clearly agreed with the value such representatives of the literati placed on historical reality and its direct, immediate representation. In an 1894 book intended for the instruction of prospective jurors, the author recalled the extraordinary impact of open trials when they were inaugurated in Spain in 1883.[65] Spectators witnessed real people, using the language real people used to describe important events and feelings. Attendance at trials provided a strong dose of reality which could be recreated to some degree, by reading newspaper reports on criminal proceedings. Those reports often featured journalists' transcriptions of the questioning of suspects and witnesses, dramatic face-to-face confrontations, and gripping summary statements delivered by both lawyers and accused.

One of the elements people evidently responded to in stories of real crimes was the role of chance. In "good" realistic fiction, chance and causality had to be presented convincingly. In real life—and in melodrama—there was no such requirement. Chance often figured as an important thematic element at the very beginning of a crime report—the corpse of the child, Pedro Bravo, in the Escorial case, was discovered in a remote area, though the odds were extremely high against its ever being found. Such events reported from real life satisfied the desire for fateful—possibly providential—interventions that realistic fiction tended to avoid.

In a piece entitled "Instant Exposures—Crime Reports" ("Instantáneas"—"Crónica negra") in *El Globo* (22 April 1896), A.O. reflected on the importance of chance in the public's reception of crime stories: "It has often been observed that one of the things that most vividly attracts people's attention and gives rise to public commentary, are the hair-raising accounts of those horrendous acts, discovered by chance, in which the anonymous victim of an anonymous killer appears." A. O. went on to describe such a discovery, deliberately—and most successfully—imitating the language of

Ponson du Terrail who, he claimed, provided the inspiration for such crime reports:

> In Leganés, between the insane asylum—a prison for bodies without souls, a palace of souls without reason—and the railroad station for Cáceres and Portugal whose proximity to the site of the crime leads one to imagine the macabre journey of an unidentified coffin: against this profoundly suggestive backdrop, chance, that implacable discoverer of the most deeply concealed mysteries, revealed in the depths of a well, floating in water the color of the waves of the river Lethe, the body of a mummified woman—a bloated naked corpse with blackened skin, and between her swollen lips her tongue, mute testimony to her wretched death by strangulation.[66]

What has come to be known as the "Rashomon Effect," familiar in fiction, was particularly compelling in crime reports. Individuals whose very lives might depend on whether their version of the event was believed put forward different versions. This "effect" generated considerable suspense as newspapers provided day by day coverage of the unfolding of new information. A case that received much press coverage in 1894 came to an end when a jury exonerated a man in Carabanchel who supposedly had kept his two sons—inexplicably missing when the father was apprehended—on bread and water in the cellar of his dwelling. The accused had denied any wrong-doing from the beginning, explaining that his sons were simply away for a short time and would confirm his account of events upon their return. Despite his explanation, over a period of several days the papers spun out a story of extreme paternal cruelty. An intricate plot to disinherit his heirs was invented. The whole story was based on nothing more—as it turned out—than circumstantial evidence: neighbors claimed to have heard cries of distress in the night. The pleasure this kind of story afforded readers no doubt lay in the freedom it gave them to construct their own versions of the truth or, if they wished, to believe the construction reporters put upon the few known facts. Such stories were only completely "written" when the cases involved were decided. When the Carabanchel case was resolved, a reporter for *La Epoca* (7 April 1894), blandly noted that it would be best for journalists not to trust their first impressions in some cases since they could easily be mistaken and perhaps cause harm to innocent people.

The appeal of many crime reports lay in the fact that, like fiction, they touched on universally moving themes and problems. As Helen Mac Gill Hughes observed: "The question 'What are human interest stories for?' will have essentially the same answer as 'What are novels for?'"[67] But news reports have an advantage over novels in several respects; for one, the very brevity and elliptical nature of some stories serve to excite the imaginations of readers. The following report, for example—laconic in its evocation of a grim domestic tragedy—was undoubtedly more haunting to some imaginations than a longer, more circumstantial fictional account might have been. It appeared in *El Correo* on April 6, 1896 and was entitled "A Repugnant Crime: A Husband Stabs His Wife and Flees" ("Crimen repugnante: Un marido puñala a su esposa y se da a la fuga"). The text read as follows:

> It appears that María Fernández called a doctor to examine her four daughters who were ill. He informed her that each girl had been brutally raped and was infected with one of the most insidious of the secret diseases. Wanting to know the identity of their assailant, María Fernández listened frozen with dread to her daughters' confession. She subsequently underwent an extremely violent scene with her husband who responded to the desolated mother's recriminations with an attempt to stab her. The court is seeing to the detention of the criminal.[68]

Kasabal offered an explanation of why people read crime reports in his regular column for *La Ilustración Ibérica* (2 February 1893), at the time when the Escorial case was breaking. He followed these remarks with instances of journalists' abuse of privacy:

> Spurred on by the desire to please its readers who seek not only information but also stories that will move them in the columns of newspapers, the daily press lends the most dramatic proportions to the least important happenings, adorning them with details and incident which border on the domain of the novel [...]. Conversations and dialogues with neighbors, with family members, with the injured—so long as they can articulate even one or two phrases—and with the prisoners, provided access to their cells is granted. Nothing escapes the reporter, who minutely describes the scene of the event and the clothes worn by those who figured in it as actors. He publicizes as much as he has been able to gather about them, their families, their past lives, their tastes and inclinations.
>
> Very interesting stories come out of all this and the public, which is exceedingly fond of them devours them, thereby exciting professional competition. This leads the worthy individuals who report on such events in fulfillment of their professional duties—despite their best intentions—to the most lamentable excesses.[69]

Once again Kasabal's objective account of why people read crime reports gave way to the obligatory reference—the pressures an insatiable public exerts on reporters merely trying to do their job.

In Chapter XV of his 1901 novel *Aventuras, inventos* y *mixtificaciones de Silvestre Paradox*, Pío Baroja satirized the late nineteenth-century's pronounced interest in crime stories. The theory his narrator offered to account for the vogue was that such stories appealed to bourgeois readers safely ensconced in their secure dwellings. More recently, Jack Katz has characterized crime narratives as "conservative genres for a conservative time. They mirror the public's paranoia over violent crime and reflect its hope that the social fabric, however badly rent, will mend itself." And, more closely echoing Baroja's insight, Katz writes, "Such is the aesthetic experience of murder—life-threatening violence as perceived by an involved, but secure, observer."[70] The increase in crime during the period of the Regency did set the conditions for the reaction which Katz suggests is possible on the part of the bourgeoisie—but the hope he referred to was not in evidence.[71]

In 1903, Pedro Dorado effectively summed up many of the ideas on this subject circulating during the last decade of the century. Limiting himself to remarks on the masses, Dorado noted that their interest in crime did not appear to stem from a desire to see justice done. If that were so, he wrote, people would not attempt to evade jury duty as most, in fact, did. It was the extraordinary nature of certain crimes that aroused interest in the masses—and here Dorado cited the crime at El Escorial as one of the three most compelling cases in recent years. Dorado believed that an interest in what is extraordinary is a sign of intellectual inferiority, an epistemological false step. Superior minds concentrate on what is ordinary and often repeated in order to adduce reliable information and form useful ideas. Unhealthy curiosity about what is unusual, a taste for thrills and morbid details, reveals moral and esthetic backwardness: it constitutes a kind of reversion to infantilism. In this connection, Dorado reminded his readers of the common person's indifference to "good" novels, "of analysis and documentation [...] which require mental effort" in favor of "novels and stories full of intrigue, with unusual happenings and scandalous plots, which are entertaining and excite emotion."[72]

Since the masses prefer what is unusual and highly dramatic, newspaper reporters capitalize on this preference by converting dramatic crimes into "novela[s] en acción" (195). Dorado provided some details on how reporters concocted such "novels." The word "concoct" aptly describes the process by which Dorado believed that facts were "spiced up," in order for them to be experienced as something rather like fiction. The experience of reading was similarly transformed metaphorically into an act of ingestion—a lower function nicely suited to the supposedly inferior esthetic sensibility of the mass consumer.

Dorado wrote that reporters "seasoned" (*aderezan*) their reports with all kinds of details, "stretched" them with the verbal equivalent of thickeners and then "served them up" to their readers (195). These metaphors were not, of course, original with Dorado. They turn up frequently in discussions of popular literature. In 1893, for example, two reporters used the same metaphors—concocting fiction-like narratives from crime reports, and dishing them up to readers—in order to emphasize the pernicious consequences: readers habituated to the diet provided them have, over the course of time, developed jaded palates which require ever more stimulating fare. Thus were blameless reporters forced to perpetuate this new and problematical mode of narrative reporting.[73]

What were the condiments thrown into the pot? Dorado wrote that reporters seasoned the "novela en acción" with all kinds of details, especially those pertaining to the protagonists. The inclusion of details, whether dramatic, humorous, horrifying, or scabrous, was often singled out as an especially effective technique that journalists used to transform crime reports into convincingly circumstantial fiction-like accounts. Often introduced under a heading like "Horrible details' ("Pormenores horribles"), such details offered a seemingly inexhaustible variety. A report filed in *La Epoca* on January 8, 1894, for example, related what happened after unknown assailants strangled D. Alejandro Bahín and his maid: "They carried their cynicism to such an extreme that once Sr. Bahín and his servant were dead, they ate up the stew which the latter had all prepared." Details such as this inserted into crime reports were undoubtedly as effective in particularizing and fixing an event or emotion in the reader's mind as were memorable, albeit more "literary" images in works of imaginative literature.[74]

Following earlier commentators, Dorado regarded Xavier de Montepin and Ponson du Terrail, popular authors of what Dorado called "novelas terroríficas," as models for crime reporters.[75] He wrote that journalists shared these novelists' aims and produced effects similar to theirs (195). The popular columnist, Kasabal, alluding in passing to the Escorial crime, had also spotted elements in newspaper crime stories which he characterized as terrorific without, however, specifying what those elements were: "The week's news has been unhappy: the child from El Escorial, the trial sessions for the crime of San Millán, the double executions in Mondonado—everything is hair-raising and terrorific, as in a novel by Anne Radcliffe, but even more gross and repugnant."[76]

The general term "terrorific" was typically used to refer to vivid, even revolting descriptions of acts of violence as well as to grotesque, macabre references to death and everything related to it—references designed to elicit the anguish and dread characteristic of Gothic novels. A reporter's circumstantial description of a woman caught by her husband *in flagrante*, trying to cut her own throat with a kitchen knife as her children looked on, was clearly thought of as terrorific. The description of the house of the supposed murderer at El Escorial as having been constructed with old coffin boards to which bits and tatters of funerary decoration still adhered, was not only terrorific but also securely within the tradition of the fearful Gothic castle, manse, or mysterious dwelling.

In their remarks on technique, neither Dorado nor other commentators on crime stories limited themselves to noting the most obvious elements—such as the inclusion of much supplementary detail, usually gruesome or repugnant—characteristic of the genre comprising the terrorific and the Gothic.

Several observers also remarked on the narrative style identified with the two French authors mentioned earlier and its appropriation by reporters. While worthwhile novels, Dorado observed, are novels of analysis and documentation, fast-paced narratives like Montepin's and Ponson du Terrail's do not pause for analysis or lengthy exposition. Suspense and plot twists draw the reader along, eliciting delight almost exclusively through an inventiveness traditionally considered attractive to the immature.[77] Reporters likewise maintained a fast pace, wrote short sentences and, in general, aimed for transparency of language.

Dorado and other like-minded observers, in effect, framed their discussion of mass reading taste in terms of the debate over the *roman romanesque* versus the highly-plotted novel—a debate which had originated in the early 1890s in France with a newspaper article by Marcel Prévost. What Prévost meant when he called for a return to the *roman romanesque* was, for the most part, imperfectly understood by the Spanish journalists and critics whose discussion of his ideas was conducted primarily in the press. In any case, the contrast between the *novela novelesca* on the one hand—which may be loosely defined as the novel of sentiment, character, poetry, or ideas—and, on the other, the novel with a complicated plot and *efectista* touches, served little useful purpose since the lines of demarcation between the two were so difficult to draw. Many novels consecrated by critics as important or even great, belonged wholly neither to one category nor the other. Moreover, those individuals who approved of the focus on finely-nuanced psychological drama in *Madame Bovary*, for example, were also capable of thrilling to the violent, melodramatic and terrorific ending of *The Idiot* or *The Kreutzer Sonata*. The *novela novelesca* discussion in Spain with its separation of novels and readers into the crude and the artful, the naive and the sophisticated, was not a literary controversy so much as a symptom of the uneasy awareness of the drift toward a culture no longer dominated by the traditional elite.[78]

The mostly bourgeois, liberal intellectuals whose comments on mass readers' taste for crime reporting have been reviewed here, made few serious attempts to understand the origins and implications of mass preferences. Critics like Leopoldo Alas, Pedro Dorado, Pompeyo Gener, Azorín, and Kasabal did contribute to a coherent definition of mass readers, representing them, as Anthony P. Cohen has put it, in terms of a "reified and/or emblematized culture."[79] The images employed to characterize the mass reading public cluster primarily around appetite and the act of eating. The appetite of the masses was depicted as insatiable, gross, undiscriminating, beastly, and as such it made claims on the commercial press which the press felt compelled to satisfy. Reporters for the commercial press served up "*platos groseros*" for the jaded palates of the public. In contrast to mass readers, the elite were by implication, self-controlled, moderate, refined and discriminating.

The role of intellectuals in defining and establishing boundaries between themselves and the masses may not have entailed conscious political goals in individual cases, but the symbols they constructed clearly proved persuasive and useful to those who did employ them for political purposes. The elite's representation of mass culture in the last decade of the nineteenth century had uses beyond "explaining" the disproportionate emphasis on crime reports in the press. It also provided ammunition to opponents of the newly-reinstituted jury system. The press's representation of the Escorial murder case illustrates aspects of the process by which the discrediting of the jury was eventually accomplished—to no small extent through reference to the images and symbols which intellectuals used in order to define the masses.

NOTES

1. The cartoon portrays the newsboy in a visored cap, his customers in top hats and bowlers. In a review of Fred Miller Robinson's *The Man In The Bowler Hat*, Oliver Reynolds quotes the author, for whom the bowler hat is "'a sign of modern times—that is to say, the time of the emerging and expanding middle classes.'" Reynolds continues: "Worn by labourer and banker alike, it is an example of the way dress-codes can cross class boundaries. An increasing uniformity of dress was, for some, merely another element in the reprehensible rise of the bourgeoisie" ("Melon Cocktail," *The Times Literary Supplement* {28 May 1993}:8). The apparent distinction made by the Spanish cartoonist between the upper-class (the wearers of top hats) and the middle-class (the bowler wearers) should perhaps allow for the possibility that the bowlers also represent some newly-literate members of the working class. If so, the cartoon is inclusive enough to accurately reflect the class make-up of readers in the 1890s. (Female readers of any class were, however, omitted by the cartoonist). For information on masculine fashion, especially bowlers and what they revealed about their owners during 1890s, see Augusto Martínez Olmedilla, *José Echegaray (El madrileño tres veces famoso) Su vida-su obra-su ambiente* (Madrid: Seaz, 1949), 181, and Juan Carlos Frías Fernández, "Niveles de vida, mentalidades colectivas y socialismo: los tipógrafos madrileños a finales del siglo XIX," *Hispania* (Madrid) 52/1 (1992):157–158.

2. "No parece aventurado afirmar, en todo caso, que la no modificación de las prácticas y principios iniciales hubiera conducido también, por otra via, a su estancamiento e ineficacia. Sin apoyo financiero público y con fondos exiguos, sin conexión con otras medidas de reforma social en las que la lectura constituyera un elemento más o una consecuencia, y con tales dosis de paternalismo o dirigismo en la determinación de las lecturas adecuadas o inadecuadas, la experiencia estaba abocada a su autocorrección o al fracaso." Antonio Viñao Frago, "A la cultura por la lectura. Las bibliotecas populares (1869–1885)," in *Clases populares, cultura, educación. Siglos XIX-XX. Coloquio Hispano-Francés* (Casa de Velázquez, Madrid, 15-17 junio de 1987), eds. Jean-Louis Guereña and Alejandre Tiana (Madrid:Casa de Velázquez UNED, 1989), 335.

3. "A partir de 1875 los intentos de renovación educativa se confunden con el *reqeneracionismo*. Pero los regeneracionistas son a la realidad capitalista española próxima a 1900 lo que los ilustrados a la realidad feudal de dos siglos antes: en absoluto cuestionan el orden económico establecido y aspiran a lo sumo a corregir el orden jurídico. Para ambos la educación resuelve los problemas sociales y rectifica las desigualdades. Entre tanto, las entidades oficiales ponen de manifiesto con su actuación que han optado, una vez mas, por arbitrar medios de control antes que de promoción. Sutil diferencia." *Clases populares, cultura, educación*, 94. See also Alejandro Tiana, "The Golden Decade of the University Extension in Spain (1898-1909): an interpretative essay," *Higher Education and Society. Historical Perspectives* (Salamanca: Universidad, 1985), 2:688-701; the same author's "La educacion popu-

lar para los institucionistas," *Manuel B. Cossío y la renovación pedagógica institucionista* (Madrid: Universidad Nacional de Educación a Distancia, 1987), 203–229; J.L. Guereña, "La projection sociale de l'Universitè à la fin du XIXe siècle: l'Extension Universitaire en Espagne," *Higher Education and Society*, 1:208–218. For descriptions of intellectuals' efforts to establish contact with the working class largely through the press, see Carlos Serrano, "Le parti socialiste espagnol et la culture (1890-1910)," *Clases populares, cultura, educación*, 457–466; María D. Gómez Molleda, *El socialismo español y los intelectuales-Cartas de líderes del movimiento obrero a Miguel de Unamuno* (Salamanca: Universidad, 1980). Paul Aubert's essay, "Culture et inculture dans l'Espagne de la Restauration: Un nouveau discours sur l'école (1909–1923)" in *Clases populares, cultura, educación*, 467–508, chronicles some significant changes in the attitudes of intellectuals toward the masses. The populist views taken by the poet, Antonio Machado, and by Miguel de Unamuno will be discussed below. See Demetrios Basdekis, "El populismo del primer Unamuno," *La crisis de Fin de Siglo: Ideología y literatura* (Barcelona: Editorial Ariel, 1975)—pp. 245–246, in particular, for Unamuno's views on Lope de Vega as "the individualized conscience of the Spanish people" ("conciencia individualizada del pueblo español").

4. See Jean-Louis Guereña, "Demande populaire d'éducation et réforme sociale," in *Clases populares, cultura, educación*, 117-126, for information on the *Comisión de Reformas Sociales*. A facsimile edition of the commission's reports appeared in 1985. See Santiago Carrillo, ed., *Reformas sociales. Información oral y escrita publicada de 1889 a 1893*, 5 vols. (Madrid: Ministerio de Trabajo y Seguridad Social, 1985). For statutes and rules of workers' associations, see Manuel Morales Muñoz, "Asociaciones obreras de instrucción en Málaga (1892–1919)," *Clases populares*, 404–405. Pere Solá's contribution to this volume,"Acerca del modelo asociativo de culturización popular," transcribes the goals (as written down in 1892) of the workers' association "Moderna Fraternidad," established in Mataró in 1879: "The idea that governed the formation of this society was solely and exclusively to propagate the culture and enlightenment necessary to young working class people in general; and in the process, by learning about and mutually sharing that knowledge which is indispensable to men and women—such as reading, writing, arithmetic, elements of mechanics, History, Human Geography—to raise the level of morality. And by counseling and helping each other in the economic crises which unfortunately abound in and embitter the life of workers—whether because of difficulties in one's line of work, or lack of work, or loss of health, or similar cases—to try to provide him or her, at such a time, with moments of pleasure and distraction. And by trying in a friendly fashion and with the appropriate cordiality, to help each other avoid directly or indirectly, the vices and pitfalls which follow upon and are inherent in frequenting cafes and gatherings and all kinds of houses or places of public diversion" ("La idea que presidió a la formación de esta sociedad fue única y exclusivamente propagar la cultura e ilustración necesaria que deben poseer los jóvenes de la clase obrera en general y al efecto, instruyéndose y difundiéndose mutuamente aquellos conocimientos indispensables al hombre, como son la lectura, la escritura, contaduría, elementos de mecánica, Historia, Geografía humana, elevar su moral; y aconsejándose y ayudándose en cualquier trance apurado que, por desgracia, abundan y amargan la vida del trabajador, ya por dificultaded en la respectiva profesión, ya por falta de trabajo o pérdida de salud, o casos análogos, procurarse al propio tiempo, ratos de solaz y distracción; y tratándose amigablemente con la debida cordialidad, afecto y respeto, evitar directa e indirectamente los vicios y escollos consecuentes e inherentes a la frecuentación de cafés y reuniones y toda clase de casas o parajes públicos de diversión") [399].

5. "¿Qué importa? ... el negocio no tiene entrañas!" From *La España Moderna* 49 (1893):204.

6. "El público inculto, que forma la mayoría, busca satisfacción a su curiosidad insana, y la prensa, que antes atiende al negocio que a la educación del público, satisface sus groseros apetitos proporcionándole platos fuertes.

Es el interés de empresa el que obliga al periódico a halagar al público, en vez de educarle, y el que obliga al periodista, por el régimen de fábrica a que se halla sujeto, a emplear las energías de su cerebro en la confección de platos que repugnan a su estómago y a su conciencia."

"Ni hay tampoco razón, sin pecar de notoria injusticia, para echar el sambenito sobre la masa indocta.

En el mismo número en que el *Heraldo* muestra tan justificados escrúpulos por tener que ocuparse en actualidad tan repugnante como el crimen de El Escorial, da cuenta de la denuncia presentada al Juzgado contra un jesuíta profesor de un colegio de niños, acusado del mismo asqueroso delito que hoy tiene al *Chato* encarcelado.

Parangone el *Heraldo* estos dos hechos, y verá que si el sentido moral se ha perdido en las clases inferiores de la sociedad, no habrá que ir a buscarle ciertamente en las que por su ilustración estaban más obligadas a dar razón de él."

7. "Ahora bien: ¿qué pide el rico en materia de producciones intelectuales? ¿La literatura seria? ¿La alta filosofía, o, en el arte de las producciones puras y severas, las altas creaciones morales? En modo alguno. La literatura divertida, los folletines, los cuentos [...]. He aquí por qué un fabricante de novelas folletinescas puede hacer una fortuna brillante y alcanzar lo que se llama una posición en el mundo, mientras que un sabio serio, así haya hecho los hermosos trabajos de Bopp o Lassen, no podría en modo alguno vivir del producto venal de sus obras."

8. "Prensa conservadora a finales del siglo XIX: *El Ancora*, de Mallorca," in *Metodología de la historia de la prensa española* (Madrid: Siglo XXI, 1982), 72-73.

9. For a cogent overview of theoretical formulations—Marxist, non-Marxist, cultural materialist—in regard to producers and consumers and relating specifically to the rise of the high-circulation press in Britain in the 1890s, see D.L. Le Mahieu, *A Culture for Democracy* (Oxford: Clarendon Press, 1988), 14–16.

10. The press's increasing dependence on advertising revenue in the eighties and nineties is dealt with briefly in María Cruz Seoane, *Historia del periodismo en España 2.El siglo XIX* (Madrid: Alianza, 1983), 291–292, and María del Carmen García Nieto, "La prensa diaria de Barcelona de 1895 a 1910," *Prensa y sociedad en España (1820-1936*), eds., Manuel Tuñon de Lara, Antonio Elorza and Manuel Pérez Ledesma (Madrid: Edicusa, 1975), 251. All histories of the nineteenth-century Spanish press note the connection between crime reporting and circulation figures. The prototypical case used to illustrate the link is known as the *Crimen de la calle de Fuencarral*, the robbery and murder of an elderly woman that took place in Madrid in 1888 and received wide coverage in the press. See, for example, Cruz Seoane, *Historia del periodismo en España*, 296–300; Henry F. Schulte, *The Spanish Press 1470-1966 Print, Power, and Politics* (Urbana, Chicago, London: University of Chicago Press, 1968), 214-215; Pedro Gómez Aparicio, *Historia del periodismo español* (Madrid: Editora Nacional, 1971), 545-566. For studies on the connection between crime reporting and revenue in the French press, see Georges O. Junosza-Zdrojewski, *Le Crime et la presse* (Jouve et Cie., Éditeurs, 1943), 208–212; for Britain, Steve Chibnall, *Law-and-Order News*: *An Analysis of Crime Reporting in the British Press* (London: Tavistock Publications, 1977). The section entitled "The Press" on pp. 241–258 of David Vincent's *Literature and Popular Culture* (Cambridge: Cambridge University Press, 1989), has an analysis of the increased importance of sales volume in the rise of the Sunday newspapers in Britain, and their appeal to a lower-middle-class readership. For the United States, see David Ray Papke, *Framing the Criminal. Crime, Cultural work and the loss of Critical Perspective 1830-1900* (Hamdon, Conn.: Archon Books, 1987), 54-74. On p.61 Papke notes that the 1874 kidnapping of four-year-old Charley Ross "became the first nineteenth-century kidnapping to attract major newspaper coverage." The following general studies of the Spanish press are not listed in the bibliography: Marc Jaryc, "Essai d'une bibliographie de l'histoire de la presse espagnole," *Bulletin du Comité Internationale des Sciences Historiques* 22 (1934); E. Fiestas and J.J. Sánchez Aranda, "Ensayo de bibliografía sobre historia del periodismo español," *Revista de Documentación de las Ciencias de la Información* VII (1983):81-197: N. González Ruiz, "Periodismo y literatura periodística en el siglo XIX," *Historia general de las literaturas hispánicas*, V (Barcelona:Editorial Vergara, 1969):148-183; Adolfo Perinat and María Isabel Marrades, *Mujer, prensa y sociedad en España 1800-1939* (Madrid:Centro de Investigaciones Sociológicas, 1980); *Prensa y sociedad en España (1820-1936)*. Eds. Manuel Tuñon de Lara, Antonio Elorza and Manuel Pérez Ledesma (Madrid: Edicusa, 1975); Marqués de Valdeiglesias, *Setenta años de periodismo. Memorias* (Madrid: Biblioteca Nueva, 1950-1952); Francisco Mateos Pérez, *Setenta y cinco años de periodismo* (Madrid: Ramón Velasco, 1923); José Luis Sastre, "*El magisterio español.*" *Un siglo de*

periodismo.(1867-1967) (Madrid: Editorial Magisterio Español, S. A., 1967); J. Timoteo Álvarez, *Restauración y prensa de masas* (Pamplona:EUNSA, 1981; Josep Francesc Valls, *Prensa y burguesía en el XIX español* (Barcelona: Anthropos, 1988); Jesús Timoteo Álvarez et al. *Historia de los medios de comunicación en España. Periodismo, imagen y publicidad (1900-1991)* (Barcelona: Ariel, 1989); Pierre Albert et al. *Historia de la prensa* (Madrid: Rialp, 1991). Specialized studies include: Luis Araujo-Costa, *Biografía de "La Época"* (Madrid: Libros y Revistas, 1946); Manuel Ortega y Gasset, "*El Imparcial*" *Biografía de un gran diario español* (Zaragoza: Librería general, 1956); Julio González Merino, *Monografía sobre "El País," diario republicano (1887-1920)* (Madrid: Escuela Oficial, 1964); Esteban Molist Pol, *El "Diario de Barcelona" (1792-1963). Su historia, sus hombres y su proyección pública* (Madrid: Editora Nacional, 1964); *Metodología de la historia de la prensa española.* Bernard Barrère et al. (Madrid: Siglo XXI, 1982); AA.VV., *Grandes periodistas olvidados* (Madrid: Fundación Banco Exterior, 1987).

11. See Jean-Louis Guereña, "Las estadísticas oficiales de la prensa," *Metodología de la historia de la prensa española*:101-107, for a discussion of the 1892 *Estadística de la prensa* in which newspapers were classified by the interests they represented, by región, and by circulation. See also J. -F.Botrel, "La iglesia católica y los medios de comunicación impresos en España de 1847 a 1917: doctrina y prácticas," *Metodología de la historia de la prensa española*:119-176. For the socialist and anarchist press, see V.M. Arbeloa's "La prensa obrera en España, 1869-1899," *Revista de Trabajo* 30 (1970):117-195, a useful listing and content analysis of periodicals.

12. The modern *El País Semanal* has a regular feature, "'Scriptóribus' Los Crímenes de 'El País Semanal,'" in which graphics containing clues to the solution of a case accompany a brief narrative that presents the essential facts of a crime. For the persistence of the "élement graphique" in most popular literature from the *aleluya* to the *novela por entregas* and the sensationalist press, see J.-F. Botrel, "Aspects de la littérature de colportage," *L'Infra-littérature en Espagne aux XIXe et XXe siècles* (Grenoble:Presses Universitaires de Grenoble, 1977), 114, note 9. Collections such as "La Sombra de Caín," published by *Ediciones Alba* attest to the enduring popularity of crime reports. Begun in 1983, its volumes (*El crimen de la calle de Fuencarral* by Lara Antonio, or *El otro crimen de la calle de Fuencarral* by Blanca Bertrand, among others), present slightly altered newspaper accounts with no notes or other scholarly apparatus.

13. "Las personas que transitaban ayer mañana por la glorieta de Santiago en Linares, vieron con asombro que un perro llevaba en la boca un niño recién nacido. La tierna criatura, que aun vivía, estaba medio devorada.

Un hombre que quiso ahuyentar al perro, tuvo que desistir de su propósito, porque el animal defendía encarnizadamente su presa.

Reunidos algunos hombres más, lograron rescatar al niño, del cual sólo quedaban la cabeza, la caja torácica y los pulmones.

Se supone que la criatura fue abandonada en el campo, donde los perros empezaron a comérsela.

La Guardia civil y la municipal buscan sin descanso a la madre desnaturalizda que tan cruelmente ha abandonado a su hijo."

14. "Cuando hace pocas semanas todo se volvía crímenes y recriminaciones, catástrofes provocadas y casuales, excitación malsana, juicios precipitados y afán de sensaciones fuertes, parecía que el orden intelectual, la pacífica literatura sobre todo, nada importaban al público, y que para España eran llegados aquellos tiempos que Max Nordau vaticina en su reciente libro *Degeneración*, en los cuales las letras han de ser despreciadas por cosa enfermiza, atávica e inútil."

15. "aficionando a la lectura a esa inmensa masa anónima que constituye el inapelable tribunal de la opinión, siempre arrebatada e impresionable, muchas veces injusto." From Juan Valero de Tornos, *España de Fin de Siglo* (Madrid: Establecimiento Tipográfico "Sucesores de Rivadeneyra," 1894), 166.

16. "Los datos que se refieren a la instrucción de la población de España son verdaderamente aterradores. Saben sólo leer.—Varones, 221.613.—Hembras, 380.392.—Total, 602.005.

Saben escribir.—Varones, 3.317.855. Hembras, 1.686.615.—Total, 5.004.470. No saben leer.—Varones. 5.067.098. Hembras, 6.878.773. Total, 11.945.871."

17. The statistics for 1900 are from Antonio Viñao Frago's "History of Literacy in Spain: Evolution, Traits, and Questions," *History of Education Quarterly* 30 (1990):584. See José A. Piqueras Arenas, "Educación popular y proceso revolucionario en España," *Clases populares, cultura, educación*, 78-79 for literacy statistics and the census. According to Harvey J. Graff, *The Legacies of Literacy. Continuities and Contradictions in Western Culture and Society* (Bloomington: Indiana University Press, 1987), 294, the middle range of European national literacy levels in 1900 was about 77 percent. France had an 80 percent literacy rate in 1901, although as François Furet and Jacques Ozouf point out in *Lire et écrire. L'alphabétisation des Français de Calvin à Jules Ferry* (Paris: Les Éditions de Minuit, 1977), 1:58, 16 percent of men and 24 percent of women over twenty years of age were illiterate—4,900,000 people out of a total population of 38,000,000. Graff has a brief but useful discussion of the press and literacy in France from mid-century to 1900 (pp.281-285), and provides similar information on England (p.333), but there is no coverage of Spain. A study conducted by the *Fundación para el Fomento de la Información Automatizada* (FUINCA), indicates that in 1993 "el porcentaje de lectores en España no llega al 60 percent"—not, however, because of illiteracy (*El País*, 26 April 1993:18). The study did not identify the reasons why 40 percent of the population does not currently read, but it is striking that this figure nearly corresponds to the percentage of Spaniards who could not read in 1900.

18. "los grupos lectores se concentraban en los núcleos urbanos y pertenecían a la burguesía—desde sus sectores más brillantes hasta los más deprimidos—o a grupos minoritarios del artesanado y los proletarios." And the subsequent quotation: "Pero tenemos que pensar también que la comunicación interpersonal o en microgrupos—lo que se contaba, lo que se leía en voz alta—, tan característica como medio de propagación de la literatura popular de tipo tradicional, tuvo que representar un papel importante en la transmisión de las informaciones y los contenidos de la novela de folletín. Y esta vía de comunicación es dificilmente mensurable." Leonardo Romero Tobar, *La novela popular española del siglo XIX* (Madrid; Fundación Juan March y Editorial Ariel, 1976), 118. See also J.-F. Botrel, "La novela por entregas: unidad de creación y consumo," in *Creación y público en la literatura española*, eds. J.-F. Botrel and S. Salaün (Madrid:Castalia, 1974), 132-136, where he identifies the newly-literate reader of *novelas por entreqas* as predominantly young, urban, and female. Recent literacy studies focus specifically on regional, class, age, and gender differences. See José A. Piqueras Arenas, "Educación popular y proceso revolucionario español," *Clases populares, cultura, educación*, 77-95; Antonio Viñao Frago, "History of Literacy in Spain: Evolution, Traits, and Questions," *History of Education Quarterly* 30 (1990):573-599. While José-Carlos Mainer in a 1974 essay remarked that information regarding the number and nature of the readers of *El Globo* or of a journal such as *Germinal*, is unavailable, in subsequent pages he characterized the reading matter of the oligarchy—the aristocracy and the upper bourgeoisie—as well as the "pequeña burguesía," providing lists of books and journals ("Literatura burguesa y pequeño-burguesa," in *Creación y público en la literatura española*, 172–173). In "Notas sobre la lectura obrera en España (1890-1930)," in *Teoría y práctica del movimiento obrero en España 1900-1936* (Valencia:Fernando Torres, ed., 1977), Mainer summarized some of the material on the reading matter editorial houses and periodicals aimed at workers which he had earlier presented in his book, *La edad de plata (1902-1939). Ensayo de interpretación de un proceso cultural* (Madrid: Cátedra, 1983), first published in 1974. In the 1977 essay he emphasized the importance of calendars and almanacs, demonstrably in great demand by workers. Finally, in summarizing the contents of the catalog of works available at the Ateneo Obrero de Barcelona in 1893, Mainer drew attention to the excellent collection of newspapers, including sixteen foreign publications (232-233). George Richard Esenwein, in *Anarchist Ideology and the Working-Class Movement in Spain, 1868-1898* (Berkeley:University of California Press, 1989), 124-133, emphasizes the importance workers placed on acquiring print culture whether directly, or indirectly through listening to readers. Esenwein notes the wide circulation of anarchist journals, newspapers and political tracts. Between 1885-1900, "no less than two dozen anarchist journals and newspapers were published" (125). See also Lily Litvak, *Musa libertaria. Arte, literatura y vida cultural del anarquismo español (1880-1913)* (Barcelona: Antoni Bosch, 1981), 439-440 where, under

the rubric "Prensa anarquista española utilizada (1880-1913)," there are 58 entries published between 1880 and 1900 alone. Harvey J. Graff's *The Legacies of Literacy*: 280ff, provides information on the reading matter of the newly-literate in France. See also James Smith Allen, *In the Public Eye: A History of Reading in Modern France, 1800-1940* (Princeton, N.J.: Princeton University Press, 1991). David Vincent, *Literacy and Popular Culture/ England 1750-1914*, 219-226, has a discussion of the reading available to that group in Britain.

19. "Cada uno de estos grupos es una cátedra donde se corrumpe el gusto y se alimentan las malas pasiones, e importaba disolverlos como a los focos de inmoralidad más disolventes." *La Ilustración Ibérica*, 11 February 1893:82. A group of Hispanists specializing in popular culture, has documented the unusually protracted coexistence in Spain of the oral with the written tradition in the collection of papers published in *L'Infra-littérature en Espagne aux XIXe-XXe siècles*. In the "Presentation," Jacques Maurice and Louis Urrutia explained the reasons for this phenomenon as follows: 1) the large number of illiterate people living in rural areas without access to libraries, clubs and other centers where reading rooms were typically provided; 2) the absence of a real industrial revolution and the tendency of a late industrialization—largely dependent on foreign capital—to accentuate the great differences and inequalities between sectors and regions of the nation, generally to the detriment of the rural masses; 3) the low number of buyers for the products of the print industry coupled with their low cultural level—an unfavorable market situation compounded by the struggle for middle-class buyers waged by the sellers of products from the dominant ideology against their republican, socialist and anarchist competitors. According to this analysis—which does not directly allude to the Church's role or to that of local or state government in advancing or retarding the interests of the rural poor—economic forces wholly beyond their control helped maintain large numbers of predominately poor, illiterate rural Spaniards within an oral tradition that only gradually gave way to change.

20. See J.-F. Botrel,"Aspects de la littérature de colportage en Espagne sous la Restauration," in *L'Infra-littérature en Espagne*, 109. In a later essay, "La Littérature du peuple dans l'Espagne contemporaine," in *Clases populares, cultura, educación*, 289, Botrel noted that a sizeable number of Spaniards went directly from an oral culture to an audio-visual one, and claimed that reading habits in twentieth-century Spain are less developed than in other European countries.

21. *Literacy and Popular Culture/ England 1750–1914*, 224. J.-F. Botrel in "La novela por entregas: unidad de creación y consumo" in *Creación y público en la literatura española*, 121, briefly discusses the transition of the newly-literate from an oral to a written tradition in connection with the kinds of graphics used to make that transition easier.

22. *Su único hijo* appeared in *El Liberal*, 5 July 1891. *Dulce y sabrosa* in *El Imparcial*, 8 June 1891. A selection from the second part of *Angel Guerra* had appeared earlier in *El Imparcial.*

23. Manuel Ortega y Gasset, "*El Imparcial.*" *Biografía de un gran periódico español* (Zaragoza: Librería general, 1956), 102. Although the serializations mentioned here may not have been successful with the general public, H.G. Wells's works were a staple of workers' libraries.

24. Romero Tobar, *La novela popular*, 204-205. José Alvarez Junco lists the *folletines* published in *El País* from 1888-1900 on p.360 of his "Racionalismo, romanticismo y moralismo en la cultura política republicana de comienzos de siglo," in *Clases populares, cultura, educación.* A surprising list for a republican paper, it excluded contemporaries like Zola and Ibsen in favor of French writers from the first half of the nineteenth century.

25. "una avalancha de cartas insultantes y amenazadoras." From M. Ortega y Gasset, "*El Imparcial*," 102.

26. "Quiso enmendar mi gusto y me dio a leer a Pereda. Era lectura lícita y la alternábamos con los folletines de Rocambole recibidos a escondidas. Diome más adelante *Pepita Jiménez*. Me aburrió." Manual Azaña, *El jardín de los frailes* (Madrid: Alianza, 1982), 14. When the students put on plays, they chose to perform the very popular Carlos Arniches: "We went along with the taste of the man in the street" ("Ibamos con el gusto callejero"), Azaña explained on p.64, lest anyone should think that Arniches represented their taste. (In *La Ilustración Ibérica y Artística* of April 7, 1894 Kasabal remarked that only the variety shows (*teatro por horas*) were drawing customers; "elegant" people were not going to the Teatro Español to see Galdós or

Echegaray.) Azaña's tastes developed along lines acceptable to the reigning cultural elite as he grew older. The tastes of other privileged young men of his class, according to Giner de los Ríos in a talk given in 1902, did not always evolve in that way: "Most of our students belong to the middle classes. They patronize the theatre, cafes, casinos; sometimes they attend the Ateneo, but seldom do they go out into the country. They go to bull-fights. They engage in no sports or physical exercise. They go on no trips or excursions. Apart from newspapers they read little, and that little usually consists of novels. They share in average measure the vices and virtues of the masculine population of our nation" ("La mayoría de nuestros estudiantes pertenece a las clases medias; hace mucha vida de teatro, de café, de casino; de Ateneo, a veces, casi ninguna de campo; va a los toros; nada de juegos ni ejercicios corporales; otro tanto de viajes y excursiones; aparte los periódicos, lee poco y esto principalmente novelas; suele tener en una proporción media, los vicios y virtudes de la masa masculina de nuestro pueblo." Qtd by José-Carlos Mainer, *La edad de plata (1902–1931. Ensayo de interpretación de un proceso cultural*, 90.

27. "Nada indica mejor el estado de un pueblo que la prensa." From J. Martínez Ruiz. *Anarquistas literarias* (Madrid: Librería de Fernando Fe, 1895), 47-48.

28. "Las novelas sangrientas, los dramas espeluznantes, lo mismo que los romances de ciego en que se narran mil crímenes, siguen aun privando. En el fondo, el pueblo pide siempre `¡más caballos!' la sangre le satisface y embriaga." From "La decadencia nacional," *Don Quijote*, 24 July 1896. Qtd by Iris Zavala in *Fin de Siglo: modernismo, 98 y bohemio* (Madrid: Cuadernos para el diálogo, 1974), 29.

29. "Esta institución de los periódicos, en una nación que hubiese estado enseñado a discurrir, habría sido muy provechosa: introducida de pronto, mecánicamente, inorgánicamente, en una nación semiafricana, rezagada de cuatro siglos, tenía que ser nociva por la misma ley que lo ha sido el Parlamento. Cerebros blandos y perezosos, sin fuerzas y sin disciplina, los que aprendían a leer, y leían (naturalmente, lo único que se ponía a su alcance todos los días y le hablaba de sus aficiones, crisis y pendencias políticas, corridas de toros, crímenes sensacionales, Lotería Nacional, escándalos y chismes de fuera o de dentro, etc.; la hoja del *periódico*), no tardaban en entregarse a ésta pasivamente abdicando en ella su facultad de pensar y acostumbrándose a no vivir sino de pensamiento hecho." From Costa's "Resumen de la información," in vol.I:216, of *Oligarquía y caciquismo como la forma actual de gobierno en España. Urgencia y modo de cambiarla* (Madrid; Ediciones de la Revista de Trabajo, 1975).

30. "'Con la relación minuciosa de estos procesos y la publicidad de los más horrendos crímenes, podrá saciarse la curiosidad morbosa de una sociedad enferma, pero no se consigue vigorizar el espíritu ni levantar la esperanza a más generosos y patrióticos ideales.'" And the passage which follows in the text: "'no se enmiendan los yerros pasados ni se hace una patria grande y vigorosa; pero en cambio se entretiene a las masas y se prepara el terreno para que arraigue y frutifique la neurosis nacional. Y váyase lo uno por lo otro.'"

31. "'Et c'est pourtant cette question qui constitue la plus grande partie du problème d'une nouvelle littérature en tant qu'expression d'un renouveau intellectuel et moral: car c'est seulement à partir des lecteurs de roman-feuilletons que l'on peut selectionner le public suffisant et nécessaire pour créer la base culturelle d'une nouvelle littérature.'" *Les Productions populaires en Espagne. 1850–1920* (Paris:Éditions du Centre Nationale de la Recherche Scientifique, 1986), 367. Salaün describes the infra-culture as representing "the cultural patrimony of a community, with its treasures, its antiquities, its arsenal of forms and of 'themes' (of functions), its panoply of tools—verbal, linguistic, rhetorical, esthetic" ("*patrimoine* culturel d'une communauté, avec ses trésors, ses antiquités, son arsenal de formes et de `thèmes' (des fonctions), sa panoplie d'outils verbaux, langagiers, rhétoriques, esthétiques)."

32. "coplas de ciegos [...] los pliegos de cordel y [...] los novelones de a cuartillo de real la entrega que sirven de pasto aun a los que no saben leer y los oyen [...]." From *En torno al casticismo* (Buenos Aires: Espasa-Calpe, 1952), 141. (Orig. publ. 1895.) Unamuno's project is summarized on p. 43: "I should like to suggest to the reader as forcefully as possible the idea that quickening the life of the mass of the people who are scattered and regionalized, must go hand in hand with opening wide the windows to Europe so that the fatherland may come into being. We must europeanize ourselves and immerse ourselves in the people. The people, the "deep" people, the people living beneath the level of history, constitute the mass [literally, the

"dough"] essential and basic to all lineages, the people are the protoplasmic matter that informs all the generations; what is differentiating and exclusionary are historical classes and institutions. And the latter can only rejuvenate themselves by plunging into the former." ("Quisiera sugerir con toda fuerza al lector la idea de que el despertar de la vida de la muchedumbre difusa y de las regiones tiene que ir de par y enlazado con el abrir de par en par las ventanas al campo europeo para que se cree la patria. Tenemos que europeizarnos y chapuzarnos en el pueblo. El pueblo, el hondo pueblo, el que vive bajo la historia, es la masa común a todas las castas, es su materia protoplásmica; lo diferenciante y excluyente son las clases e instituciones históricas. Y estas sólo se remozan zambulléndose en aquél."

33. "Hay que buscar la causa de nuestro atraso en otra parte: en el estado intelectual de la masa; en esa infancia del pueblo, sencillo y manso o bravío, ilustrado y comsciente nunca." And the following citation: "Con el alma estremecida, con el espíritu sediento de cultura y grandeza, nos quedamos atados a nuestra roca, soñando que la gente española despierta al fin y que, olvidando divisiones, se resuelve a la magna, pero relativamente fácil tarea de instaurarlo todo en la patria." Qdt from her response to Joaquín Costa in the latter's *Oligarquía y caciquismo*, 2:296, 298.

34. "The History of Literacy in Spain: Evolution, Traits and Questions," 595. Nearly every essay in *Clases populares, cultura, educación* provides information on popular education. In "Le parti socialiste espagnole et la culture (1890-1910)," 466, Carlos Serrano calls for studies of "sociabilité populaire" focusing on the taverns where workers spent much of their time. In this connection, he claims that the workers' libraries at the end of the nineteenth century only answered the needs of a minority within the working class.

35. "No hay ya puerta por entre cuyas rendijas no mire el ojo inquisitivo del periodista, no hay dolor que no profane, ni cosa alguna pública o privada que no cuente a la indiferente y poco piadosa multitud. ¡Triste cosa es pensar que nuestra fama, nuestro crédito, nuestras desgracias se han de vender por unos cuantos céntimos en la plaza pública!" From "La prensa periódica," 204.

36. "—Qué quiere usted, don Manuel. La fiera nos pide más carne, más noticias, y no hay otro remedio que dárselas—dijo el primero de los dos, vivaracho y simpático.

—Agotado tenemos ya el filón—indicó el segundo—; pero como es necesario servir al público diariamente, ayer le di yo reseña exacta de lo que come Nazarín, y una interesante noticia de los malos partos que tuvo su madre.

—Pero hijos míos—dijo Flórez, con más bondad que enojo—, vuestra información nos va a volver locos a todos. Habéis dicho mil cosas inconvenientes, otras que no le importan a nadie [...]

—Servimos al público.

—Pero ¿no sería mejor que le serviráis dirigiéndole, que dejándoos arrastrar por su novelería caprichosa y malsana?

—¡Ah don Manuel! No somos nosotros, pobres reporteros, los que encendemos la hoguera. Nos mandan llevar cuanto combustible se encuentra, troncos bien secos si los hay; si no, leña verde, para que estalle, y hasta paja, si no encontramos otra cosa." *Obras Completas* (Madrid:Aguilar, 1950), 5:1809b-1810a.

37. In 1893 Varela, son of doña Luciana, victim of the *crimen de la calle de Fuencarral*, was living with a woman who fell to her death from their balcony. Varela became a suspect in the case and was put in the *Cárcel-Modelo*. *La Correspondencia de España*, 7 March 1893, ran a piece called "Crimen de la Calle de Carretas" (site of the new alleged crime) in which the public was informed of how much Varela paid for his cell 'six *reales* per day" ("seis reales diarios"), and what he ate the day before: "two sole filets, one serving of veal with green peas, olives, pastries, and a half bottle of wine, which is all that the rules permit" ("dos lenguados, una ración de ternera con guisantes, aceitunas, pastas y medio cuartillo de vino, que es lo más que tolera el reglamento." In the section entitled "A Little of Everything" ("De todo un poco") from *Madrid Cómico*, 15 May 1894, Luis Taboada made fun of reports on Julián García's eating habits: "May God repay the newspapers; thanks to them we receive as many reports as we could possibly need regarding the *Chato*'s health, which is good, thanks be to God [...] he eats up two stews, a sausage, a potato omelette and other trifles at a single sitting. After he eats, he rests, and there you have him like clock-work until the afternoon when he eats another two

stews, etc., provided there is someone to pay for them" ("Dios se lo pague a los periódicos; merced a ellos recibimos cuantos informes podíamos necesitar acerca de la salud del *Chato*, que es buena, a Dios gracias [...] se come dos cocidos, un chorizo, una tortilla y otras frioleras, de una sola sentada. Después de comer se echa a descansar, y ya le tienen ustedes como un reloj hasta la tarde, en que volvería a comerse otros dos cocidos, etc., si hubiese quien se los pagara.")

38. *El País*, 9 March 1893, ran an article on the trial of Fray Eulogio Aguirre, accused of having abused Rafaela Roldán, a six-year-old girl. The paper noted that the monastery in which the friar resided had been stoned by irate neighbors. *El Correo*, 10 March 1896, in the section, "Tribunales," noted that a jury had found Joaquín Coderch guilty of sexual molestation (*abusos deshonestos*) against the person of Josefa Fernández Marino, age six. The court of law (*tribunal de derecho*) imposed a sentence of three years on this individual who was a five-time offender.

39. Two examples follow, both from *El Correo*. First, from Sevilla on July 14, 1895: "An individual tried to abuse a nine-year-old girl at Ruiseñor street by getting her drunk on brandy. A neighbor woman called the police, and the individual was taken to jail, followed by people who wanted to lynch him." ("Embriagándola con aguardiente, quiso abusar un sujeto, en la calle de Ruiseñor, de una niña de nueve años. Una vecina llamó a la policía, y el sujeto fue a la cárcel, queriéndole lynchar la gente cuando lo llevaban preso"). Also from *El Correo*, 22 July 1895: "Three youths ranging in age from eighteen to twenty years were detained at the Mediodía station for having abused a boy of twelve. All three have gone to jail." ("En la estación del Mediodía han sido detenidos tres mozalbetes de diez y ocho a veinte años, por haber abusado de un niño de doce. Los tres han ingresado en la cárcel"). This brief notice was entitled, "What Society Has Come To!" ("¡Cómo está la sociedad!").

40. "Yo confieso que no he podido leer sin emoción lo que el marido de la mujer herida en la calle de San José ha dicho a uno de mis compañeros que le interrogaba acerca de su conducta futura si su mujer salía del horrible trance en que se hallaba.

—Yo—, contestó aquel desgraciado,—quizá la perdonaría, porque la he querido mucho; pero después de lo que han dicho los periódicos es imposible que vuelva a reunirme con ella."

41. "En el triste caso a que me refiero no puede estar en manera alguna la compasión al lado del autor del crimen y de su familia, que no inspira las menores simpatías; pero creo que nadie tiene el derecho de atormentar al que ha caído bajo el poder de la justicia, que le hará expiar con arreglo a la ley su horrible crimen." So far as I can judge, Leopoldo Alas was the only other person who referred to the press's ill treatment of Julián García. On January 5, 1895 in *La Ilustración Ibérica*, 10, he wrote in connection with the unfavorable reviews Galdós had received for *Los condenados*, that: "the author of *Realidad* has been treated by some people only a little less cruelly than was the Chato of the famous trial at El Escorial" ("se ha tratado por algunos al autor de *Realidad* poco menos cruelmente que al Chato del famoso proceso del Escorial").

42. In his May 15, 1894 column for *Madrid Cómico*, Luis Taboada spoofed the "personas finas" whose tastes for scabrous details provided by public trials had to be satisfied in the Escorial case with what the press chose to print. If the trial were public, wrote Taboada, " by now many hundreds of us refined people would be at El Escorial in order to find out all the details about the intimate lives of the *Chato*'s sisters [...] but we have to content ourselves with what the press chooses to tell us, and God only knows what juicy items it has kept under wraps" ("a estas horas estaríamos en El Escorial muchos cientos de personas finas para enterarnos de todos los detalles referentes a la vida íntima de las hermanas del *Chato* [...] pero hay que conformarse con lo que quiera decirnos la prensa, y sabe Dios las cosas sabrosas que ésta se habrá callado"). "Refined" people, especially women, were often singled out as being assiduous spectators at criminal trials in nineteenth-century Spain. On February 6, 1895, for example, *El Día* reported on a *Tribunal Supremo* session in which the court was considering an appeal brought by Julián García's lawyer. The reporter noted, tongue in cheek, that among the spectators, "were representatives of the beautiful sex fond of studies pertaining to religion and morality" ("tenía representación el bello sexo aficionado a estudios de religión y moral").

43. Jacques Maurice in "Remarques sur la poésie dans les journeaux anarchistes espagnols a la fin du XIXe siècle," *L'Infra-littérature en Espagne*, 125, alluded to anarchist parents' concern with preserving the innocence of their daughters. See also Pere Solá, "Acerca del modelo

asociativo de culturización popular de la Restauración," in *Clases populares, cultura, educación*, 398–399, on the importance ascribed to "automoderación" with respect to gambling, drinking, and related matters in workers' centers, societies, and associations.

44. *New Grub Street* (Boston: Houghton Mifflin Company, 1962), 298.

45. Mary S. Hartman. *Victorian Murderesses: a True History of Thirteen Respectable French and English Women Accused of Unspeakable Crimes* (New York:Schocken Book, 1977), 272, note 15. References to the liberating effects of the press on women in Spain are uncommon while its disruptive effects on unsophisticated female readers are frequently noted—newspaper reading by the latter group undermined authority. In her 1882 novel about female tobacco workers (*cigarreras*) in Galicia, Emilia Pardo Bazán emphasized the role of newspapers in fanning their republican ardor. The factory owners reacted by prohibiting the women from reading them in the workplace (*La tribuna. Obras Completas* (Madrid:Aguilar, 1956), 2:147-148). Javier de Burgos spoofed the supposed consequences of lower-class women's reading of newspapers in his zarzuela of 1896, *Las mujeres*—it threatened male dominance.

46. *La Ilustración Ibérica*, 1 April 1893:194. Following the publicity surrounding the Escorial crime there were indeed reports of other sexual abuse cases involving young boys typically entitled "Otro crimen de El Escorial," or "Otro Chato." The reality of "copy-cat" crimes was unquestioned. In 1893 the *Revista de Legislación y Jurisprudencia* 83 (1893):622–624, published a translation of an article by Paul Aubry—author of *La Contagion du meurtre: Étude d'antropologie criminelle* (1888)—in which Aubry asserted that detailed press accounts of crimes lead people to commit crimes. At a time when terrorism was in the news, Aubry added that workers, who lived in a milieu characterized by alcohol abuse, were especially likely to be aroused to violence when exposed to reports of terrorist attacks. Even responsible people, those who live in a state of equilibrium, are affected by crime reports. But as for evil individuals (*malos*): "In the streets, it is not possible to escape this source of suggestion. Much more dangerous than the suggestiveness of pornographic images, they pursue us everywhere. Once an evil individual is affected by the idea of homicide, habituated, so to speak, to the sight of blood and to the emotion of viewing a corpse, and is in possession of knowledge as to the easiest way to get rid of an enemy, he will not hesitate for an instant, when the occasion presents itself, to commit one of these crimes called crimes of passion, or of whatever kind it may be" ("No es posible escapar en la calle a esta sugestión, mucho más peligrosa que la de las imágenes pornográficas; por todas partes nos persigue. Una vez penetrado el individuo malo de la idea del homicidio, habituado, por decirlo así, a la vista de la sangre y a la emoción del cadáver, y conocedor de la manera más fácil de desembarazarse de un enemigo, no titubeará un instante, cuando la ocasión se le presente, en cometer uno de estos delitos llamados pasionales o de cualquier otra clase" ("De la influencia contagiosa de la publicidad de los hechos criminales":623). A review by S. of the second Spanish edition of Aubry's book appeared in the *Revista de Legislación y Jurisprudencia* 84 (1894):425. The reviewer noted that Aubry's ideas on the contagion of murder as a result of the publicity surrounding homicides were widely accepted. Aubry's solution to the problems presented by press coverage of crime was to limit such coverage to the bare minimum needed to inform the public of the occurrence of a homicide, its victim or victims, the outcome of a subsequent trial, etc.

47. "La excesiva publicidad es causa primordial de multitud de delitos y aun de crímenes." Baldomero Lois and E. Alonso y Orera. *Páginas de actualidad* (Madrid: Imprenta de Enrique F. de Rojas, 1895), 1:181.

48. The first passage: "Todos padecemos, aunque en grado distinto, la superstición de la letra de molde, y todos somos dados a la imitación; pero los más inclinados a ésta y los que más intensamente sufren aquélla son los inferiores, los de personalidad menos acentuada, los de menor auto inhibición y más propensos a ejecutar determinado género de acciones." The second passage: "Y esa sugestión la encuentra muy a menudo en los relatos y descripciones de los periódicos. ¡Cuánta culpa, pocas veces directamente voluntaria, claro está, no debe atribuirse a estos, siempre que nos encontramos con una repetición extraña y alarmante, con una de esas *razzie* de crímenes por celos, de amantes homicidas por haber sido desdeñados, de suicidios en pareja!" The third passage: "Convirtiendo los delitos que se prestan a ello en asunto de novela folletinesca, de las que el pueblo devora con febril avidez, contribuyen maravillosa-

mente a mantener vivo y en tensión fortísima el fuego de nuestras pasiones salvajes." "La psicología popular ante los crímenes llamativos," *La Lectura* (1903):189–200. The passages quoted are from p.199 of the essay.

49. "Una infeliz madre de dos niños pequeños, excitada por los minuciosos detalles que publican los periódicos acerca de la desgraciada muerte del niño del Escorial, ha perdido la razón, aterrada ante la idea de que los pedazos queridos de su alma pudieran sufrir igual suerte que el desgraciado Pedrín. Su manía es ver al Chato en todos los que se acercan a sus hijos y gritar aterrada que se los quieren matar." Kasabal in *La Ilustración Ibérica*, 1 April 1893:194. The unnamed mother mentioned above illustrated the argument made by the reporter for *El Heraldo* on April 6, 1893 to the effect that newspaper crime reports could have a real effect on people: "there you have the case of the woman driven mad by the fear that her children would be sexually attacked and murdered like the boy at El Escorial" ("ahí está el hecho de esa mujer dementada por el temor de que sus hijos fueran estrupados y asesinados como el niño de El Escorial"). The point he wanted to make was that newspapers might have such an effect, "But the novel? What novels would the *Chato* or the *Carabanchel* have had at the head of their beds? What drama could have served to pervert the killers of Albalate or the murderers responsible for the Fuencarral crime? What maleficent work of literature could have caused the conscience of Vásquez Varela to slacken? ("¿Pero la novela? ¿Qué novelas tendrían a la cabecera de su cama el *Chato* o el *Carabanchel*? ¿Con qué drama se habrán pervertido los asesinos de Albalate o los asesinos de la calle del Ferrocarril? ¿Qué literatura maléfica habrá relajado la conciencia de Vázquez Varela?"). The reporter did not explain why imaginative fiction, unlike crime reports, did not lead to pernicious effects. Meanwhile, on August 25, 1895 in *El Liberal*, José de la Loma denied that mothers were afraid—as was rumored—to take their children to El Escorial for a summer holiday. All references to the reactions of mothers to the Escorial crime stressed fear to the exclusion of all other responses.

50. "Ante el jurado se ha visto en el Tribunal de los Assises de los Bajos Pirineos, la causa instruída por parricidio contra Fernando Segura, natural de Valcarlos (Navarra).

El día 27 de Septiembre un niño encontró, medio enterrado en un monte cercano, el cadáver de Catalina Segura, hija mayor del acusado, que presentaba tres heridas graves en la cabeza, producidas con instrumento contundente.

El matador fue el padre de Catalina, el móvil del crimen la deshonra de la hija de Fernando Segura, que ya había dado a luz, y nuevamente se hallaba en cinta [sic].

Ante el Tribunal ha declarado que no quiso matarla, sino castigarla; que si después la enterró fue para ocultar su deshonra y su crimen, y que su mujer fue quien le ayudó a transportar el cadáver de su hija.

El Jurado dictó veredicto de inculpabilidad, y el Tribunal de derecho absolvió a Segura, que inmediatamente fue puesto en libertad."

51. *Black Swine in the Sewers of Hampstead* (New York: Viking Penguin, 1989), 60.

52. *Annales:Économies, sociétés, civilisations* 46/5 (septembre-octobre 1991):1172. "L'activité proprement intellectuelle du parti se réduit à peu. Une collection éditoriale, créé en 1895, diffuse en traduction des ouvrages de Marx et d'Engels. Les journaux socialistes alimentent avec parsimonie des rubriques à partir de 1893 à caractère littéraire, scientifique et culturel. Le número spécial annuel de la revue *El Socialista*, publié à l'occasion du premier mai, est exclusivement consacré aux problèmes culturels." In one of the essays, "Le parti socialiste espagnol et la culture (1890-1910)," in the collection under review (*Clase populares, cultura, educación*), Carlos Serrano writes: "In the final analysis, everything indicates that during the first ten years, at least, of its existence, the Spanish Socialist Party had enough to do in diffusing the rudimentary doctrinal knowledge of which the small groups of its first militants had need, without wanting or being able to launch itself into more complex intellectual adventures, and not until about 1900 did it begin to expand its cultural activities" ("Au bout du compte, tout montre que pendant les dix premières années de son existence au moins, le parti socialiste espagnol eut assez à faire en diffusant les rudiments de doctrine dont avaient besoin les noyaux réduits de ses premiers militants, sans vouloir ou sans pouvoir se lancer dans des aventures intellectuelles plus complexes, et ce n'est que vers 1900 qu'il commence à élargir ses activités culturelles"[460]). Gérard Brey's article, "Ideología y acontecimiento en la poesía de un periódico obrero de Cadiz: El proletario" (1902-1903)" in *Metodología de la historia de la*

prensa española, noted, however, that in the newspaper he studied, "'theoretical' articles, of a more or less Utopian character, occupy much more space than concrete news on the workers' movement" ("los artículos 'teóricos,' de carácter más o menos utópico, ocupan una superficie mucho más importante que las noticias concretas sobre el movimiento obrero" [57]). He speculated that this may have been so because there was little hope that the strikes occupying the news would be of much benefit to workers. He also notes that other anarchist papers, such as *Tierra y Libertad* in Madrid, gave more space to reporting events.

53. J.L. Roca León in *Vicente Blasco Ibáñez* (Valencia: Ediciones Prometeo, 1967), referred approvingly to the literary nature of Blasco's paper: "The literary orientation that the director of *El Pueblo* gives to his publication shows that he is not only a political man but also one of the literati. Not a day goes by in which a story does not appear next to a political article or a piece of local news" ("Que el director de *El Pueblo* no es sólo un político, sino un literato, lo demuestra la orientación literaria que da a su publicación. No hay día en que junto al artículo político, a las noticias locales, no aparezca un cuento" [135]). There were also articles on music. Concepción Iglesias in *Blasco Ibáñez. Un novelista para el mundo* (Spain: Silex, 1985), described the content of the paper: "There are two fixed sections in the paper: 'Today's News,' commentaries on current political affairs, written by Blasco Ibáñez himself, and another entitled 'The Story of the Day,' which was of literary interest" ("En el periódico hay dos secciones fijas: una con comentarios de actualidad política—'Lo del día'—, de la que se ocupa Blasco Ibáñez personalmente, y una segunda de interés literario, titulada 'El cuento del día'" [76,77]).

54. "Da la impresión de que la extensión real de los conocimientos y la mentalidad científica les interesa menos que la referencia global al mundo de la ciencia como garante del proyecto político." From p.356 of "Racionalismo, romanticismo y moralismo en la cultura política republicana de comienzos de siglo" in *Clases populares, cultura, educación.*

55. A writer for *El Globo*, August 29 1891, in an article called "La ciencia tratada por Wanderer," noted that Wanderer had been corrected on different occasions in *El Heraldo de Madrid*, in *El Resumen*, and in *La Justicia*: "Today, unfortunately, it's our turn to take on the thankless task of refuting the errors of Wanderer" ("Hoy, por desgracia, nos toca a nosotros el turno en la ingrata tarea de refutar los errores de Wanderer." Manuel Ortega y Gasset in "*El Imparcial." Biografía de un gran periódico español*, 119, described Wanderer, whose name was Manuel Alhama Montes: "the creator of the section in the paper called 'Around the World,' an amusing showcase of scientific curiosities, he in turn created in Spain the genre which deals with surprising novelties in the realm of material progress, and he naturally went on to include all the unusual things on earth, in the sea, and in the air; that is to say that he infused into the great public the spirit of Jules Verne whose fascinating Utopias were converted one by one, into real advances" ("creador en el periódico de la sección, 'Alrededor del Mundo,' divertido muestrario de curiosidades científicas, creó a su vez en España el género de la novedad sorprendente en el terreno del progreso material y acogió con natural asociación las rarezas todas de tierra, mar y aire; es decir que incorporó al gran público el espíritu de Julio Verne, cuyas utopías fascinadoras convirtiéronse, punto por punto, en positivos adelantos"). Whatever may be said of Wanderer's shortcomings, the relative paucity of scientific material published in Spain at the time made it all the more important that the spirit and, even better, the works of Jules Verne be made available to Spaniards. See Rubén Benítez, "La novela científica en España: Ramón Cajal [sic] y el Conde de Jimeno," *Revista de Estudios Hispánicos* Ríos Piedras, Puerto Rico VI (1979):26, for Verne's decisive influence on Spain's most distinguished scientist. Cajal's speech before the *Academia de Ciencias Exactas, Físicas y Naturales* on December 5, 1897, entitled *Reglas y Consejos sobre investigación científica*, and later published as *Los tónicos de la voluntad*, spelled out what he saw as the deficiencies of Spanish culture specifically as they affected the study of science.

56. "Y el mal parece que se agrava y cunde; es cada día mayor la ignorancia y, la peor de todas, la que se ignora a sí misma, la de la semiciencia presumida. Y a todo esto, mucho denigrar la frivolidad francesa y poner por los suelos al utilísimo Larouse [sic], fuente casi única de información de algunos de nuestros conspicuos. ¡Y gracias!, porque los que los critican y zahieren no han pasado de Wanderer." *En torno al casticismo* :138.

57. "El libro si está bien editado, con impresión clara, satinado papel y bonitos grabados, es adquirido, a lo sumo, como un mueble, como un objeto precioso, como un *bibelot* que se coloca

para adorno de una mesa, o en una *étagère*. Se compra cual chuchería de lujo. Se abre a ratos perdidos, se hojea rápidamente y se cierra sin leerlo." The second passage quoted: "Hoy la crónica, el artículo humorístico, es la obra literaria señaladamente popular. Hay muchísima gente que recuerda todos las artículos de Taboada; y en cambio, no conoce, ni por los títulos ninguna de las novelas de Galdós." *El Heraldo de Madrid*, 28 February 1893.

58. *Obras completas* (Madrid: Aguilera, 1947), 3:1183b. The fears of the literati concerning the low numbers of novel readers may have been exaggerated. Cheap novels were available in the late nineties. According to the *zarzuela*, *La Chula*, 19–20, market vendors included books by eminent novelists among the items they sold in the plaza del Lavapiés, a working-class neighborhood:

"Lighters from
Bazas de la Unión
and, at ten *céntimos* apiece, books
by Clarín, Zola, and by Galdós."
("Mecheros procedentes
del Bazas de la Unión
y a diez céntimos libros
Clarín, de Zola y de Galdós").

59. Iris Zavala, *Fin de Siglo: modernismo, 98 y bohemia*, 21-22.

60. "La prensa grande, como se la llama en la jerga del oficio a la de gran circulación, no ha de privarse espontáneamente de un elemento de tan seguros resultados como el de satisfacer la voracidad pública y sostener por ende sus millares de lectores, excitando la fantasía del pueblo con sus relatos ampulosos, hiperbólicos y lúgubres." *El Globo*, 21 January 1894.

61. For a brief discussion of the apparent taste of cultivated readers for crime and mystery stories, see Romero Tobar, *La novela popular española del siglo XIX*, 113–118. He provides evidence of such tastes both from historical figures and from fictional characters.

62. *Waverley* (London: J.M. Dent and Sons, Ltd., 1915), 7.

63. "*Un journal est la pharmacie de l'âme*, il contient à la fois les calmants, les toniques et les excitantes.—Autre avantage: il remène au naturel, à la verité simple, car la fidélité de l'impression est sa première, son unique règle." *Journal intime* (Lausanne:Éditions l'Age d'Homme, 1976), 1:208.

64. "Nous sommes, je crois, à la veille d'étudier les êtres et les choses directement, sans transposition aucune. Les mémoires seront la littérature de l'avenir." Jules Huret, *Enquête sur l'évolution littéraire* (Paris: Bibliotèque Charpentier, 1891), 227.

65. Ventura Barcáiztegui y Orfila, *Estudio teórico-práctico del concepto de la culpabilidad, medios probatorios y veredictos ante el tribunal del jurado* (San Sebastián: Imprenta de "La Voz de Guipúzcoa,"), 8. Criminal jury trials were a popular entertainment wherever juries were found in the nineteenth century. Marcus Gleisser in *Juries and Justice* (South Brunswick: A.S. Barnes and Company, 1968), 30, quotes an anonymous writer who characterized the early American jury trial as a form of melodrama which had the added advantage of being real.

66. "En Leganés, entre el manicomio, prisión de cuerpos sin alma, palacio de almas sin razón, y la estación del ferrocarril a Cáceres y Portugal, que por su proximidad al lugar del suceso, hace pensar en el viaje macabro de un ataúd ignorado, ante esa decoración tan hondamente sugestiva, la casualidad, la implacable delatora de los más recónditos misterios, descubre en el fondo de un pozo, flotando sobre las aguas obscuras, del color de las aguas del Leteo, el cadáver momificado ya de una mujer, desnudo el cuerpo tumefacto, negruzca la tez, hinchados los labios y cogida entre ellos la lengua, muda acusadora de la estrangulación infame."

67. *News and the Human Interest Story* (Chicago: University of Chicago Press, 1940), 255.

68. "Parece que hallándose enfermas las cuatro hijas que tiene este matrimonio, María Fernández llamó a un médico, por quien supo que habían sido víctimas de un brutal atentado y contagiadas de una de las más peligrosas enfermedades secretas; y queriendo saber el nombre del que las hubiese atropellado, María Fernández escuchó aterida la confesión de sus hijas y tuvo a continuación una escena violentísima con su marido, que respondió con una cuchillada a las recriminaciones de la desolada madre. El juzgado se ocupa de la detención del criminal."

69. La prensa diaria, llevada por el afán de complacer al público, que desea hallar en las columnas de los periódicos no sólo la información que le entere, sino el relato que le conmueva,

da al menor suceso las más dramáticas proporciones, adornándole con detalles e incidentes que llegan a los dominios *de la novela* [...].

Conferencias y diálogos con los vecinos, con los individuos de la familia, con los heridos, si pueden articular una palabra, con los presos, si se puede llegar hasta su calabazo. Nada perdona el *reporter*, que describe minuciosamente el teatro del suceso, los trajes de los personajes que en él han figurado como actores, y que lanza a la publicidad cuantos antecedentes ha podido reunir acerca de ellos, de sus familias, de su vida pasada, de sus gustos y de sus inclinaciones.

Con esto se hacen relatos muy interesantes, y el público, aficionadísimo a ellos, los devora, excitando así la competencia del reporterismo, que lleva, sin querer, a las dignas personas que le ejercen en cumplimiento de un deber profesional a los más lamentables extravíos."

70. *Seductions of Crime: Moral and Sensual Attractions in Doing Evil* (New York: Basic Books, 1988), 241, 73.

71. At about the same time Baroja's novel was written, Pedro Dorado Montero published an article,"La criminalidad," in *Nuestro Tiempo* (Mayo 1902):815-833, in which he confirmed the increase in crime, noting, however, that statistical data were inadequate. See Alicia Fiestas Loza, "Codificación procesal y estado de la administración de justicia (1875-1915)," in *La España de la Restauración: Política, economía, legislación y cultura* (Madrid: Siglo XXI, 1985), 413-433. For a study of crime and punishment from the eighteenth to the twentieth century along the lines of Foucault's work on the subject, see Pedro Trinidad Fernández, *La defensa de la sociedad* (Madrid: Alianza, 1991), especially pp, 204–210 for information on crime statistics in the nineteenth century. The *Revista de los Tribunales y de Legislación Universal* 30 (15 de Febrero de 1896):107–110, published statistics on crime in Italy, France, Austria, Germany, England, Belgium, and Spain. The last available figures for Spain had been published in 1894 and referred to 1893. The statistics provided record the number of trials, declared mistrials, convictions, recidivists, and so on, but do not analyze the crimes committed. Three years earlier, in the same publication (26 [23 y 30 de Septiembre de 1893]:297), the *fiscal* of the *Tribunal Supremo* had regretted the inability of the Ministry of Justice to gather crime statistics for the nation because of the lack of funds.

72. "de análisis y documentación [que] requieren esfuerzo mental"; "novelas y cuentos de intrigas, de sucesos raros, de escandalosos enredos, que emocionen y entretengan." From *La Lectura*, 194. Further page references to Dorado's essay appear in the text.

73. "K," "El Afán de dramatizar," in *La Correspondencia de España*, 31 January 1893:1, and Kasabal, in *La Ilustración Ibérica*, 11 February 1893:1.

74. "Llevaron a tal extremo su cinismo que una vez muertos el Sr. Bahín y su sirvienta, se comieron el cocido que éstos tenían preparado." Another example from *El Heraldo de Madrid*, 10 February 1893, of the kinds of details meted out by reporters to their readers:

"In the hamlet of Pedregal a cat has killed a four-month-old baby. The baby's parents went off to the fields, leaving him in bed, and the cat began to play with the poor infant, tearing his nasal cartilage and covering his face with scratches. The baby positioned himself in such a way that he died of asfyxiation. The cat also ate three fingers of his right hand" ("En el caserío de Pedregal ha matado un gato a un niño de cuatro meses. Los padres de éste se marcharon al campo, dejándole en la cama, y el gato empezó a jugar con el pobre niño, rompiéndole el cartílago de la nariz y llenándole la cara de arañazos. La criatura se colocó de tal modo, que falleció por asfixia. El gato se comió, además, tres dedos de la mano derecha"). The inclusion of what Kasabal refers to below as gross and repugnant details was common in the reporting of this period and serves again to underscore the sharp division between what was permissible in the press as opposed to what was allowed in "polite" literature, as well as to indicate the continuity between traditional terrorific literature and the press.

75. A.O., for example, writing in *El Globo* on April 22, 1896, noted the similarity: "The most recent crime to excite people's morbid curiosity seems as if it came out of a chapter inspired by the abominable muse of the novel without literature in the dishevelled fantasy of Ponson du Terrail" ("Y por cierto que el último crimen que mantiene la morbosa curiosidad de las gentes, parece uno de los capítulos que la musa abominable de la novela sin literatura inspiró a la desgreñada fantasía de Ponson du Terrail"). As for translated or native versions of the literature of terror or the Gothic, José F. Montesinos in his *Introducción a una historia de la*

novela en España en el siglo XIX. Seguida de un esbozo de una bibliografía española de traducciones de novelas (1800-1850) (Valencia: Editorial Castalia, 1955), 72-73, found scant evidence of Gothic novels translated into Spanish up to the mid-century point. The National Union Catalogue lists *El vampiro o, la sangre de las víctimas*, published in Madrid in 1843 by the Oficina del Establecimiento Central. Attributed to Byron, it is probably John W. Polidori's 1819 novel, *The Vampyre*. Juan Ignacio Ferreras, *Los orígenes de la novela decimonónica 1800–1830* (Madrid: Taurus, 1973), 243-264, presents a perfunctory definition and history of the "novela de terror" up to 1830. The principal Spanish contribution to the genre noted by Ferreras is the twelve-volume 1831 edition of *Galería fúnebre de espectros y sombras ensangrentadas* by Pérez Zaragoza Godínez. See also Ferreras' *La novela por entregas 1840–1900* (Madrid: Taurus, 1972), 293-304, whose section entitled "La novela de crímenes" records the intense editorial interest from the 1870s on to the end of the century in journalistic accounts of contemporary crimes. Romero Tobar in *La novela popular*:50-51 provides several references to crime fiction in the last quarter of the nineteenth century.

76. "La semana ha sido infausta: el niño del Escorial, las sesiones del juicio por el crimen de San Millán, las dobles ejecuciones en Mondonado—todo es espeluznante y terrorífico como en una novela de Ana Radcliffe; pero más grosero y repugnante." From *La Ilustración Ibérica*, 4 March 1893.

77. David Punter in *The Literature of Terror. A History of Gothic Fictions from 1765 to the Present Day* (London: Longman, 1980), notes the role the Gothic played in the general development of the "novel of plot" (403). He credits J.M.S. Tompkins, author of *The Popular Novel in England, 1770–1800* (1932), with establishing the relationship between complex plotting and the Gothic: "It is to the Gothic, she claims, that we owe the entire apparatus of novelistic suspense; it is only for the Gothic writers that complexity of plotting was necessary, because it was only for them that the process of suspense and release was an essential fictional mechanism" (16).

78. See the discussion of the *novela novelesca* in D.J. O'Connor, "The Idea of the Poetic Novel," (Ph.D. diss., "Leopoldo Alas and The Spanish Realist Novel. 1876–1890" (University of California, Berkeley, 1982), 120–181.

79. In his article "Culture As Identity: An Anthropologist's View," *New Literary History* 24:1 (1993), Cohen presents the thinking behind current notions of people as active agents in the creation of culture. The phrase "Culture as identity," he writes, "refers to the attempt to represent the person or group in terms of a reified and/or emblematized culture." He then connects the attribution of identity to a person or a group with social and political processes in terms that seem applicable to the Spanish elite's defining of the masses in the 1890s: "Culture, in this view, is the means by which we make meaning, and with which we make the world meaningful to ourselves and ourselves meaningful to the world. Its vehicle is the symbol [...] symbols are inherently meaningless, they are not lexical; they do not have a truth value. They are pragmatic devices which are invested with meaning through social processes of one kind or another. They are potent resources in the arenas of politics and identity" (195–197).

Chapter Two

Fictionalizing the Escorial Crime

According to Domingo Blanco in *El Imparcial* on May 12, 1894, when José de las Cuevas, Julián García's lawyer, delivered his closing arguments, he devoted half an hour to an analysis of the press's role in forming public opinion on the case. He charged that the press had conducted the pre-trial investigation, the trial itself, and now wanted to dictate the sentence. Rodrigo, writing for *El Heraldo* on the same date, paraphrased Juana's lawyer, Díez Enríquez: "He believes—like his colleagues—that the summation is more like a novel than a summation" ("Cree que el sumario tiene más de novela que de tal, en lo cual coincide con sus compañeros"). Since the summation cannot be consulted, having been converted to paper pulp at the beginning of the Civil War, it is impossible to gauge the accuracy of Díez Enríquez' remarks. That the other lawyers for the defense shared his opinion may indicate nothing more than their joint frustration at press coverage unfavorable to their clients. On the other hand, complaints about the improper formation or construction—in effect the fictionalizing of the summations—were not uncommon, outside as well as inside Spain.

SUMARIO OR NOVEL?

In an 1898 study of French Superior Criminal Courts, it was noted that at the reading of an indictment, "The law wanted a summary but a novel was provided instead."[1] And in Spain, Díaz Cobeña, the lawyer for the director of the *Cárcel-Modelo*, José Millán Astray, accused of improperly allowing Vázquez Varela—the man suspected of his mother's murder in the famous Fuencarral case—to come and go freely from jail, made the same charge. Referring to the notorious 1888 case, he wrote: "This crime, reduced to its proper proportions would scarcely have provided material for a week's news;

but it was necessary to take advantage of the occasion it offered in order to lend variety to the news. And so, thanks to the tireless imaginative efforts poured into the columns of reporters, little by little a kind of installment novel emerged which would be laughable if it had not had such fatal consequences for my client." Not only did the press fabricate a novel for the delectation of readers and indirectly influence the magistrates who tried the case; in addition, Díaz Cobeña charged, the newspapers directly influenced the way the summary was conducted by supplying information to the court and by rigging the testimony of witnesses.[2]

Press coverage of crime in which imagined details as well as information gleaned from a variety of sources were fictionalized or novelized had drawn criticism since the practice became wide-spread in the eighteenth century.[3] The voices of those who considered themselves victimized by these practices were seldom heard. Lawyers, on the other hand, often protested not only in oral presentations at the conclusions of trials, as in the Fuencarral and Escorial cases, but also in newspaper articles and essays included in the legal literature.

The two men accused in the Escorial and Fuencarral crimes did attempt to reach the public directly. Perhaps they genuinely believed in the power of public opinion to change their status; or, possibly, caught up by the publicizing process, they felt compelled to present their stories in their own words. Julián García, who could neither read nor write, had a letter written for him following the November 15, 1895 decision on an appeal made in his case before the *Tribunal Supremo*. The letter was published in a Madrid newspaper on November 18. *El Nacional*, on November 19, described its contents. Julián "complains (poor fellow) about his acrimonious treatment by the press, together with its failure to make public certain details favorable to him" ("se lamenta (¡pobrecito!) de la acritud con que la prensa le ha tratado, y de que no se hayan hecho públicos ciertos detalles que le favorecen"). Julián swore that he was innocent and concluded thus: "'The public [...] wanted a guilty party in this trial as in many others, and I was gratuitously assigned the role'" ("'El público [...] buscaba para esta causa, como para otras muchas, un criminal, y ese papel se me adjudica a mí graciosamente'").

Julián, writing after the court's decision had been handed down, may have hoped, by proclaiming his innocence publicly, to improve his chances of winning a pardon. José Vásquez Varela, on the other hand, appealed to public opinion in the apparent hope that it would affect a pending court decision. He published a pamphlet entitled *Mi justificación* a few days before the *Tribunal Supremo* was to decide his appeal in the so-called crime of the Calle de Carretas. (Six years after his mother's murder on the Calle de Fuencarral, he was accused of having pushed his mistress off their apartment balcony to her death.) In his regular column for the *Revista de Tribunales*, Angel Ossorio y Gallardo characterized Varela's attempt as a "*coup de théâtre* staged for the public's benefit only a matter of days before the decision which would decide his fate was to be handed down" ("golpe teatral al pueblo días antes de la sentencia que para él había de ser decisiva de su suerte").[4] In any event, despite their apparent failure to alter public opinion, the letter and the pamphlet indicate that the two men were aware of their roles as players in a public spectacle. By writing their own scripts they attempted—unsuccessfully—to break out of the parts that the press had assigned to them.

In the Escorial case, since the summary is missing, reporters' representations of the circumstances are all that remain, thus making any comparison between their versions of the case and the lawyers' and defendants' versions difficult to assess. What is evident is that press accounts did not merely fascinate a reading public accustomed to similar fare in the popular fiction they consumed: those depictions also seemed wholly plausible, and were largely responsible for the public outrage following the jury's verdict which found Julián guilty of homicide rather than murder, thereby dictating a sentence of *reclusion temporal* (from twelve years and a day to twenty years). See the *Código Penal of 1870,* 70–71 for sentences and gradations within those sentences, pages 84–85 for tables describing time to be served for sentences handed down. Julián was later sentenced to *cadena perpetua*, limited to thirty years and considered next to the death penalty in severity (69). Julián's lawyer believed that the rural Gothic horror story concocted by reporters had convicted an innocent man. Judging from the newspaper accounts, there was, in fact, no real evidence against him.

GRISLY DETAILS

When people all over Spain who had read about the discovery of Pedro Bravo's corpse on February 10, 1893, opened the February 13 edition of *El Imparcial*, they read the following more circumstantial account of "The Discovery" ("El encuentro"):

> Bernabé Pastor, a guard from the School of Mining Engineers, and an adjutant, José Larrañaga, were patrolling the mountain when Pastor called out from the height of the Risco to his companion down below:
>
> "Come up. There's a dead child here."
>
> Larrañaga climbed up, and saw a very small child lying face down on the ground.
>
> Both men wondered whether it might be the missing child so anxiously sought by the inhabitants and authorities from El Escorial. While Bernabé remained on the spot in order to prevent the child from becoming food for the eagles, vultures and other birds of prey which abound at those altitudes, the adjutant descended the mountain to report their discovery to the magistrate.

> In a short while, the latter having appeared with a forensic physician and a pair of Civil Guards—all of whom had made the climb with considerable difficulty—the examination of the child's corpse commenced.
>
> His head was cradled on his right hand, as if death had surprised him while he slept. The other arm was stretched out and both hands were clenched as if the fingernails were dug into the palms.

A detailed description of his clothing followed, then:

> The child's parents, who came as soon as they were informed of the discovery, identified their son amidst moving transports of grief.
>
> All the inhabitants of El Escorial also climbed up to view the cadaver.
>
> When the magistrate ordered the body to be turned over everyone present drew back in horror.
>
> Where the child's eyes had been there were now two cavities filled with nests of worms.
>
> The rest of the body showed no sign of decomposition.[5]

In his article the *Imparcial* reporter, Hernández y Bermúdez, wrote that the forensic physicians had subsequently discovered that the boy had been strangled, and was, as well, the victim of a "beastly attack," ("brutales daños"). Throughout the reporting of the case, the image of the boy's vulnerable body was kept before the public. The reporter for *El Imparcial* provided a detailed account of the very thorough autopsy—on February 13 he reported that the child's tongue and larynx had been cut out—juxtaposing the scientific mutilation of the child's corpse with his parent's anxiety over the delay in burying his rapidly decomposing body. On February 14, Pedrín's body was finally wrapped in a sheet and placed in a white box with blue ribbons hanging from it. Many townspeople accompanied the funeral procession to the cemetery and threw earth on the coffin.

The reporter's attention to the grisly details of the autopsy—the forensic physicians' assumption, for example, that the child's eyes had been gouged out—undoubtedly drew many readers. (This assumption, amounting to nothing more than conjecture, was unsuccessfully contested at the trial by the lawyer defending Crisanto Jorge.) Several reporters were quick to speculate that this must have been done in order to prevent identification of the assailant or assailants when the child was released, but that plan was no doubt abandoned later in favor of killing him outright. Particularizing details of this kind increased the public's receptivity to the skillful development of the themes implicit, or apparently implicit, in the case. The handling of these themes unquestionably explains the crime's great impact.

As the passage quoted above demonstrates, the reporter showed considerable expertise in the use of fictional techniques intended to intensify the emotional appeal of his narration of events, the depiction of participants, and the significance of their participation in those events. The *Imparcial* reporter established a vivid and meaningful visual reference with his placement of the human figures on different planes—Pastor and the dead child up above, Larrañaga below—and the birds of prey circling high over all. The parents' and villagers' difficult climb up from the town and Royal Monastery to the height where the body lay—a high place in this context inevitably suggesting a sacrificial site—to make the identification, turns into a moment of sheer horror when the body is turned over and the onlookers see the empty eye sockets swarming with worms. The reporter's preceding description of the child lying with his head cradled in his right hand as if he were asleep increases the shock of this discovery. The scene is alive with movement. The guards go up and down, the villagers ascend the mountain-side, everyone draws back in horror. In a few crisply written lines, the reporter suggested the theme of human sacrifice, tapped fears of gloomy mountain heights (this was at a time in Spain when Alpinism had not yet transformed most peoples' aversion to mountains), and introduced the kind of gruesome detail that makes the contemplation of death thrilling. With the single exception of the reporter for *El Heraldo de Madrid*, whose copy normally seemed designed to convey what was known and nothing more, the other journalists covering the case, like the reporter for *El Imparcial* in the passage quoted here, clearly set about to exploit certain themes, and as they did so used all the resources contemporary fiction had to offer.

INVENTION: FALSE REPORTS

The most obvious way in which some reporters fictionalized their coverage of this case was simply to invent material. Eduardo Rosón, of *El País*, at one point chided the reporter for *La Correspondencia de España*, who had either himself fabricated two pieces of false information, or had reported unsubstantiated rumors. He wrote that the house of the accused murderer was built from old coffin boards, and that parents at the Escorial, frightened by this revelation, no longer allowed their children to play outdoors.

On March 10, one month after the child's body was discovered, C. Ballesteros (not the paper's regular correspondent for the Escorial case) reported in *El Heraldo de Madrid* that the accused murderer had, in all likelihood, admitted the crime the night before in confession to D. Leonardo Novel. The alleged confession and its content formed the basis for a long article in which the reporter's pious faith in the essential uprightness of human nature carried the underlying message. The priest, however, denied that Julián had confessed to the crime and announced his intention to take the reporter to court.

False, sensationalist reports with no essential bearing on the facts of the case were, apparently, soon forgotten. Reporting a confession that amounted to mere speculation on the reporter's part was, however, inadmissible. Inventing facts of this kind could provoke the worst of all possible reactions in the public, as an earlier, similar instance demonstrated. Several years before, when a journalist for *El Imparcial* attributed testimony to a suspect in the case concerning the crime of the Calle de Fuencarral—testimony that turned out to be false—the "public condemned the fraud so resolutely that within a very few days there was a downpour of thousands of cancellations of subscriptions to the paper. Sales declined and the paper was vilified in the streets. It was the worst crisis *El Imparcial* had been through since 1879."[6]

While false reports were, for the most part, exposed and corrected, it was more difficult to curtail some reporters' tendency to print rumors. Several rumors which found their way into print early in the coverage of the case, contributed to the invention of a lurid subplot involving the sisters of the alleged murderer. A few days after Julián García had been accused of the crime, the reporter for *El País* wrote that a rumor considered highly credible was circulating in the town according to which Francisca (Julián's eighteen-year-old sister) had had two babies whom she had buried shortly after their birth in the patio adjacent to the house. People were also saying that they had seen her leave the town pregnant and return sometime later without any baby. Excavation of the patio finally put an end to this rumor.

UNSOURCED DIALOGUE AND RECREATION OF SCENES

The novelistic technique especially favored by reporters in their coverage of the Escorial case was dialogue (unsourced for the most part) based on declarations and testimony given at the pre-trial investigations in 1893 and at the trial in 1894, neither of which was open to the public. Under pressure to satisfy readers avid for details, correspondents produced highly-dramatized versions of what had transpired before the examining magistrate and in court, embroidering them as each saw fit. Some journalists made it clear that the observations and dialogues they reported amounted to a reconstruction of what had actually been said and done; others did not. So, for example, in February 1893, the reporter for *El Imparcial*, who had not been present, wrote in reference to the accused murderer's protestation of innocence at one of the pre-trial hearings: "his pretended indignation was transparently artificial" ("se trasparentaba el artificio en su pretendida indignación").[7]

There were few attempts to reproduce the language of the individuals involved in the case. Everyone—from the well-educated, prestigious lawyers and magistrates from Madrid to the often illiterate local defendants—was represented as expressing himself or herself in standard Castilian. Occasionally, for the amusement of his urban readers, a reporter would note a colorful expression, the use of a malapropism by one of the uneducated Escorial witnesses, or indicate that a euphemism was being substituted for an unprintable word. On May 9, 1894, for example, Domingo Blanco headed one of his sections "Las 'sinángulas,'" in humorous reference to a word coined by a local witness. The word which the witness meant to use was *sonámbulas*, in the sense of diviner or fortune-teller. Julián's lawyer, Sr. Cuevas, in the course of interviewing the same witness, asked why Pedrín's parents had gone on the *romería de San Antonio*. The witness answered, "Well, if the priest is mistaken about the child being dead, and if he's not mistaken, he is alive" ("—Pues si el cura se equivoca en que el niño estaba muerto, y si no se equivoca, está vivo"). At which surprising and nonsensical statement, Blanco reported, the court must have laughed.

Reporters were normally allowed access to prisoners in their cells. The resulting interviews were rich with piquant details, dramatic confrontations, and opinions expressed by the reporters concerning the veracity of their interlocutors. Journalists readily seized the opportunity to relay false or slanted information based on their private interviews as can be gathered by subsequent clarifications and retractions. Prevailing journalistic ethics did not prevent the reporter from *El Imparcial* on February 25 from advising Juana, the eleven-year-old sister of the accused murderer, at the beginning of an interview in the cell she shared with her two sisters, "If you will tell me something important, I won't tell anybody" ("Si me cuentas algo importante no se lo diré a nadie"). The reporter's presentation of the ensuing cat and mouse game with a clever child was more dramatic, no doubt, for many readers than an equivalent fictional encounter might have been. A man's life, after all, was hanging on testimony, formal and informal, such as hers. To what extent the reporter enhanced the drama of this interview with Juana by exaggerating the wit of her repartee cannot be determined. Juana was, however, consistently represented as unusually smart by the reporters who interviewed her—a "monstrous" trait insofar as her intelligence did not appear to be in harmony with her age and body.

Juana prompted one of two effectively imagined scenes presented by reporters in the pre-trial coverage. Until February 20 when Julián García's brother-in-law accused him of the crime, Juana was the sole accuser. Since she was only eleven years old, there were doubts about her understanding of the circumstances and the consequences of her accusation. The frequent changes she made in her story were unsettling, but, above all, it was difficult to understand how—as she claimed—the sisters could have been unaware of Pedrín's presence in the loft. Her capacity to bear witness was yet to be decided legally when *El Heraldo de Madrid* and *La Correspondencia de Madrid* revealed that Juana had had a transforming experience at the house of the bailiff (*alguacil*) where she had been taken on the morning of February 21. Mestre Martínez reported it for *La Correspondencia de España* in language consecrated by the *folletín*, emphasizing a theme that pervaded early interpretations of the defendants' nature—their accessibility to universally prized human and religious values. He wrote:

> This morning Pedro, the bailiff, took Juana Valle, the Chato's half-sister, to his house, and there before an image of the Virgin they knelt down together. After they had prayed, he urged the child to tell him all she knew.
>
> Upon which the child, impressed by the power of religion, and not daring to lie after having lifted up her prayers to the Virgin, said:
>
> "I saw Julián when he took Pedrín into the house, and I also saw him when he put him in the loft, where I saw the child for several days. But I was afraid to say so for fear *El Chato* would punish me." After this concrete statement, the bailiff took the child before the magistrate, where she repeated the same story. Then she knelt and said, weeping: "But I am not guilty of anything!"
>
> The belief that the sisters were aware of the crime has been confirmed. [8]

The scene transcribed here was especially significant in view of Juana's lack of religious instruction and reputed ignorance of even the most commonly-repeated prayers. It appeared to corroborate the notion that at the core of our flawed human nature lies an innate responsiveness to religious truth and sentiment. Of significance to modern readers—and, no doubt, to some contemporaries as well—is the likelihood that what may have been a coercive action on the part of the bailiff, was represented by the reporter as an exemplary religious transformation.

On March 1, *El País* and *El Imparcial* reported on the testimony given the day before by Pedrín's father and aunt. Under the epigraph, "Intuiciones," Hernández y Bermúdez of *El Imparcial* created a dramatic scene, developing the motifs of chance and coincidence essential to effective crime reporting during this period. He provided dialogue charged with transparent irony, and ended with a genuinely chilling image of the concealed figure of Julián, looking down from a window into the patio at Pedrín's father who had come there in search of clues to his son's disappearance. What follows is a complete transcription of the section in question:

> Fate disposed matters otherwise; and its inscrutable designs did not permit the child, Pedro Bravo, to be delivered from martyrdom.
>
> On December 26, Pedrín's father and one of his aunts walked around the house of the Chatos. Possessed by a vague suspicion, they stood for a few moments against the wall behind which the child lay hidden, but not even one sob betrayed his presence there.
>
> Today both of them lament the excessive trust which one of them invoked to dissuade the other from the strong suspicions she harbored as she hearkened to a supernatural intuition, an impulse of the heart—to one of those presentiments which resemble divinations.
>
> That day—the 26th—the child's father and aunt were walking in the vicinity of the Romeral pass searching for the poor creature when they saw *El*

> *Chato* resting against a wall and observing them with meaningful concentration.
>
> Julián approached them, and after listening to their laments, told them that it was useless to look for the child around there since he had already looked that same day and the day before. He had roamed around the Romeral and the heights around it with no results at all.
>
> Pedrín's relatives were disheartened at this sad news, but it did not make them stop searching.
>
> They had scarcely left the *Chato* when he suddenly took off in the direction of his house. He jumped easily over the low wall that encloses the patio and entered the house through the stable window.
>
> His maneuver did not pass unnoticed by the aunt who pointed it out to her brother-in-law, adding: 'This *Chato* gives me the willies.'
>
> "Don't be unfair," the boy's father replied. "That poor family is incapable of harming anyone. Besides, what good would it do them to kidnap my son if they know that we are as poor as they are?"
>
> "Never mind that," replied the aunt. "My heart tells me that that *Chato* is a bad sort, and that we ought to watch the house and, if necessary, search it."
>
> "Well, just to convince you that your fears are misplaced, I'm going to do what you want."
>
> And so saying, the father jumped over the wall into the corral beside the Chato's house. He examined every corner of it. He searched the lean-to shed and looked under the straw which covered it. He peered into the house through the two low windows that opened onto the patio, crying out all the while, "Pedrín! Pedrín!"
>
> Since he did not notice anything unusual, nor did the slightest cry answer his repeated calls, the boy's father came out saying, "You can see there's no one there."
>
> Meanwhile, hidden from view in the loft, the *Chato* watched the hapless father search for his son.
>
> The child probably did not call out because Julián had gagged him.
>
> Now the victim's family recounts the incident, filled with regret that because of their blind trust they suppressed the instincts directing their steps to the house of crime.[9]

In this passage, as in his description of the discovery of Pedrín's body, Hernández y Bermúdez displays the ability shared by many nineteenth-century reporters to make his account visually convincing and compelling. There is no doubt at any point as to where his interlocutors are in relation to each other, to Julián, or to the García family's corral and house. Their carefully described movements in this scene seem to reflect the forebodings, intuitions, and uncertainties which the dead boy's relatives express. And, most effective of all, Eugenio Bravo's Christian forbearance (the reporter suggests) is mocked by the devilishly nimble Julián as he looks down from the loft window and monitors the father's search for signs of his son.

The fabrication of sensational material, the imaginative reconstruction of dialogue and of scenes, were all put to the service of a theme with universal appeal. This theme, evoking nothing less than the problem of evil, stemmed from the indisputable facts: the sexual abuse and eventual murder of the blonde, blue-eyed Pedrín Bravo. The child's disappearance at the site of one of Spain's most impressive religious monuments lent special gravity to the protests of believers. How, asked the correspondent for *El Imparcial* on February 13, 1893 shortly after the crime was discovered, could God have permitted such an outrage? The victimization of a child so young he could not yet distinguish good from evil was nearly unthinkable. And Luis Bonafoux, in a long article for *El Globo* written on May 15, 1894 at the conclusion of the trial, again asked why a child of three had had to undergo unspeakable torment: "What kind of God is it who permits wickedness of such enormity?" ("¿Qué Dios es ese que consiente tamañas iniquidades?").

THE CHILD VICTIM

Several reporters attempted to contextualize the Escorial murder for their readers by referring to the brutal rape and murder of the child, Cecilia Combates, in Toulouse in 1848. Literary representations of the mistreatment and even the murder of children had appeared recently in Spain. In 1890 the popular novelist Armando Palacio Valdés had published *La espuma*, a novel which included sensational descriptions of child abuse. In this novel, Rosa Coote lashed her five-year-old child with a whip, then applied vinegar to the cuts. She made her kneel for hours on end on hard peas scattered over the floor. She forced her to wear shoes too small for her feet. She refused to give her water and rubbed nettles on her skin. She plunged her daughter's head down into the opening of the toilet hole until the child, half-asphyxiated, fainted. And, finally, she burned the child's buttocks with a candle. This last act of torture, discovered by a neighbor, led to the child's removal from her mother.

In 1893, the year Pedrín's body was found, Palacio Valdés published *El Maestrante*. Even crueler parental mistreatment and torture in this novel led eventually to the death of the abused child. Palacio Valdés had based his account of child abuse on a real case, that of the Duquesa de Castro-Enríquez who was accused of cruelty to a servant girl. (Although she was brought to trial, her lawyer managed to get the trial postponed indefinitely.)[10] The case had been extensively reported in the press and was fresh in the public's recollection. In all these instances—real and fictional—the victim was a girl. As for Pedrín, at three and one-half years of age he not only lacked intellectual development and moral discernment; he was, in addition, not yet clearly defined sexually. The practice of dressing small boys in girl's clothing, common at this time, contributed to perceptions of sexual ambiguity or indeterminacy. The reporter for *El Imparcial* (19 February 1893) chose to remark on the items of girl's clothing that Pedrín, too young as yet to wear completely masculine dress, was wearing when his body was found. The resulting image is that of a child whose gender was still ambiguous:

> His clothes were hiked up to his chin, making it appear that he had rolled down the slope. He was wearing a girl's long drawers, a white woolen overskirt, a red garment with black checks on top of that, and a black overcoat. He had an ash-colored stocking on his left foot. The right foot had none.
>
> One of his white boots was found some 16 meters above the body, the other to the right of it. The missing stocking was found 86 meters off—again above the body—and his beret, which was red, was recovered at a distance of 98 meters from the corpse.[11]

The drawing of Pedrín which appeared in *El País* on February 24, was not based on a photograph for none had ever been taken of the child. Several journalists wrote that he was said to have resembled his surviving siblings: chubby and beautiful (*hermoso*), with blonde hair and blue eyes. Rosón in *El País* on February 18 reported that when the child accompanied his mother and aunt as they went about the town selling fruit and vegetables "the customers all petted him because of his extraordinary beauty and precociousness," ("por su extraordinario hermosura y precocidad, [fue] objeto de las caricias de todas las parroquianas").

Although Pedrín's alleged confinement in the loft of the García family's house was unproven—and would never be proven—reporters did not hesitate to describe his long period of sequestration in that place, which was said to be dark, cold, and filthy. Consciously or not, reporters emphasized a theme that Peter Brooks has identified as important to the structure of melodrama and Manuel Aguirre to that of horror literature—that of claustration. Aguirre writes: "The world is defined in horror literature as *space* and, furthermore, as a *closed space*." Hence the labyrinths, prisons, caves, catacombs, and other enclosed spaces characteristic of that fiction.[12] The image of a child—represented as angelically beautiful and innocent—confined in such a space, did indeed provide material for even the least fertile imagination to build on.

El Heraldo de Madrid, in its report of Francisca García's declaration before the examining magistrate on February 23, provided the most detailed description of the child's purported confinement. Although Francisca later retracted her statement, it fixed an image of Pedrín in the loft to which the reporters on the case frequently returned when they wanted to evoke the child's suffering. The detail of Pedrín crying for his mother was, in particular, often repeated.

Francisca's statement, presented as a direct quotation, was, of course, based on a second-hand account of what she had said:

On December 26—that is to say—on the day after the child, Pedro, disappeared, I was alone in the house. I heard a weak voice calling out "Mama," and not knowing where it was coming from, I looked around the house to see whether a child had gotten in. I then heard a moan which made me look up, and I saw that next to the ladder, in the loft, there was a child who would have fallen if I hadn't stopped him, because he was trying to throw himself down.

Julián appeared while I was asking the child who had brought him there, and when he saw me speaking to him, my brother began to insult me, threatening to kill me if I revealed what I had seen.

I understood the brutal act which my brother had committed, and I first told my sister, Concha, about it, and then María and her husband, Crisanto. We all agreed to keep the secret.

I was not able to sleep one single night, since the child was in a corner of the loft which was directly above the room we girls slept in. The moans and weeping of that poor creature continually sounded in our ears; but our brother, who slept up above, threatened us if we asked him about what was happening. For several days we heard what sounded like the words and moans of someone who was dying, but we could do nothing to help him. Many times my sisters and I wept over his terrible misfortune; but in order to save our brother, we didn't dare reveal it.

In the mornings, Julián went out and got a glass of milk and a roll. That was all the food he gave to Pedro—and he didn't give him that every day.

One day Julián brought home more milk than usual, and invited us to have some milk with rice. Not one of us wanted to have any.

On the night of January 9, we heard a lot of noise in the loft. I believe that that was the day my brother killed him. At about midnight, we heard someone tap lightly at the door.

We drew back frightened, but Julián opened the door, and in walked a person called Isidoro. I don't know his last name, but I can describe him.

Isidoro and my brother talked together in the kitchen—about what, I don't know.[13]

Reporters were skeptical about Francisca's protestations of pity for the child and her claim that she had not been able to sleep for over a month. Nonetheless, they drew often on her testimony in their depiction of Pedrín in the loft, adding sometimes that Pedrín was bound and lightly clothed despite the frigid temperatures. Their descriptions suggested once again the helplessness and vulnerability of a child not yet clearly defined as male.

CHILD SEXUAL ABUSE

The journalist for *El Imparcial* who had described Pedrín's clothing when the child was found as being hiked up to his chin, repeated the reference in a subsequent report. He did not connect it to the child's fall down the steep embankment; instead, he mentioned it as a way of alluding to Pedrín's having been sodomized, and especially, to the shame of being thus violated.

According to the Spanish penal code, rape (*violación*) only applied to females. Pederasty (*pederastia*)—on occasion, passive pederasty (*pederastia pasiva*)—was the term commonly used by reporters to refer to what had happened to Pedrín. The term forcible sodomy was not available to them and reporters did not paraphrase the act, for example, as sodomy imposed by force. Rosón, exceptionally, called it rape (*violación*). He wrote: " [Crisanto] has declared that his brother-in-law, Julián, presumed an idiot, and a near imbecile, was the perpetrator of the kidnapping, rape and murder" ("declara [Crisanto] que el autor del secuestro, violación y robo de *Pedrín* es su cuñado Julián, el supuesto idiota, el cuasi imbécil" (*El País*, 22 February 1893). Rosón repeated the term on March 2, after which it did not appear again. Whether it was described as an assault (*atropello*), or pederasty, the act allegedly committed against Pedrín fell into the category of sexual abuse (*abusos deshonestos*), defined as lascivious acts directed against a person of either sex, which do not culminate in carnal knowledge (*acceso carnal*), do not have copulation as their object, and are effected through force, intimidation, incapacity or unconsciousness on the part of the victim, or when the victim is under twelve years of age.[14]

Public outrage at the act Pedrín was allegedly subjected to may have been compounded by the ambiguity involved in his having undergone acts of sodomy not quite clearly as a boy or as a girl, but rather—because of his extreme youth—as a creature of an as yet ambiguously perceived sexuality. While the sexual abuse of a boy was clearly unacceptable, the sexual abuse and/or rape of an underage girl probably seemed more deserving of condemnation to many Spaniards. Langle Rubio, writing in 1911, described the perpetrators of rape and sexual abuse and the girls they victimized in terms that leave no doubt about the special gravity of these acts and the extreme emotions they elicited:

> a truly serious crime is committed when a man attacks an innocent girl, pitilessly tearing off the veil of her purity. Those degenerates who, after having exhausted all the possibilities available to their effeminate natures, stimulate and satiate their perverted desires with young girls; those corrupt valetudinarians, pariahs from all sound love, who slather their repugnant slobber on the alabaster bodies of candorous virgins not yet seasoned by passion's banquets—such men deserve far more than scorn. They deserve the unforgiving persecution of a battle waged by the law, by morality, by religion, by the consciences of honorable people.[15]

Langle Rubio also noted that whereas in Italy men who forcibly sodomized males were prosecuted for rape, a crime which entailed a more serious penalty than *abusos deshonestos*,

> Our laws, following quite different paths, have not yet opened up to similar reforms, and thus we are presented with the absurdity and the injustice of a situation in which the same penalty (imprisonment to the medium and maximum degree) is imposed on the individual who goes to the farthest limits of carnal and unnatural perversion by making a male the object of his reprehensible assault, as on the individual who causes offense with less serious obscene behavior. And the same penalty is levied on the individual who behaves in a repugnant and obscene way with a woman, but without actually raping her, as on the person who fails to show proper respect for the honor due to the female sex.[16]

There was potential ambivalence concerning the interpretation of the act committed against Pedrín, given possibly ambiguous perceptions of his sexuality. There was undeniable ambivalence in the Penal Code which, as Langle Rubio suggested, stemmed from the hypocrisy of a society which preferred not to acknowledge certain aspects of some criminal sexual acts.

Julián García was sentenced to four years imprisonment for repeated acts of pederasty performed on Pedro Bravo. Those who clamored for the death penalty in his case, demanded it as punishment for both the sexual abuse and the murder of the child. In the hundreds of columns that reporters dedicated to the Escorial crime there were a number of explicit and implicit calls for severe punishment for Pedrín's sexual tormentor. No one, however, converted these calls into a journalistic crusade for legal reform. No one who wrote about the case in the major legal journals argued that the four-year sentence given to Julián García for sexual abuse was inadequate and should be increased. While there was no concerted effort to change the law, there were spontaneous movements towards popular justice, including lynching, in this case and in others where sexual abuse alone had taken place.

Some recent historians of domestic child abuse and of the sexual abuse of children by individuals other than parents, have argued that during the 1890s people were unable to conceptualize this phenomenon in ways that might have led to meaningful social and legal action. It was not for lack of information. Readers of newspapers in Spain, just as elsewhere in Western Europe, Britain and the United States, knew that child sexual abuse existed. And Spaniards interested in social and legal reform would have been aware through law journal articles and reports of changes taking place—especially since the late 1880s—in child protection legislation, notably in France, Britain and the United States.[17] There was no lack of evidence that child sexual abuse was far from being an isolated phenomenon, that children needed legal protection, and that existing penalties should be reviewed.

In *Postcards from the End of the World. Child Abuse in Freud's Vienna*, Larry Wolff reviews and analyzes the cultural implications of several cases of child abuse reported in the Viennese press. He observes that while child abuse was visible at the turn of the century, it subsequently disappeared from public awareness for decades. In order to explain this puzzling development, Wolff argues that people (here his reference is apparently restricted to the Viennese) at the *fin de siècle* were incapable of thinking about acts which they perceived as monstrous and incredible, especially when carried out by parents.[18] And what of those individuals who might be expected to have overcome deeply ingrained aversions to such thoughts? Wolff and others have devoted many pages to speculation as to why Freud abandoned his position on the real prevalence of child abuse as set out in "The Aetiology of Hysteria" of 1896. Even Freud, according to his apologists, was reluctant, indeed, incapable of entertaining certain notions.[19]

Some of the notions that Larry Wolff singles out as having blocked construction of a context for meaningful discussion of the sexual abuse of children are: conflicting views about the nature of children; the sanctity and inviolable privacy of the home; the sentimentalization of the family, which implied the unquestioned authority of the father and the idealization of maternal love.[20] All but the first item refer specifically to difficulties in thinking about the domestic sexual abuse of children. The primary concern here, with respect to the Escorial case, is with instances of sexual abuse of children by people other than parents or family members. It is clear that the monstrousness of the act and of the individual who committed it is what reporters most often chose to underline.

Occasionally, reporters noted the physical damage to children, as in the case of an eight-year-old boy who was sodomized not long after the Escorial crime appeared in the papers, and who suffered serious injury as a result: seldom did they speculate about violated innocence and potential psychological damage.[21] The Escorial case was exceptional in this respect. Reporters emphasized not only the attacker's beastliness but also Pedro Bravo's pathetic plight as a child whose innocence had been violated, perhaps because they were intent upon drawing as strong a contrast as possible for the melodramatic effects they were after, perhaps out of genuine conviction.

Not all Spaniards accepted the idea that children were by nature innocent. Certain educators of the young, especially anarchists and those influenced by Rousseau and by the German philosopher, Karl Christian Friedrich Krause, may have assumed the innocence of children, but Catholics could scarcely subscribe to such a notion except as a sentimental affirmation of the relative innocence of the very young. Non-Catholics could find themselves in agreement—if not with the dogma of original sin—at least with a belief in the child's atavistic bent towards wrong-doing. The Catalonian poet, Joaquín María Bartrina, who was a Darwinist, asserted, for example, that: "The child, even more than present-day savages, represents primitive man. He has no language; his powers of reason are almost non-existent; he acts instinctively; his one rule of behavior is caprice; his inclinations are towards evil rather than good."[22]

The question of innocence was significant first of all, because its absence allowed for the possibility that the child had initiated or had been complicit in the seduction. But if innocent children suffered sexual abuse, it was possible to think that their innocence had been lost, or even that they had not registered the significance of the acts, and thus might not suffer any consequences from such acts in the future. The following remarks voiced by Kasabal in *La Ilustración Ibérica* of May 26, 1894, are typical of the way reporters framed the question of Pedrín's innocence, i.e., they lamented its violation, condemned the society that failed to protect children by severely punishing child molesters and killers, and sympathized with the plight of fearful mothers:

> It is a miserable society that does not surround its innocent and candorous children—the very images on earth of the angels in Heaven—with all possible protection! How corrupt and degenerate is that people that does not aid and protect such innocence by severely punishing the barbarian who manhandles it! In such a society, mothers would not dare let their beloved children leave their sides; and the cross raised on the height of Avante [sic], where Pedrín's mutilated corpse was found, would be an eternal emblem of ignominy if it did not also call to memory a severe and exemplary punishment.[23]

Kasabal wrote about the need for society to protect children. What protection existed at the time in Spain? Twelve days after Pedrín's body was discovered, on February 22, 1893, the *fiscal* of the *Tribunal Supremo*, Martínez del Campo, had a circular published in the *Gaceta* which was directed to the provincial and municipal judiciary. It reminded them of the law of July 26, 1878, promulgated for the protection of children. That law dealt primarily with the exploitation of child workers and the abduction of children to be recruited as mendicants. It did not deal directly with the sexual abuse of children. The circular may have been issued because of the initial suspicion that Pedro Bravo had been kidnapped and taken to Madrid to join the ranks of child beggars. On May 17, 1894 *El País* reported recent figures—as of 1891—that 165,492 children in Spain lived by begging or prostitution, "vilely exploited, it must be supposed, by an equal number of families sunk in misery and vice" ("vilmente explotadas, y debe suponerse, por otras tantas familias sumidas en la miseria y en el vicio." In the event, there was little else but this law in regard to the legal protection of children.

The only preventive child protection law on the books which did allude to the possibility of sexual abuse was article 171 of the Civil Code: "The courts may deprive parents of *patria potestad*, or suspend it, if they treat their children with excessive harshness, or give them orders, or advice, or set an example which corrupt them. In these cases, parents may also be deprived of the use of their children's goods, or appropriate measures may be taken to favor the children's interests."[24] Theoretically, children could be removed from abusive parents, but, as Pedro Armengol y Cornet pointed out in his 1895 essay calling for reform of this article, the law was seldom invoked. This was so, in part, because children removed from their parents would have been cast out into the streets: there was no provision to provide for their placement in foster homes, or in state or municipal institutions.[25]

Changing conditions required that this ineffectual law be reformed once it became apparent, in Spain as in other Western countries, that more than a few parents engaged in criminal behavior and that they encouraged their children to engage in criminal behavior as well. Armengol y Cornet conceded that the traditional probity and respectability of many a domestic hearth no longer existed. In recent years,

> deeds and trials have clearly and repeatedly shown that habitual drunkenness, domestic scandals, instigations to vagrancy, mendicancy and stealing, and parents' complete abandonment to evil instincts constitute an extremely grave danger to the morals of their children; and that in many instances the latter cover up the thefts committed by the parents who demand that their offspring bring home the booty they reap from their thefts and pilfering.[26]

The reform which Armengol y Cornet advocated did not come about. Meanwhile, the penalties for child sexual abuse were so light relative to those for rape, as to recommend it as the sexual crime of preference.

The Escorial case opens up an aspect of child abuse that Wolff and some other historians of crime and sexual abuse of children in the late nineteenth century, such as George K. Behlmer and Benjamin F. Martin, either did not discuss or merely alluded to in passing; namely, the sexual molestation of girls and boys by the clergy. At the time, the *El País* reporter, Eduardo Rosón, brought it up only to drop it—hinting that the Church was exerting pressure to suppress discussion.

It seems likely that then as now, children molested by the clergy were often unable to comprehend or interpret what had happened to them, much less act upon it. Ramón Pérez de Ayala's recollection of young boys (including himself) who were unwillingly subjected to sexual fondling illustrates the puzzlement and powerlessness many children doubtless felt in such a situation. In his novelistic depiction of life at a Jesuit boarding school, *A.M.D.G.*—published in 1910 and later banned in Spain—the author described what had happened to him and his fellow students at the hands of a lay brother in charge of the infirmary at the Jesuit school in Gijón in the mid-1890s. And in a footnote, the author added that in 1905 a student from the school had revealed to him that Brother Echevarría (his real name) was still pursuing his "tactile interests" in boys who appear to have recounted what had taken place only to each other. The adult Pérez de Ayala clearly thought that the act imposed on him was wrong: at the time, other boys subjected to the same treatment kept it to themselves, or, if they talked about it, masked their embarrassment and discomfort with laughter and jokes.[27]

If boys and girls, subject to the authority and control of clerics, often may not have known how to think about sexual mistreatment at their hands, the parents, relatives and neighbors of sexually abused children, do not seem to have had any difficulty in assigning culpability for sexual abuse. They did, on the other hand, have difficulty obtaining legal redress. The question must then be asked: Who were the molesters and who were the individuals representing the power of Church and State who neglected to reform the laws or prosecute offenders—even to the extent that the inadequate laws of the time provided for? The press provided sufficient evidence of public awareness and willingness to act on cases involving molestation by laymen and clergy alike. It seems legitimate then to ask whether the force of consecrated ideas about the family prevented Spaniards in the 1890s from conceptualizing child sexual abuse, or whether they were stymied and silenced in their real attempts to obtain legal redress by the power of Church and State.

The press reported several cases of offenses committed by clerical molesters during the years from 1894 to 1896. A story from *El Socialista* of May 11, 1894 reported charges of sexual molestation brought against a Jesuit who taught at a boy's secondary school. Another report from *El Socialista* of June 5, 1896 referred to a priest's rape of a young girl in his charge:

> A poor mother with a daughter in the Ciempozuelos insane asylum has denounced in a newspaper the scandalous fact that the unfortunate inmate was attacked and raped, and she has accused the *padre* director of said establishment of the shameful crime. Although the heartbroken mother has appealed to the courts and has been able to prove the rape, it does not appear that the forces of justice are very determined to expose the guilty party. But one must not think ill of the courts of justice. It is by now well known that they are incorruptible.[28]

El Socialista reported a case of clerical sexual misconduct in Huesca in 1896.[29] In another instance, referred to in Chapter I, irate neighbors were reported to have stoned the residence of a priest accused of sexual molestation. This kind of anecdotal evidence indicates that individuals were not reluctant to come forth, assert publicly that a sexual crime had been committed, and then seek legal redress. Indeed—although clerics were not involved in this instance—in the Escorial case, when a young girl accused Julián García in court of having made improper sexual advances to her in an isolated place, he replied that that was impossible. If he had done so, he said, she would have told her parents, who would have promptly had him charged. In France, according to Benjamin F. Martin, sexual molestation of female minors appears to have been reported readily enough.[30] In the absence of reliable statistical information, it is impossible to know whether such was the case in Spain also. Newspaper reports quoted here and below suggest that successful prosecutions may not have been numerous, especially when the clergy was involved.

In America the historian, Henry Charles Lea, in later editions of his *History of Sacerdotal Celibacy in the Christian Church* (first published in 1867), drew primarily from Italian and French sources in his discussion of hurdles the Church put up to foil prosecution of priests for sexual misconduct and crimes. Lea's interest was focused mainly on concubinage and the seduction of female penitents. While he referred to several specific cases in which female minors had been seduced, he did not place minors in a separate category for the purposes of his discussion. In a review of statistical evidence for criminal sexual behavior among French priests from 1861 to 1879, he did remark on the number of cases of sexual misconduct which took place in educational institutions—a fairly clear indication that the victims were minors, and that they included boys as well as girls.[31]

Finally, in this connection, it must be asked why the examining magistrate in the Escorial case did not question the monks. Eduardo Rosón of *El País* was the only journalist to ask publicly for an investigation of the monastery. He claimed, however, that he was not the only reporter who thought that the monks should be investigated. In a report which appeared on February 20, 1893 in *El País*, Rosón wrote that the principal problem with Julián García's defense was that he could not remember where he was on December 25 nor could he find any witnesses to establish his whereabouts on the day of Pedrín's disappearance. Rosón noted that although Julián was so poor he often went without food, the doctors who performed the autopsy on Pedrín's body stated that he had been fed milk. The child was, in fact by the doctors' account, as chubby when his body was found as he was when he disappeared over a month earlier. How could Julián have bought milk at 80 *céntimos* per liter? Rosón also wondered why, since Julián's house was close up against neighboring dwellings and there was no physical sign that the child had been gagged, no one in the vicinity had heard unusual sounds coming from the storage loft. At this point he referred to the memory loss caused by excessive masturbation, a practice Julián was known to engage in. Perhaps the accused man had a legitimate alibi which he simply could not remember. In short, Rosón concluded, it seemed unlikely that Julián had kept the child in his house: Pedrín must have been confined in a large building, perhaps one away from the town, inaccessible to spying neighbors. Speculation along the lines he then suggested did not appear elsewhere:

> If it were possible to engage in another kind of speculation suggested by the very nature of this repugnant crime, one would be led to think of men accustomed to a certain kind of comfortable, tranquil life—men forced for a variety of reasons to a life of involuntary abstinence.

> Certain maladies are common in such men; satiriasis, for example, which is infrequent in the working classes, often leads these men to commit the most horrendous acts against nature.
>
> This must be taken into account. One must bear in mind the terrible stories of children raped in France by their preceptors—all of them men who fit the above conditions.
>
> Why is the worthy magistrate, Sr. Estirado, so obsessive in following only one lead? Why—without abandoning it altogether—doesn't he consider other paths of investigation, if only to examine all the possibilities and entertain all conjectures, even those that seem most absurd?
>
> Sometimes in life, there is nothing so unlikely as reality.
>
> In conclusion.
>
> Let it be remembered that, according to Concha, Julián's sister, during those first moments after she realized that Pedrín was lost, his mother concentrated her search precisely in a place which up to now has not been investigated at all.[32]

On February 26, Rosón again raised questions about the examining magistrate's refusal to investigate the monastery adding, "And let me say for the record, that I do not want to excite again the wrath of *El Meneo Católico*" ("Y conste que no quiero excitar nuevamente las iras de *El Meneo Católico* "). (The publication named here has not been located in lists of Catholic papers or newspapers from the nineteenth century.) There was, in any case, no further reference to an alleged attempt on the part of the clergy to block an investigation.

A story about a pederast and a child killer who was also a monk would not have been implausible either in popular literary tradition or in reality. The figure of the "malevolent monk" represented a perennial cache of sensationalistic material in fiction. In fact, a scandal involving priests and young girls at a convent boarding school in Lisbon received considerable attention in the Spanish press in the early 1890s.[33] In any case, for reasons that cannot be uncovered now, the examining magistrate did not choose to investigate the monks. This failure allowed Rosón to conjecture later that Julián may have been set up by the real perpetrator of the crimes.

The prosecution of sexual abusers of children in Spain in the 1890s was clearly perceived as inadequate. The blame lay with a Church which protected clergy, and with the state (as represented by a civil or criminal court) which hindered prosecution of offenders. There was a generalized indifference to the reform of child protection laws and to the imposition of more severe penalties for child abuse. People who may have felt that they had little or no recourse to the law took the law into their own hands by threatening to lynch the offender or, at the least, by inflicting physical damage of some kind.

SUPPORTERS OF LYNCH LAW

Whether committed against boys or girls, the sexual abuse of children elicited public wrath that occasionally verged on lawlessness. The townspeople of El Escorial had not believed Julián García capable of committing the crimes of which he was accused until his brother-in-law, Crisanto Jorge, implicated him in the course of a long confession on February 20. The people abruptly turned against him, as *El Imparcial* reported two days later: "Public indignation against the *Chato* is such, that rumors circulated in the morning that the jail was going to be stormed and the prisoner lynched. The captain of the Civil Guard sent reinforcements, but the jailor, D. Cándido López, asked that they be sent away as he would answer for the safety of the defendants" ("La indignación pública contra el *Chato* es tal, que por la mañana circuló la especie de que iba a ser asaltada la cárcel y linchado el preso. El capitán de la Guardia civil envió fuerza al establecimiento, pero el director D. Cándido López la rogó que se retirase, pues respondía de la seguridad de los detenidos").

On May 15, 1894, the day after the jury delivered its verdict in the Escorial case, Luis Bonafoux wrote a long article on the decision for *El Globo*. He quoted a piece from the *New York Herald* written in 1893, shortly after the Escorial crime became known: "'In Spain the *Chato* will be tried before a court of law. In the United States he would be executed in jail'" ("'En España se juzgará al *Chato* ante los tribunales. En los Estados Unidos se le ejecutaría en la prisión'"). Bonafoux, who blamed Julián's lawyer, José de las Cuevas, for persuading the jury that there was not enough evidence to ask for the death penalty, concluded: "Delivering the executioner of the child, Pedrín, from death, has been a great *lawyerly* triumph, Sr. Cuevas, a great triumph beyond any question. But I am convinced that, as a *man*, you will ask yourself at some moment or other—as I ask now—whether you are not guilty for having rejected the recommendation made by the *New York Herald* ..." ("Gran triunfo de *abogado*, señor Cuevas, gran triunfo ha sido, sin duda, el liberar de la muerte al verdugo del niño Pedrín. Pero yo tengo la convicción de que usted, en cuanto *hombre*, se preguntará alguna vez, como me pregunto yo, si no es reo de no haber contribuído a realizar la recomendación, del *New York Herald...*").

One year later, on July 14, 1895, *El Correo* reported that a man in Seville attempted to sexually abuse a nine-year-old girl after plying her with brandy, and was nearly lynched on the way to jail. This and other similar incidents should not be taken to indicate that only nameless faces in unruly crowds favored lynching. In 1892, before Bonafoux publicly condoned vigilante justice, a book advocating Lynch law had appeared in Spain, and occasioned considerable discussion on the subject. The criminologist Constancio Bernaldo de Quirós noted in 1898 that the book's arguments had been refuted by F.

Cuervo, and that Dorado Montero had published an article, "intended to demonstrate that Lynch law may be a reassuring sign of a country's moral state; but not always, and it does, on the other hand, always constitute a barbarous index of regression to a primitive form of administering justice which must be restrained even when its motives are those of the highest moral law."[34]

Discussion was still alive in 1903 when Emilia Pardo Bazán commented on the recent lynching in Russia of a man who had raped a little girl. She posed the following question to the readers of her regular column in *La Ilustración Artística* on August 31:

> What do you think of Lynch Law? Insofar as it reveals forcefulness and a concept of justice, it does not displease me. There are crimes that are so offensive and anger us so, that punishment has to be immediate, like the blow with which we respond to a serious and shameful affront.
>
> Do those who take advantage of their superior strength and attack the young—do the bestial molesters of children deserve anything but lynching? I shall never think otherwise. The indignation felt at the first moment, which later loses intensity, is the best counseller and the surest judge: in such cases emotion is a better teacher and a more certain guide than all the formulistic legalities of a long and tedious trial. And emotion—in cases like those which are frequently narrated in the press and which generally end in a mistrial or light penalties—would call for the rope, for the garrote, for something as exemplary as what is called for in that strong nation so full of sap, which has solved the problem of how to get to one's destination by the shortest route [...].[35]

Many Spaniards doubtless shared Pardo Bazán's admiration for direct action based on moral outrage as well as her frustration at the failures of the justice system and the inequities in the penal code. Furthermore, sexual abusers of children and the members of the race subjected to mob violence in the United States had in common the "degeneracy" ascribed to them by a variety of contemporary criminologists, anthropologists and other authoritative figures. It is possible that a number of Spaniards more or less consciously associated the perceived bestial, "degenerate" nature of men who raped children with the similarly bestial nature of the "degenerate" race whose punishment by lynch mobs in the United States required no elaborate justification.

DEGENERATION AND ATAVISM: EPILEPSY, AND CRIMINALITY

One aspect of the case—the accused man's supposed degeneracy—was, in fact, a basic element in the story line gradually being constructed by journalists, a story which began with the fatal encounter of an innocent child with a depraved criminal. Few readers had to be convinced of the child's inexperience and innocence, but how were Julián's degeneracy and depravity established? Notions regarding physical and moral degeneracy were pervasive in the early nineties. There was, moreover, considerable press attention devoted to sexual vice, in particular, in 1893 and 1894—publicity which doubtless intensified concern over the dangers posed to children by degenerate adults.

A significant index of that concern was the founding of the *Asociación de los Padres de Familia* in early 1893. The Marqués de Comillas served as president while many notables figured on the membership list. *El Día* of April 2, 1893 noted the extent of the association's governmental and institutional support: "Its statues having been approved by the Civil Government, the Society has received expressions of support and sympathy from the Ministry of Justice, the Governor of the province, examining magistrates, and a large number of important people." ("Aprobados los estatutos por el gobierno civil, la Sociedad ha recibido adhesiones y manifestaciones de simpatía del ministerio de Gracia y Justicia, gobernador de la provincia, jueces de instrucción y gran número de personas de importancia"). In February 1893, when the Escorial case began to appear in the newspapers, the association was involved in the prosecution of the impresario who permitted a notorious group of transvestites to hold balls at the Liceo Rius. The extremely active association instigated prosecutions against everyone from belly-dancers to the owners of brothels who employed child prostitutes, to abortionists, earning much coverage in the press and, presumably, causing some alarm through interviews apprising the public of what they considered to be serious offenses against morality.[36]

Newspaper readers as much as readers of journals and books would have been aware of the connection between degeneracy and contemporary theories of criminology. Articles on this subject were appearing in the press well before Emilia Pardo Bazán's series entitled "The New Burning Question" ("La nueva cuestión palpitante") ran in *El Imparcial* from May through December of 1894. The primary purpose of her articles was to present a critical review of the implications of Lombroso's and Max Nordau's ideas for the future of art. But the newspaper-reading public had already had abundant opportunity to become familiar with the general lines of Lombroso's ideas, in particular. Furthermore, despite the skepticism expressed in some of the articles dealing with the new ideas—a skepticism many people may have shared—the new school of criminal anthropology was duly represented in courts trying criminal cases.[37]

Ideas in circulation at the time encompassing degeneration, atavism, epilepsy and criminal behavior, thus figured prominently in how reporters sketched in the background to the encounter of the child and the defective individual living outside the bounds of normal humanity. Reporters discovered at the outset that the alleged murderer was an illiterate, often-unemployed man of twenty, who suffered from epileptic seizures. Because of his malady and the nature of the crime, it was not difficult to represent him as a bestial degenerate, even as a monster. At the outset, on February 16, Hernández y Bermúdez, the reporter for *El Imparcial*, wrote: "If anthropologists of the Lombroso school were consulted, they would say that he was a criminal, because his appearance, and his public and private acts correspond fully to the picture they have drawn of delinquent epileptics" ("Si se consultase a los antropólogos de la escuela de Lombroso, dirían que era criminal, porque su aspecto y sus actos públicos y privados entran de lleno en el cuadro en que se incluye a los epilépticos delincuentes").

In the beginning, reporters portrayed him as unintelligent, almost to the point of idiocy, rather than as an obviously dangerous delinquent. His narrow forehead held meaning for adepts of Lombroso and for those versed in phrenology, a discipline whose findings still retained some legal validity. A phrenologist evaluated the youngest member of the family, Juana, precisely in order to determine whether, at eleven years of age, she had the necessary intelligence to testify in court; normally testimony from a child under twelve was not admitted in evidence.

Before Julián was accused of the sexual attack and murder of Pedro Bravo by his brother-in-law, Crisanto Jorge, on February 20, reporters emphasized his lack of intelligence. On February 16, the reporter for *El Imparcial* wrote that at Julián's second interview with the examining magistrate:

> The suspect contradicts himself at every moment because, as he says, he can't remember what he said before.
>
> When the judge asks questions designed to reveal what he did on the 25th and the 26th, he thinks he's being asked about the theft of the wood for which he is currently being held prisoner.
>
> He is so obtuse that one cannot question him indirectly or with any delicacy because he opens his mouth, gives a stupid look, and then says, "I don't understand."[38]

As an epileptic, Julián was suspected of being sexually aberrant. Rosón, in an *El País* dispatch of February 20, confirmed that suspicion, suggesting further, that Julián's frequent indulgence in masturbation accounted, in part, for his apparent denseness: "Julián is completely dedicated to a solitary pleasure that atrofies the memory and dulls the senses. And still they ask him in minute detail to recount everything he did on a particular day two months ago" ("Julián se entrega por completo a un placer solitario que atrofia la memoria y embota todos los sentidos. Y sin embargo, a Julián se le pregunta detalle por detalles, todo lo que hizo hace dos meses y en determinado día"). Rosón also noted that Julián was said to be indifferent to women. However, during the trial, according to *El Ideal* on May 8, 1894, Julián was asked whether he "liked" men and animals, to which he replied: "No sir. That's what woman are for—to get pleasure out of them" ("No señor: para eso están las mujeres, para gozar de ellas").

Two reports offered information on Julián's epilepsy. Rosón wrote on February 18, that Julián had suffered seizures since childhood. He added that as a result of becoming eligible for possible military service, his illness was identified and he was placed under observation for seven months in the Military Hospital in Madrid. Nothing, apparently, in the way of treatment resulted from his stay there. A detailed explanation of Julián's malady, based on the journalist's interview with the suspect the day before, appeared in *La Correspondencia de España* on February 19. According to the reporter, Julián had suffered attacks for twelve years:

> Fate, or an evil influence, as he says, was the cause of his epilepsy.
>
> Once, when he was a boy, he was going down the road with another fellow. Just for fun his companion threw a rock at a pair of oxen.
>
> The driver became angry and, without pausing to commend himself to God or to the devil, and without noticing who had thrown the rock, he went after Julián, dealing him such a tremendous blow that he left him unconscious. From that moment, he has suffered off and on from this terrible malady.
>
> "The only piece of luck I ever had," he ended by saying, "was when I drew lots for the service. I drew the highest number. But it didn't do me any good because I would have gotten off anyway due to my sickness."[39]

It was his temperament and his malady which provided the strongest case against Julián in the opinion of the reporters who interviewed him on February 17, 1893. As Rosón wrote on the day following Crisanto Jorge's accusation: "There were a lot of clues that implicated him, to be sure; but it is also true that not one of them came remotely close to constituting proof against him. They were attributable to chance, to unusual coincidences, to that inexplicable *I know not what*, that an honorable man sometimes has trailing after him, and which degrades him and tears his honor to shreds, however blameless he may be" ("Indicios había muchos contra él sí, es cierto; pero también no lo es menos, que éstos no podían ni remotamente constituir prueba; atribuíanse a fatalidades, a extrañas coincidencias, a ese *no sé qué* inexplicable, que a veces el hombre honrado arrastra consigo hasta degradarle y hacer girones su honor, por intachable que éste parezca").

On February 21, Mestre Martínez in *La Correspondencia de España* reviewed the townspeople's former opinion of Julián. He noted that no one had considered him capable of committing the crime he was now accused of, and that everyone had censured the examining magistrate for pursuing the investigation of such an individual. There was only one reservation concerning his character: "Despite his honorable background, Julián García was, according to neighbors, refractory to work and his ideal consisted in doing as little as possible" ("Julián García, sin embargo de los buenos antecedentes que respecto a su honradez tenía, no se recatan la gentes de asegurar que era refractario al trabajo y su bello ideal consistía en hacer lo menos posible").

The examining magistrate's decision not to look for any other leads in the case compelled journalists to provide readers avid for information with as many details as could be dredged up on the habits and conduct of the sole suspect. Regarding his appearance, according to Rosón, it was unexceptionable, though there is a suggestion of bodily disproportion—difficult to interpret because of the reporter's telegraphic style—in the following passage. Rosón described him thus on February 18:

> The man detained up to now due to strong suspicions that he might be the author of the crime, is about twenty-five [sic] years old, not very tall or robust, he would almost be a giant if he filled out his frame.
>
> In spite of his twenty-four years [sic], he is almost beardless, with light down above his upper lip. His thick, short dark hair grows down over his temples, revealing an extremely narrow forehead.
>
> He wears a blue shirt and trousers, and black rope sandals.[40]

POVERTY OF THE DEFENDANTS

All the reporters noted that the García family was extremely poor. The condition of unskilled day workers such as Julián and his sisters living in towns in the adjacent province of Avila, was repeatedly described in nearly identical fashion by the informants for the volume of *Reformas sociales* published in 1892. In general terms, they were described thus: "The condition of these day-laborers is, without any doubt, the most discouraging and perhaps the most difficult to remedy of any which has been observed among the workers in the province" ("El estado de estos *jornaleros* es, sin duda alguna, el más desconsolador y quizás el de más difícil remedio entre los que se ofrecen al reseñar el que alcanzan las clases trabajadoras de la provincia").[41] On February 18, *El Imparcial* wrote of the García family: "Many days they go without eating, but when they earn something they make up for their enforced abstinence " ("Muchos días los pasan sin comer, pero cuando ganan algo se resarcen de las abstinencias que por necesidad padecen"). Rosón in *El País* also on February 18, informed readers about Julián's work habits:

> Since he is extremely poor, he looks for whatever work he can get; he has served as kitchen help at the Hotel Miranda, as a municipal worker on the roads, as a mason, etc., etc. When there is no work, and his and his family's needs are pressing, he goes into the woods and steals fagots which he sells in the town. There have been times when he has walked six or seven leagues in order to gather a pile of mushrooms which no one wanted to buy.[42]

If this description of Julián's willingness to work is to be believed, it is worth speculating as to why Enrique Sepúlveda on May 16, 1894, wrote in *El Día* that Julián García and Crisanto Jorge were "vagos *ab initio*." Evidently, Sepúlveda (and perhaps others) thought of day laborers, *jornaleros*, who comprised a large percentage of the work force, as being little better than vagrants, with all the pejorative connotations which that term suggested.

Theft, according to a report in *Reformas sociales* on adjacent Avila province, was one of the two principal vices of the workers in the region—the other was drunkenness. The latter was attributed to poor nutrition, the former to entrenched tradition, and to the existence of " uncultivated public lands which are a constant incitement to the fraudulent cutting of wood and of improper grazing" ("montes públicos, que les excita constantemente a la corta fraudulenta de leñas y al pastoreo abusivo [...]").[43] *El Imparcial* informed readers on February 14, that the place where Pedrín was found had been ceded by the town (El Escorial) to the School of Forestry one year earlier, making it out-of-bounds to shepherds, wood and charcoal gatherers. Impoverished poachers, (*merodeadores*) like Julián were not deterred, however, from occasional forays into the woodlands or *montes públicos*. In effect, Julián was in jail waiting to be charged with stealing wood (nine *arrobas* of *carbonilla*, according to *El Imparcial* on February 21) when Pedrín's body was found. On September 29, 1893, after being tried in the *Audiencia* in Madrid, Julián was sentenced to two months and one day of incarceration for the theft. (A few years earlier, according to an informant for *Reformas sociales*, the worth of a load of wood was about 50 *céntimos*.)[44] He began to serve his sentence in the *Cárcel-Modelo* of Madrid, but he was later transferred to the jail at El Escorial for reasons of health. There is no indication in any of the newspaper accounts that Julián was condemned by the townspeople for occasionally stealing wood or charcoal.

DIVERSIONS OF THE ACCUSED

Questioning as to his activities in December, 1892 and in January and February of 1893, revealed that like most *jornaleros*, Julián spent much of his time in taverns. On several occasions during that period, friends went to his house to play cards (*julepe* and *mus*) and drink wine. At least twice while Pedrín was allegedly confined in the attic or loft, friends stayed for the night after an evening of gambling.

Ramiro Mestre Martínez, who took over for Fernando M. Lanuza at *La Correspondencia de España* after February 20, was the most assiduous in finding out and presenting details concerning Julián's daily life as well as some of its high-points. He revealed that Julián was not without ambition; he aspired to be a bull-fighter. According to friends, Julián had not missed a *corrida de novillos* in any town in the vicinity since he was twelve. In his report of February 28, Mestre Martínez included a notice directed to a well-known journalist—popular for his reviews of bullfights in *El Liberal* and *El Imparcial*—clearly in response to a query about Julián's prowess in the bull-ring:

> For Mariano de Cavia:
>
> I have just been authorized to publish the name of the bullfighter whose entourage included the *Chato*.
>
> His name is Master José García, and he is at the disposition of impresarios. He has no agent.
>
> I have spoken with him at length about the *Chato's* aptitude for bullfighting.
>
> "He would never have amounted to anything," he said, "because he had legs in the form of a violin and he was forever falling down."[45]

Despite this unflattering portrait, Julián's strength and agility were clearly illustrated by three noteworthy incidents which Mestre Martínez described in the February 27 edition of *La Correspondencia de España*. The first one had taken place three years earlier:

> As part of the festivities which were held three years ago in El Escorial de Abajo to celebrate the opening of the market, a *cucaña* had been placed in the middle of the plaza. It was so high that not one of the boys dared to climb it, even though the prize which had been hung up on top consisted of a ham and a purse with a few *pesetas* in it.
>
> Then Julián García said to them; "You're no good for anything—I'll go up." And without further ado, he climbed up the slippery pole, and took possession of the prize.
>
> This created great enthusiasm, and those present regaled him with cigars and wine.[46]

The second event took place on December 23, 1892, two days before Pedrín disappeared. Julián challenged a professional runner (*andarín de oficio*), to a race from the plaza de la Constitución to the casa del Pollo in the Escorial de Abajo—and won.

Finally—an incident that had taken place the year before, when some men who were working alongside Julián threw his shoes into a nearby well:

> He went down into the well for them, using a rope. When he was at the bottom and was ready to come out with his shoes, his comrades pulled the rope up. He exclaimed: "I don't care if you make fun of me. I'll climb up without the rope even if it kills me."
>
> Within moments, to everyone's surprise, he managed to get out by climbing up as nimbly as if he were a cat.[47]

Julián's enormous appetite was the individualizing trait which the reporter for *La Correspondencia de España* attributed to Julián at the outset. Lanuza wrote of Julián on February 19:

> Gluttony is his overriding passion.
>
> According to him, when he worked in the kitchen of the Hotel Miranda at El Escorial—the only time in his life when he was able to eat until he was full—he had daily attacks of colic because of his gluttony. He never gets tired of wolfing down food nor does he ever feel any repugnance for it, no matter how heavy it is.[48]

The other reporters on the scene also wrote about his preoccupation with food and need for large amounts of it—he was capable of eating two stews (*cocidos*) at one sitting, they noted. Their handling of his appetite, insatiable by his own account, was not wholly unsympathetic, perhaps because as professional journalists they were familiar at first hand with wide-spread urban and rural poverty in Spain. In a review of Luis Fatás's *La mortalidad de los niños en Madrid* in *El Globo* of June 26, 1903, the reviewer recounted a grim anecdote revelatory of the deprivation in which many people lived at the time:

> Spaniards belong to a race that does not eat, and—at the same time—the toll on their bodies exacted by work is enormous. There are areas where, if someone falls ill, three things are taken to him at the same time: chocolate, a doctor, and a priest. The priest, because, most often there's no time for anything else; the doctor, to certify his death; and chocolate, so that the sick man *won't leave this world without having ever tasted it*.[49]

On February 17, Hernández y Bermúdez for *El Imparcial* wrote that Julián could easily go for three days without eating, but that when he worked at the Hotel Miranda and devoured everything in sight, if asked whether he was hungry, he would reply that he was not, that he ate out of sheer love of eating. And then "he would laugh like an idiot."

The account cited above represented Julián as a stereotypical dim-witted country bumpkin. From a similar perspective, Rosón of *El País* on March 2 headed one of his paragraphs dealing with Julián's gluttony, "A True Story" ("Auténtico"), as if to tip off his readers that a tall tale was coming. He then described a tavern scene recounted to him by a "reliable witness." Someone wagered that Julián could not eat twenty-eight Extremadura sausages at one sitting. Julián accepted the challenge and, while his companions watched, he calmly ate all but one. When his friends, seeing that he was going to devour them all, begged to split the last one, he reluctantly agreed. The feat caused widespread disbelief, and so—to counter it—Julián soon after ate *five dozen meatballs* (*bartolillos*).

One of the last references to Julián's appetite—by now represented as Gargantuan—appeared in *La Correspondencia de España*, on March 2. Julián had dreamed about a sheep which he wanted to eat ("un carnero al cual deseaba comer").

Details of this kind about Julián's personal life provided grotesque, humorous relief (and pumped up copy) for the main narrative, which had gathered momentum on February 20—the day on which Crisanto Jorge accused his brother-in-law of Pedrín's murder. Until that date these details may have suggested to some readers that Julián was unfortunate, but—except for his malady—not much out of the ordinary; a man unluckily singled out by the examining magistrate whose reluctance to follow any other leads in the case remained unexplained.

CONFRONTATION WITH THE BEAST

After February 20, the day of Crisanto's accusation, reporters who had previously characterized Julián as presenting signs of moral imbecility, now saw evidence of animal cunning and astuteness. Emphasizing the animality they attributed to him, they described him as an atavistic throwback to a primitive, almost monstrous state. On February 21, Rosón wrote that the crime demonstrated "that there are human beings capable of acts which are so cruel and repugnant as to cause reason to recoil, because one does not dare even to imagine that man can go beyond the beast, that the being chosen by the Creator can become a monster" ("Demuestra cómo hay seres humanos capaces de cometer actos tan crueles y repugnantes que la razón repele, porque no se atreve a suponer siquiera que el hombre deje atrás a la bestia, que el ser elegido por el Creador se convierta en monstruo"). For Rosón, the confrontation (*careo*) with Crisanto Jorge was a turning point. During that confrontation, Julián became: "a jackel baring its teeth to its enemy, evading his moves in order to throw itself on him and destroy him " ("un chacal que enseña los dientes a su enemigo y esquiva sus movimientos para lanzarse sobre él y destrozarle [...]").

All the reporters wrote about Julián's violent behavior in his confrontation with Crisanto. It must be remembered that they were not present: presumably, the secretary, who accompanied the examining magistrate in order to take down the proceedings, recounted the scene to them. The story they then told, describing a man's reversion to an animal state, was a staple of terrorific literature. The scientific literature of the period similarly offered vivid descriptions of the dramatic transformation of man to beast characteristic of the degenerate about to commit a criminal act: "The moral imbecile becoming brutish suddenly on occasion betrays the fangs of the wolf or the spring of the tiger [...]," wrote a specialist on crime and degeneration in

1902.[50] The reporter for *La Correspondencia de España*, again conjuring up a picture of primitivism through references to Julián's ape-like stance and resemblance to members of a race generally deemed inferior and itself atavistic, described him thus on February 24, 1893: "He is about one meter, seventy five centimeters tall. While his forehead is sunken and narrow, the back of his head is larger. His eyes are small and his face resembles that of a Hottentot. He has a habit of biting his lips, and walks with his head bent forward" ("Su estatura será próximamente de un metro setenta y cinco centímetros, tiene la frente deprimida y estrecha, la cabeza en su parte posterior abultada, ojos pequeños; el aspecto de su semblante semeja al del hotentote, y tiene la costumbre de morderse algún tanto los labios; al andar inclina un poco la cabeza hacia adelante"). The reporter for *El Imparcial* on the same day referred to him as "this savage" ("este salvaje"), "this man-monkey" ("este hombre mono"). He was said to have subjected his child victim to "hyena-like cruelties and punishments worthy of the Inquisition" ("crueldades de hiena y castigos inquisitoriales"). The reiterated appeal to deeply-held fears—dread of savages and the uncivilized, of animality—no doubt struck a responsive chord in readers.

Eduardo Rosón was the journalist who succeeded best in objectifying the repugnance that Julián and his alleged sexual attack on Pedrín had provoked in the public. On February 25, under the heading "Stains" ("Manchas"), he described the mat (*estera*) taken from the loft in Julián's house, and assumed to have served as a kind of pallet for Pedrín: "The medical experts have again examined the mat which served as a bed of torture for the child, Pedrín. They have found the excrement of an adult, and stains characteristic of the horrendous, brutal attacks to which the unfortunate child was subjected" ("Los peritos médicos han examinado nuevamente la estera que ha servido de lecho de tortura al niño Pedrín; han encontrado escrementos [sic] de persona mayor y manchas características del horrendo y brutal atropello cometido con el desgraciado niño." It is hardly surprising, in view of Rosón's graphic description, that the Escorial crime, more than any other crime of the *fin de siglo*, was referred to as "asqueroso" and "repugnante." The repulsive sights and odors reporters (especially Rosón and Mestre Martínez) conjured up, were striking even in an era when crime reporters did not stint on their presentation of such details.

Thirteen days after Pedrín's body was found, and three days after Julián was accused of the crime by his brother-in-law, Rosón at last appeared to be convinced of his guilt. Only the day before, he had written that Julián was an ordinary *campesino*, with nothing at all to mark him as unusual. But subsequently, (February 24), he went on to speculate: "It is impossible to tell from his appearance whether he provides an example of neurosis, as they say, a type which may be confirmed by applying Lombroso's doctrines, an imbecile converted by disgusting vices into a brute, or a hardened, able criminal—

'gallows bait'—who has revealed himself as such at the appropriate psychological moment" ("No se puede colegirse de su aspecto si es un caso de neurosis, como dan en decir, un tipo de estudio que se preste a las comprobaciones de las doctrinas lombrosistas, un imbécil embrutecido por vicios asquerosos, o un criminal empedernido y hábil `carne de horca,' que se ha revelado como tal en el momento psicológico"). His puzzlement gave way to some measure of certainty regarding Julián's guilt, but his conviction was short-lived; by February 26, nagging questions surfaced once again to trouble his mind.

Rosón, Mestre Martínez and Hernández y Bermúdez had all depicted Julián first, as almost imbecilic, then, as a creature capable of animal cunning. In either case, he was represented as a man whose moral responsibility could not be established with certainty. After Crisanto's accusation and the confrontation between the two men, the same reporters began to view Julián in a different light. Hernández y Bermúdez on February 26 wrote that Julián refused to confess to the crime in the belief that his refusal would save him from the garrote: "No one who examines him closely, however, will be deceived. His cynicism betrays the criminal he is. His cunning shows through the mask of stupidity behind which he tries to hide" ("No engañará, sin embargo a nadie que de cerca le examine. Su cinismo denuncia al hombre criminal; su astucia trasparéntase a través de la máscara hipócrita de estúpido con que pretende ocultarse").

On February 28 the reporter for *El Imparcial* claimed to have observed a significant transformation in Julián. If he earlier feigned stupidity out of a kind of "astucia" that could still be ascribed to animal cunning, Hernández y Bermúdez now saw him as an intelligent, fully self-conscious individual:

> The *Chato* is revealing an astonishing perspicacity, discussing everything put before him with powerful arguments and surprising sophistry—as if the hours of solitude spent in his cell had given him time to reflect on the very grave situation in which he finds himself, and as if this constant meditation had sharpened his mental faculties. He is no longer the uncouth man who hung his head in confusion at the overwhelming charges brought against him, but rather a thinking being who has realized the importance his attitude may take on in the progress of the trial.[51]

Mestre Martínez made similar observations on February 24:

> Today a radical change in the way the *Chato* expresses himself has been observed.
>
> He has denied the accusations made against him, not with monosyllables or short sentences, but with relative verbosity.
>
> It seems that since his brother-in-law Crisanto hurled the terrible accusation against him, he has undergone a complete metamorphosis.[52]

MEDICO-LEGAL VIEWS OF EPILEPSY AND CRIMINAL RESPONSIBILITY

Reporters thus appeared to waver between representing Julián as a depraved, degenerate criminal acting on brutal impulses triggered by epilepsy, or as a rational criminal, responsible for his acts. When Julián's lawyer called a doctor to testify at the trial in May 1894 on the degeneracy and consequent possible lack of responsibility of the members of the García family, newspaper accounts of his testimony indicate that it had little impact on the jurors. The doctor, Fernando Calatraveño y Valladares, author of two books—*Ensayos médico-literarios* (1884), and *El hipnotismo al alcance de todas las inteligencias* (1888)—testified first that Juana was an hysteric and could not be held responsible for her words or actions. He claimed that her intelligence was only apparent, her suggestibility great. He said as much of the other sisters. Julián, he stated, was an "histero-epileptic, with brain deformation" ("histero-epiléptico, de cerebro deformado"), the type of individual who, in the course of time, as legal medicine progressed, would be found to be without criminal responsibility. Domingo Blanco, who had replaced Hernández y Bermúdez for *El Imparcial*, reconstructed the following exchanges in court on May 10, 1894:

> The prosecutor, Sr. Pico, asks: "Is it possible for the effects of epilepsy to last in a criminal throughout the forty days during which he is committing the crime?"
>
> Calatraveño: "There are periods of relief, but they never lead to a state of normalcy. The brain of an epileptic is like a stick of dynamite; it is always dangerous, and when it is jostled it explodes."
>
> Presiding Magistrate: "Sr. Calatraveño, there must be different degrees of seriousness in hysteria, since there is scarcely a family in one's acquaintance that does not number hysterics among its members."
>
> Calatraveño: "There is no question but that this illness like all others, has different degrees of seriousness. There are gradations ranging from the capricious young woman who refuses food, and the girl who enjoys eating the plaster she scrapes off the walls, to the individual who has convulsions."
>
> Presiding Magistrate: "What we need to verify here is whether epileptics are capable of committing crimes during periods of relative tranquility."
>
> Calatraveño: "It is possible that they may possess a will of their own in periods of calm, but it is always attenuated."[53]

Dr. Calatraveño's testimony evidently did not convince the jury that it should attribute attenuated responsibility to Julián because of his malady. Reporters' representation of Julián during the pre-trial investigation as a dangerous degenerate may have sharpened the public's (and the jury's) desire to hold him fully accountable so that he would receive the severest penalty possible. But it was also the case that by the mid-nineties, courts were becoming reluctant to accept the testimony of medical experts supporting decisions of irresponsibility or attenuated criminal responsibility.

In a review of a lecture, "Madness and the Courts" ("La locura ante los Tribunales"), given by the eminent Dr. Ots y Esquerdo before the *Academia médico-quirúrgica* and published in *El Imparcial* on January 27, 1894, Esquerdo was quoted on the reluctance to accept determinations of irresponsibility, so frequently attested to by magistrates. He claimed that it stemmed from testimony given in recent trials in which doctors who had been swayed by Lombroso's theories saw all criminals as mad, and therefore irresponsible. In fact, wrote the reviewer, the reaction against such determinations of irresponsibility was so great that in professional medical journals it was said that if a lawyer wanted a client declared sane, he needed only to present to the court an affidavit of mental alienation signed by an alienist (*médico alienista*). In an attempt to counter the impression that there was universal resistance to expert medical counsel, Esquerdo recalled a recent decision in which a man who had killed his fiancée was declared not responsible because he suffered from "epilepsia alcohólica." Esquerdo's recommendation, according to the reviewer, was that doctors should limit themselves to informing the court about the accused person's medical history, and to the current evaluation of his or her mental state. That information would make possible a rational determination of attenuated responsibility, if warranted.

In the published version of his lecture, Esquerdo summarized current European medical and legal thought on criminal responsibility in epileptics. Esquerdo's own position coincided with that of the well-known Parisian forensic physician, Charles Vibert. Epileptics incurred responsibility, according to Vibert, for acts committed when not undergoing a seizure, and for acts committed with full consciousness which were retained in the epileptic's memory.[54] With regard to the Escorial case, the loss of the court records makes it impossible to determine whether criminal responsibility was, in fact, seriously at issue. It was not so represented by the press during the trial, nor did it figure prominently in post-trial commentaries.

The nearly blank page reporters wrote on as they fashioned their versions of the accused murderer had little on it at the outset but the words "poor" and "epileptic." The discovery of Pedrín Bravo's body high above the Royal Monastery of El Escorial with its suggestions of sacrifice and ritual murder, also suggested a killer whose evil nature must prove unfathomable to ordinary people. It was difficult, however, to attribute convincingly much more than gross animality and a degeneracy marked by his malady to Julián García. Most of what reporters discovered about Julián's life, as set out above, cast him in the familiar mold of the uncouth, rural male who traditionally used animals, family members, and defenseless children to satisfy uncomplicated sexual needs. Resourceful journalists, intent on demonizing the accused man, found ways to represent Julián indirectly as something more than brutish by turning to the conventions of Gothic fiction.

NOTES

1. Qtd in Ruth Harris, *Murders and Madness. Medicine, Law, and Society in the "Fin de Siècle"* (Oxford:Clarendon Press, 1989), 131.

2. "Este crimen, pues, reducido a sus condiciones propias, apenas hubiese dado juego para una sola semana; pero era necesario aprovechar la ocasión para dar variedad a los periódicos, y entonces fue cuando empezó a realizarse en sus columnas ese incansable trabajo de imaginación, merced al cual fue creándose poco a poco una especie de novela por entregas, de la que habría motivo para reírse si no hubiera tenido resultados tan funestos para mi defendido." "D. Luis Díaz Cobeña. Notas biográficas," *Colección de trabajos forenses y noticias biográficas de los más notables abogados de España y de las repúblicas de la América Latina* (Madrid: Centro Editorial de Góngora, 1897), 88-89.

3. See Frank Harris, *Presentation of Crime in Newspapers. A Study of Methods in Newspaper Research* (Hanover, N. H.: Sociological Press, 1932), 3. See also Joel Black, *The Aesthetics of Murder. A Study in Romantic Literature and Contemporary Culture* (Baltimore and London: The Johns Hopkins University Press, 1991), 33ff. for a discussion of the problematic conflation of journalistic and literary treatments of crime.

4. "Crónica de Tribunales," *Revista de los Tribunales y de Legislación Universal* 27 (22 de septiembre de 1894): 661. According to Ossorio, the pamphlet was received with absolute indifference by the press and by the public. Varela's pamphlet paraphrased the strong defense made at his trial and emphasized the contradictory evidence of the forensic experts. It also quoted letters from the woman he was accused of murdering which clearly revealed her suicidal tendencies. In short, it was a serious attempt to inform and change public opinion. Nonetheless, as Ossorio pointed out, the public's mind was made up: Varela was the embodiment of vice. The climate of opinion in the early nineties which fostered the emergence (discussed below), of the *Asociación de los Padres de Familia*—veritable watch-dogs of Christian morality—was inimical to Varela who was considered a monster of immorality. In *La Chair de l'autre. Le crime passionnel au XIXe siècle* (Paris: Olivier Orban, 1986), 312, Joëlle Guillais has noted that in the course of criminal trials, some accused, unable to recognize themselves in what was being said of them, wrote exculpatory accounts of their actions. But since such accounts lacked judicial value they ultimately served to underscore the powerlessness of their authors. Sarah Maza observed in her article, "Domestic Melodrama as Political Ideology: The Case of the Comte de Sanois," *American Historical Review* 94 (December 1989):1255, that in the eighteenth century trial briefs were sold by the thousands: "many of the most successful trial briefs were first-person narratives, analogous to novelistic memoires and allegedly written by the defendants. Readers, however, were well aware of the real authors." Maza argues that the effect of such memoirs (often written in a deliberately melodramatic style) was to engage a broad reading public in questions which related intimate private concerns to the public sphere.

5. "Iban recorriendo la sierra el guarda de la Escuela de Ingenieros de minas Bernabé Pastor y el capataz José Larrañaga cuando aquél gritó desde lo alto del Risco al último que iba por abajo:

—Sube, que hay aquí un niño muerto.

Larrañaga ascendió al sitio en que estaba su compañero y entonces vio tendido boca abajo a un niño muy pequeño.

Ambos pensaron si sería el que con tanto afán buscaban las autoridades y vecinos de El Escorial, y mientras Bernabé se quedó custodiándolo para librarle de ser pasto de las águilas, los buitres y demás aves de rapiña que abunan [sic] por aquellas alturas, el capataz bajó a dar cuenta del hallazgo al juez.

A poco presentóse éste con el médico forense y una pareja de la guardia civil, quienes lograron con mucho trabajo llegar a aquel sitio, y se procedía al reconocimiento del niño.

Tenía éste la cabecita apoyada en la mano derecha, como si durmiendo le hubiera sorprendido la muerte. El otro brazo estaba extendido y ambas manos cual si las uñas se hubieran incrustado en las palmas."

The second passage quoted:

"Los padres del niño, que se presentaron en cuanto tuvieron noticia del suceso, reconocieron a su hijo en medio de conmovedores trasportes de dolor.

Todos los habitantes de El Escorial subieron también a ver el cadáver.

Al levantarlo, por orden del juez, cuantos habían acudido retrocedieron horrorizados.

La criatura tenía por ojos dos cuencas convertidas en nidos de gusanos.

El resto del cuerpo no acusaba la menor señal de descomposición."

6. "el público castigó el fraude con tan unánime repulsa que en pocos días llovieron a miles las bajas de suscripción, decayó la venta y se escarneció en las calles al periódico. Fue la crisis más grave corrida por *El Imparcial* desde 1879." M. Ortega y Gasset, "*El Imparcial*," 60.

7. *El Imparcial*, 24 February 1893. The practice described here lives on in modern newspapers as well as in journalistic non-fiction. In a review of Byron Burrough's *Vendetta*, John Taylor wrote: "The author shows an appalling disregard for technique. In the beginning, scenes are organized around reconstructed dialogue and heavy-handed novelistic devices, with no attribution of sources either on the page or in an appendix. We get passages such as: 'You don't threaten me!' Bob Smith's angular face was red and trembling as he tore into the Safra man across the table. 'Nobody threatens me!' But as the book progresses, Mr. Burrough grows impatient with this approach, or else finds it inappropriate, since he starts to rely more on narrative summary and direct quotations from subjects he interviewed, with traditional newspaper-type attribution. But now and again, when the mood grips him, he swerves back into unsourced reconstruction." *The New York Times Book Review*, 21 June 1992, Book Review section.

8. "Esta mañana, el alguacil Pedro llevó a la niña Juana Valle, cohermana del *Chato*, a su casa, y allí, ante un imagen de la Virgen, se arrodillaron, y después de rezar invitó a la niña a que dijera cuanto supiese.

Entonces la niña, impresionada por la idea religiosa y no atreviéndose a mentir, después de haber elevado ante la Virgen sus plegarias, dijo:

—Yo vi cuando Julián entró en su casa a Pedrín, y vi también cuando lo entró en el desván, en donde he visto al niño durante varios días; pero no me he atrevido a decirlo, por miedo a que me castigase el *Chato*. Después de esta concreta declaración, el alguacil llevó a la niña ante el juez, y allí repitió lo mismo. Después se arrodilló y dijo, llorando:

—¡Pero yo no tengo la culpa de nada!

Confírmase la creencia de que las hermanas del *Chato* no ignoraban el crimen."

9. "La fatalidad dispuso las cosas de otro modo, y el niño Pedro Bravo no se libró del martirio por extraños designios de la suerte.

El día 26 de diciembre el padre de Pedrín y una tía de éste rondaron la casa de los *Chatos*, impulsados por leve sospecha, permanecieron breves instantes junto a la pared tras la cual encontrábase oculta la criatura, y ni un sollazo de ésta vino a denunciarles su presencia en aquel sitio.

Hoy ambos lamentan la excesiva confianza a que uno de ellos se entregara disuadiendo a la otra de las suspicacias excesivas que abrigó entonces, obedeciendo a una intuición sobrenatural, a un impulso del corazón, a un presentimiento de esos que se confunden con las adivinaciones.

En ese día 26 iban el padre y la tía del niño por la puerta del Romeral buscando a la pobre criatura, cuando vieron al *Chato* recostado en una tapia y observándoles con atención significativa.

Julián se acercó a ellos, y después de escuchar sus lamentaciones díjoles era inútil que buscaran al niño por aquellos lugares, pues ya él habíalo hecho el mismo día y el anterior, recorriendo el Romeral y los cerros que lo rodean sin obtener resultado alguno positivo.

Los individuos de la familia de Pedrín quedaron descorazonados al oir tan tristes nuevas; pero no por eso desistieron de proseguir en sus pesquisas e indagaciones.

Apenas se separaron del *Chato*, éste salió presuroso en dirección a su casa, saltó ligero la tapia que cierra el patio y se introdujo en el interior de la edificación por la ventana de la cuadra.

La maniobra no pasó inadvertida para la tía del niño, y así se lo hizo observar a su cuñado, que la acompañaba, añadiendo:

—Ese *Chato* me da mala espina.

—No seas maliciosa—repuso el padre;—esa pobre familia es incapaz de hacer daño a nadie. Además, ¿qué adelantaría con secuestrar a mi niño, si sabe que somos tan desgraciados como ella?

—No importa—replicó la tía—el corazón me dice que ese *Chato* es un malvado, y debíamos observar su casa y, si es preciso, registrarla.

—Pues para que te convenzas de que tus temores no tienen razón de ser, voy a complacerte.

Y diciendo esto, el padre del niño saltó por encima de la tapia al corral de la casa del *Chato*, examinó bien todos los rincones, registró el cobertizo removiendo la paja de que se hallaba tapizado y miró al interior de la casa por las dos ventanas bajas que dan al patio, sin cesar de gritar: '¡Pedrín! ¡Pedrín!'

Como nada de particular advirtiera ni el más pequeño grito contestara a sus repetidos llamamientos, el padre del niño salió diciendo:

—Ya ves como no está aquí.

Entre tanto el *Chato*, puesto en acecho, observaba desde el desván las operaciones del infeliz padre.

El niño no debió de responder, entonces, sin duda porque Julián le pondría una mordaza para evitarlo.

Ahora la familia del [sic] víctima refiere el suceso, lamentándose que su confianza le cegara hasta el extremo de acallar los impulsos que dirigieron sus pasos a la casa del crimen."

10. See Robert W. Kern, *Liberals, Reformers and Caciques in Restoration Spain 1875-1909* (Albuquerque: University of New Mexico Press, 1974), 80; and Jesús Tobio Fernández, *Las ideas sociales de Concepción Arenal* (Madrid: CSIS, 1954), 117 for this episode.

11. "Las ropitas habíansele subido hasta la barba de modo que parecía que había descendido resbalando por la pendiente. Hallábase vestido con pantalón de niña, un refajo de bayeta blanca, una bata encarnada a cuadros negros y un gabancito negro. El pie izquierdo cubríalo con media de color ceniza. El derecho lo tenía desnudo.

A unos 16 metros más arriba del cadáver fue encontrado uno de los brodequines blancos, a la derecha el otro. La media que le faltaba se halló a 86 metros de distancia, siempre más arriba que el cadáver, y la boina, que era encarnada, recogióse a 98 metros de aquel punto."

12. Peter Brooks, *The Melodramatic Imagination. Balzac, Henry James, Melodrama, and the Mode of Excess* (New Haven: Yale University Press, 1976), 50; Manuel Aguirre, *The Closed Space. Horror Literature and Western Symbolism* (Manchester: Manchester University Press, 1990), 2.

13. "El 26 de Diciembre, o sea el día siguiente al de la desaparición del niño Pedro, me hallaba yo sola en casa. Oi una voz débil que decía 'mamá,' y sin saber de dónde salía, busqué por la casa a ver si en ella había entrado algún niño. Un quejido que oi luego me hizo levantar la vista, y vi que junto a la escalera, en el desván, había un niño, que si no le impido se cae, pues trataba de arrojarse desde la altura.

Julián se presentó cuando yo estaba preguntando al niño quién lo había llevado allí, y al verme con él, mi hermano empezó a insultarme, amenazándome de muerte si llegaba a revelar lo que había visto.

Yo comprendí el hecho brutal que mi hermano había cometido, y lo comuniqué primero a mi hermana Concha, y luego a María y su marido Crisanto. Todos acordamos guardar el secreto.

Durante las noches no he podido un solo día conciliar el sueño, pues el niño se hallaba en el rincón del desván que corresponde al cuarto en que nosotras dormíamos. Contínuamente llegan a nuestros oídos los quejidos y llanto de aquella pobre criatura; pero nuestro hermano dormía arriba y nos amenazaba si le hacíamos reflexiones acerca de esto. Varios días oíamos como voces y quejidos de un moribundo, pero no podíamos socorrerle. Muchos ratos, yo y mis hermanas, llorábamos aquella desgracia; pero por salvar a nuestro hermano nada nos atrevíamos a revelar.

Por la mañana, Julián salía y traía un vaso de leche y un bollo. Era el único alimento que le daba a Pedro, y esto, no todos los días.

Un día trajo Julián más leche que de ordinario, y nos convidó a comer un arroz con leche. Ninguna de nosotras quiso probarlo.

El día 9 de Enero, por la noche, oímos gran ruido en el tablado. Creo que fue el día en que mi hermano cometió el asesinato. A eso de las doce oimos unos ligeros golpes dados en la puerta de casa.

Nos sobrecogimos, pero Julián abrió la puerta y entró por ella un sujeto llamado Isidoro. Ignoro el apellido, pero daré las señas suyas.

Isidoro y mi hermano hablaron en la cocina, ignoro de qué."

14. Art. 454 of the 1870 *Código Penal.*

15. "es que se comete un verdadero crimen atropellando a una niña inocente, rasgando sin piedad el velo de su pureza. Esos degenerados que después de apurar todos los recursos de la molicie, despiertan y sacian sus extraviados deseos con tiernas criaturas; esos seres valetudinarios, corrumpidos, parias del sano amor, que impregnan con su baba repugnante el cuerpo alabastrino de la virgen candorosa y aun no sazonada por el festín de las pasiones, no es sólo desprecio lo que merecen, no: es persecución implacable, guerra de las leyes, de la moral, de las religiones, de las conciencias honradas." Emilio Langle Rubio, *La Mujer en el Derecho Penal* (Madrid: Hijos de Reus, 1911), 94.

16. Langle Rubio, 95. The *Código Penal* of 1870 (*Artículo* 454) provided that *abusos deshonestos* be punished by "The penalty of prison and corrective detention and exile for six months and one day to six years" ("Las penas de presidio y prisión correccional y destierro [que] durarán de seis meses y un día a seis años." The sentence could be served in the jurisdiction where the case was tried. Rape (*Artículo* 453) was punished by "reclusión temporal," i.e., confinement for twelve years and one day to twenty years in a prison in or outside of the peninsula. The following news items are useful in comparing the Escorial sentence to sentences for homicide and sexual abuse of children handed down in contemporary Spain. In 1988 a twenty-seven year-old truck driver abducted a ten year-old boy who was riding his bicycle near Argentona. The older man put the boy in the truck, taped his mouth and threatened him with a knife. After driving to a secluded place, he removed the gag and put a plastic bag over the boy's head, tearing a small hole in it to expose the boy's mouth. The man then obliged the boy to fellate him, after which he penetrated him anally. Two years later the *Audiencia* of Barcelona sentenced the man to three years and four months of prison for abduction and *abusos deshonestos*. From *El País* 28 July 1990. The second example: "The Provincial Court in Lérida on July 11, 1989 condemned Jové to 10 years and four months in prison for homicide and sexual abuse" ("La Audiencia Provincial de Lérida condenó el 11 de Julio de 1989 a Jové a 10 años y cuatro meses de prisión por homicidio y abusos deshonestos") [*El País* 22 July 1990]. The victim of the seventeen-year-old Jové—the latter's legal status as a minor constituted an attenuating circumstance—was an eight-year-old boy. In 1990 the *Tribunal Supremo* added thirteen years to the sentence after determining that the aggravating circumstance of *alevosía* applied. Julián had received twenty-one years for homicide and *abusos deshonestos* ninety-five years earlier—twice the number Jové was originally sentenced to serve.

17. For a discussion of child protection laws in Spain in the nineties interested Spaniards could have read Pedro Armengol y Cornet, "Cuestiones relacionadas con la infancia y los menores," *Revista de los Tribunales y de Legislación Universal* 29 (8 de Junio de 1895):354-360. For a brief retrospective view which included France they could have consulted M. Hudry-Menos, "La protección a la infancia," *Boletín de la Institución Libre de Enseñanza* 22 (1898):194-198. Hudry-Menos' article indicates how little had been done up to 1898 to ensure the physical and moral safety of children. Armengol, in the article cited above, referred to the heart-breaking reports of the French criminologists, Bonjean and Joly, regarding the harm parents did to their children. He also referred to the French law of 1889 which permitted the state to remove children from the home and make them its wards. I am not aware of studies of the history of child abuse or of child protection legislation in Spain. The discussion of the latter in Fernando Alvarez-Uría, *Miserables y locos. Medicina mental y orden social en la España*

del siglo XIX, prólogo de Robert Castel (Barcelona: Tusquets Editores, 1983), 334-353, deals primarily with the period after 1900. For modern reviews of child protection legislation in Britain, see pp.363-365 of Deborah Gorham, "The 'Maiden Tribute of Modern Babylon' Re-Examined: Child Prostitution and the Idea of Childhood in Late-Victorian England," *Victorian Studies* 21 (Spring 1978), and George K. Behlmer's *Child Abuse and Moral Reform in England, 1870-1908* (Stanford, California: Stanford University Press, 1982), 157-160. See also Nigel Parton, *The Politics of Child Abuse* (New York: St. Martin's Press, 1985), which chronicles the history of the public's awareness of child abuse in England and of state intervention on behalf of children; Harry Ferguson, "Rethinking child protection practices: a case for history," in *Taking Child Abuse Seriously: Contemporary Issues in Child Protection Theory and Practice* (London: Unwin Hyman, 1990), 121-142. Ferguson's essay studies a case history which engaged inspectors of the National Society for the Prevention of Cruelty to Children in London between 1891 and 1898. Ian Hacking on pp. 264-266 of "The Making and Molding of Child Abuse," *Critical Inquiry* 17 (Winter 1991), analyzes movements designed to deal with child abuse in Britain and the United States from the 1870s to the turn of the century.

18. Larry Wolff, *Postcards from the End of the World. Child Abuse in Freud's Vienna* (New York: Atheneum, 1988), 60; 76–77. The last chapter of Behlmer's *Child Abuse and Moral Reform in England 1870–1908*, "The 'Discovery' of Child Abuse," notes that in late nineteenth-century England child abuse had not been "medicalized," and as a result, the injuries of battered children were not the focus of attention. Private philanthropists, not doctors, were most active in dealing with the problem, and their concern, above all, was to remove children from homes where they were in danger. Behlmer points to the later publicizing of child abuse in the mass media as an important factor in increasing awareness. Yet, he acknowledges that the "curious decline of public interest in child abuse between 1914 and the early 1960's" requires some explanation. He proposes the impact of two world wars, economic preoccupations, and changing views about the removal of children from their families as key factors (225–226). Jeffrey Moussaieff Masson provides useful information on medico-legal investigations of child abuse in nineteenth-century France in "Freud at the Paris Morgue" from *The Assault on Truth: Freud's Suppression of the Seduction Theory* (New York: HarperPerennial, 1992), 14–54. Spaniards such as Armengol y Cornet who were interested in legal developments concerning children in contemporary Europe, Britain, and America, would probably have been familiar with this material which was available to them in the medical and legal journal literature. Ian Hacking's essay, "The Making and Molding of Child Abuse," insists that a framework which establishes what is abnormal and what is normal had to come into being in order for us to conceive of child abuse as we now do (287). Cruelty may not have been "medicalized" at the turn of the century but the Escorial coverage indicates that it was "anthropologized." The public learned that at least some brutal, ferocious attacks against children were made by animal-like throwbacks to our primate cousins. With adequate data at hand, it might be possible to show that in the general perception, informed above all by the press and popular literature, parents (especially middle and upper class parents) as well as clergy were exempted from possible inclusion in the category of atavistic criminals. Linda Gordon, in her *Heroes of Their Own Lives: The History and Politics of Family Violence 1880–1960* (New York: Penguin, 1988 and London: Virago, 1989), shows how a sample real child abuse case might have been treated at different periods characterized by different mentalities since the "discovery" of child abuse in Britain in the 1870s.

19. Wolff's discussion on pp.204–217 provides commentary on the work of Freud's critics and supporters, including Marianne Krüll's *Freud and His Father* (1979), Alice Miller's *Thou Shalt Not Be Aware: Society's Betrayal of the Child* (1985), and Jeffrey Moussaieff Masson's *The Assault on Truth: Freud's Suppression of the Seduction Theory* (Orig. Publ. 1984).

20. See Wolff's Chapters 2 and 3, in particular, for material on the innocence of children and maternal love respectively.

21. Entitled "Otro 'Chato' de El Escorial," the article, which appeared in *El Correo* on October 7, 1894, began:

"In Algeciras a horrible attack has taken place with circumstances analogous to those in the unfortunately famous case of the crime at El Escorial.

A seven-year-old boy named José Díaz Bayarren, son of a telegraph operator, fell sick.

His mother called the doctor, Sr. Morán, who made a diagnosis of peritonitis. During the course of the treatment, the doctor observed certain unusual symptoms which obliged him to make a more thorough examination whereupon he clarified the origin of the ailment. The child had been brutally assaulted" ("En Algeciras ha ocurrido un horroroso atropello, en el cual concurren análogas circunstancias al del tristemente célebre crimen de El Escorial.

Se trata de un niño de siete años, llamado José Díaz Bayarren, hijo de un ordenanza de telégrafos, que cayó enfermo.

Su madre avisó al médico Sr. Morán, quien diagnosticó el padecimiento de peritonitis.

Durante el curso de la enfermedad, observó raras manifestaciones, que le obligaron a ampliar el reconocimiento. Entonces puso en claro el origen del mal. El pobre niño había sido brutalmente atropellado.") Despite his grave condition, the child was able to identify his assailant in a line-up.

22. From Bartrina's notes for a lecture on "La América precolombina" in *Obras en prosa y verso*, ed. J. Sardá (Barcelona, Madrid: Texidó y Parera, 1881), 162. The former journalist turned novelist and short story writer, Pedro Antonio de Alarcón, presented an unforgettable portrait of a sexually perverse little boy in his story "La comendadora," dated 1868. The legal writer, Pedro Armengol y Cornet, did believe in the innocence of children—innocence in the sense of a *tabula rasa* which once written on for ill could never be reinscribed for the good. In his "Cuestiones relacionadas con la infancia y los menores," he wrote of the harm abusive parents cause: "it cannot be repaired, for once innocence is lost, and bad habits have taken root, passions excited so early in life are not capable of being reconstituted" ("es de imposible reparación, puesto que la inocencia perdida, los malos hábitos arraigados, las pasiones excitadas tan temprano, no son susceptibles de reconstitución") [400]. Armengol y Cornet put more emphasis on the influence of environment than was the case among the most orthodox followers of the Italian school of anthropological criminology. In an 1899 lecture delivered before the Child Study Department of the National Education Association meeting in Los Angeles ("Status of Child Study in Europe" *The Pedagogical Seminary*, vol. 6 (Worcester, Mass.: J.H. Orpha, 1899), 378), Will S. Monroe commented on differences of opinion on this point and provided brief accounts of the activities, research, and recent conferences relating to children in most European countries. Spain was not included. Monroe referred to the views on juvenile crime of Lino Ferriani. See also Patrizia Guarnieri for a discussion of Ferriani's and others' views on children's "strong instinct toward evil," in *A Case of Child Murder. Law and Science in Nineteenth-Century Tuscany*, Trans. Claudia Mièville (Cambridge, U. K.: Polity Press), 66–67.

23. "¡Menguada sociedad la que no rodea de todas las protecciones posibles al niño inocente y candoroso, imagen en la tierra de los ángeles del cielo! ¡Pueblo corrompido y degenerado el que no ampara y protege esa inocencia castigando severamente al bárbaro que la marchita! En esa sociedad, en ese pueblo, las madres no se atreverían a apartar de su regazo a los hijos de sus entrañas, y la cruz levantada en el cerro Avante [sic], donde se encontró el mutilado cadáver del niño Pedrín, sería un eterno madero de ignominia si al mismo tiempo que el repugnante crimen no se pudiesen recordar el severo y ejemplar castigo."

24. "Los tribunales podrán privar a los padres de la patria potestad, o suspender el ejercicio de ésta, si tratasen a sus hijos con dureza excesiva, o les dieren órdenes, consejos o ejemplos corruptores. En estos casos, podrán asimismo privar a los padres, total o parcialmente, del usufructo de los bienes del hijo, o adoptar las providencias que estimen convenientes a los intereses de éste."

25. "Cuestiones relacionadas con la infancia [...]," 354–356.

26. "los hechos y los procesos vinieron a justificar, que en repetidas ocasiones, la borrachera habitual, los escándalos domésticos, la instigación a la vagancia, la mendacidad y el hurto, el abandono completo a los malos instintos por parte de los padres, constituían un gravísimo peligro para la moralidad de los hijos, y que en muchos casos éstos eran los encubridores de las raterías cometidas por sus padres y que éstos exigían a sus rapazuelos que volvieran a casa con el fruto de su rapiña y merodeo." From his article, "Una gran deficiencia del Código civil," reprinted in the *Revista de los Tribunales y de Legislación Universal* 29 (22 de Junio 1895):398.

27. Ramón Pérez de Ayala, *A.M.D.G.* (Madrid: Biblioteca Renacimiento, 1911), 173. On pp. 11–13 of his edition of *A.M.D.G.* (Madrid: Cátedra:, 1983), Andrés Amorós notes that

publication of the novel was not permitted in Spain after the edition of 1931. During the Franco period, the *Obras completas* of Pérez de Ayala were published with the understanding that *A.M.D.G.* would not be included.

28. "Una pobre madre que tenía recluída a una hija suya en el manicomio de Ciempozuelos denuncia en un periódico el hecho escandaloso de haber sido atropellada y violada aquella infeliz reclusa, y culpa de tan vergonzoso delito al padre director de dicho establecimiento. Aunque la desolada madre ha recorrido a los Tribunales y ha podido comprobar la violación, no parece que pone gran empeño la justicia en descubrir al culpable. Pero no hay que pensar mal de los Tribunales de justicia. Porque ya se sabe que esos [sic] son incorruptibles."

29. The story carried by *El Socialista*, 26 July 1896, informed readers that two priests, D. Ramón Palacios and an unidentified colleague, had fled Huesca with a young girl, with passports under assumed names issued from the Mexican consulate, and 3,400 pesetas. Indirect evidence indicates that the clergy did not often appear in secular courts. *La Época*, 22 December 1894, carried an article under the rubric "Gaceta de los Tribunales" about a priest who had been charged with "disrespect" ("desacato") by the *Asociación de los Padres de la Familia*. He had allegedly written an anonymous pamphlet condemning the Popes. The reporter observed that since it was so rare to see a priest on the bench many people had jammed the Salesas, i.e., the court, to hear his defense.

30. *Crime and Criminal Justice Under the Third Republic. The Shame of Marianne* (Baton Rouge: Louisiana State University Press, 1990), 35–38. Martin theorizes that the high incidence of girl molestation in France may have been related to the relatively common middle and upper class practice of contracting arranged marriages, although he notes that commission of this felony cut across class lines (35).

31. *The History of Sacerdotal Celibacy in the Christian Church* (New York: Russell and Russell, 1957), 573.

32. "Si fuera posible hacer otra suerte de suposiciones deducidas de la naturaleza misma del repugnante crimen, habría que pensar en hombres acomodados a cierta clase de vida, regalados, tranquilos, forzados por tales o cuales causas a involuntaria abstinencia.

Hay enfermedades frecuentes en hombres de estas condiciones; la *satiriasis*, poco común en las clases proletarias, por ejemplo, que les conduce frenéticos a realizar los más horrendos atentados contra la naturaleza.

Es preciso fijarse en esto, recordar las tremendas historias de jóvenes violados en Francia por sus preceptores, hombres todos de aquellas precitadas condiciones.

¿Por qué razón el digno juez Sr. Estirado, se obsesiona en seguir una pista única y, sin abandonarla, no emprender otros derroteros, siquiera para examinar todas las probabilidades de acierto y ensayar todas las conjeturas, hasta las más absurdas?

A veces, en la vida, no hay nada tan inverosímil como la realidad.

Para terminar.

Recuérdese que según Concha, la hermana de Julián, en los primeros momentos en que se advirtió la falta de Pedrín, la madre de éste dirigía todas sus pesquisas hacia donde hasta ahora no se han hecho investigaciones de ninguna especie."

33. For entries on the "malevolent" monk, see Ann B. Tracy, *The Gothic Novel, 1790-1830; Plot Summaries and Index to Motifs* (Lexington: University Presses of Kentucky, 1981).

34. "encaminado a demostrar que el Linch law puede ser un síntoma consolador de la moralidad de un país; mas no siempre, y siempre en cambio índice bárbaro de retroceso a la forma primitiva de administrar justicia, que sería necesario corregir aún cuando su móvil sea derecho del más moral y real." Constancio Bernaldo de Quirós, *Las nuevas teorías de la criminalidad* (Madrid: Hijos de Reus, 1898), 175-176. The book in favor of Lynch law, authored by González Lanuza, was *La ley de Linch en los Estados Unidos*, published in Havana in 1892.

35. "¿Qué opinan ustedes de la ley de Lynch? A mí no me disgusta en cuanto revela energías y concepto de la justicia; porque hay crímenes que de tal manera ofenden y soliviantan, que parece que el castigo ha de ser inmediato, como el golpe con que se responde a grave y bochornosa afrenta.

Los que prevalidos de su fuerza, atropellan a la niñez; los bestiales ultrajadores de criaturas, ¿merecen acaso, otra cosa que el linchamiento? Jamás lo creeré. La indignación del primer instante, que se debilita después, es la mejor consejera y el juez más recto: en tales casos el sentimiento enseña mejor que y guía más certeramente que todas las legalidades formulistas del enjuiciamiento largo y pesado. Y el sentimiento, en hechos como los que frecuentemente narra la prensa, y que por lo general se desenlazan con sobreseimientos o penas leves, dictaría la cuerda, dictaría el garrote, dictaría algo tan ejemplar como lo que practica esa nación fuerte y llena de savia que ha resuelto el problema de ir a todas partes por el camino más corto [...]."

36. The press reported a number of protests against pornography in Madrid during the summer and fall of 1894. On August 28, 1894, *El Correo* reported that the *gobernador* had ordered a sweep of pornography vendors on Recoletos (a principal thoroughfare), "including a crackdown on the vendors whose descriptive language obliges modest women to stop their ears" ("alcanzando la represión a los vendedores que con sus calificativos obligan a taparse los oídos a todas las mujeres pudorosas"). *El Correo* added: "But the governor will not get very far in this campaign, because it is clear that the police, left to themselves, are inclined to the greatest passivity" ("Mas poco adelantará el gobernador en esta campaña, si no desplega constancia, porque está visto que la policía, entregada a sí misma, propende a vivir en la mayor pasividad"). On September 4, 1894, Monte Amor in *La Época*, wrote that: "An illustrious lady urges us to call the attention of the authorities to the scandalous sale of pornographic books, and even of certain publications whose contents are shouted out by the vendors" ("Una dama ilustre nos excita a que llamemos la atención de las autoridades sobre la escandalosa venta de libros pornográficos, y hasta de ciertas publicaciones cuyo texto anuncian los vendedores a grito pelado"). The reporter noted that the Conde de Canga-Argüelles had recently addressed this matter in the Senate—unfortunately to no particular effect—and that it did, indeed, merit serious attention. Finally, on November 6, 1894, in a piece called "Los gritos pornográficos," *El Correo* reported: "Security police, by order of the Civil Governor yesterday detained a fair number of vendors of pornographic prints and books in the Puerta del Sol and several other centrally-located streets. We applaud this campaign undertaken by the Duke of Tamames and we recommend it be used against those who hawk publications with scandalous titles, and those who sell an unusual-looking item called `Maüser Pistols' which they use to cause particular annoyance to decent women" ("Los agentes del cuerpo de Seguridad, por orden del gobernador civil, detuvieron ayer en la Puerta del Sol y varias calles céntricas buen número de vendedores de estampas y libros pornográficos. Aplaudimos esta campaña emprendida por el duque de Tamames, y le recomendamos a los que pregonan publicaciones con títulos escandalosos y a los que expenden una mercancía de raro aspecto que llaman `Fusiles Maüser' con la que ponen especial empeño en molestar a las señoras").

37. For a contemporary account of the new trends in criminology, see Constancio Bernaldo de Quirós, *Las nuevas teorías de la criminalidad*. Pages 157–176 of the 1898 edition—which contains some material on Spain not included in later editions—deal specifically with the development of criminology and related disciplines in Spain. In his preface, Bernaldo listed two other works similar to his: Dorado Montero's *Antropología criminal en Italia* and Aramburu's *La nueva ciencia penal*, both published ten years earlier and concerned with the development of criminal anthropology (excluding criminal sociology) in Italy, but not in Spain. Many articles on criminology by followers of Lombroso appeared in the nineties in journals such as *La España Moderna*. Enrico Ferri was a particularly assiduous contributor. In 1894, *La escuela de criminología positivista* by Lombroso, Ferri, Garofalo and Fioretti, came out in Madrid published by the editorial house of *La España Moderna*. Excerpts and occasional reviews of new work in criminology also appeared in the press. Meanwhile, Max Nordau's *Entartung* was published in Berlin in 1893, the French translation, *Dégénérescence*, appeared in Paris in 1894, and the two-volume Spanish translation by Nicolás Salmerón y García, *Degeneración*, was published in Madrid in 1902. For a modern account of ideas about degeneracy during the period in question, see Luis Maristany, *El gabinete del doctor Lombroso. Delincuencia y fin de siglo en España* (Barcelona: Anagrama, 1973). Also see Daniel Pick, *Faces of Degeneration. A European Disorder, c.1848–c. 1918* (Cambridge: Cambridge University Press, 1989), in which the concept of degeneration is studied in relation to "the broad crisis of liberal social optimism in the face of revolution" (67).

38. "El detenido se contradice a cada paso, porque, según manifiesta, no se acuerda de lo que dijo anteriormente.

Le dirige el juez preguntas encaminadas al descubrimiento de lo que hizo en los días 25 y 26 y él cree que alude al hurto por el cual se encuentra preso.

Su entendimiento es tan obtuso, que para interrogarle no se puede andar con rodeos y delicadezas, porque abre la boca, mira estúpidamente y luego dice:

—No entiendo."

39. "La fatalidad, o la *mala sombra*, como él dice, fue la causa de la epilepsia.

Cuando era muchacho, iba por la carretera acompañado por otro mozalbete. Éste por jugar, tiró una piedra a una pareja de bueyes. El mayoral se enfadó, y sin encomendarse a Dios ni al diablo, y sin fijarse en quién había sido, arremetió contra Julián, dándole tan tremendo garrotazo, que le dejó privado de sentido. Desde entonces, con mayor o menor intermitencia, padece tan terrible mal.

—La única suerte que he tenido—dijo al terminar—fue cuando me sortearon. Saqué el número más alto; pero de nada me sirvió, porque me hubiera librado por mi enfermedad."

40. "El detenido hasta ahora, por existir vehementes sospechas de que sea el autor del crimen es un hombre de unos veinticinco [sic] años de edad, de escasa estura [sic] su cuerpo, de complexión poco robusta, no guarda relación con su talla [sic] si ésta guardáse paridad con aquélla, Julián García sería un cuasi gigante.

A pesar de sus veinticuatro [sic] años es casi imberbe [sic] ligero bozo apunta en su labio, su pelo negro corto y recio le cubre hasta la [sic] sienes, dejándole una frente sumamente estrecha.

Viste blusa y pantalón azul y calza alpargata negra."

41. "Memoria de la Comisión Provincial de Avila," *Reformas sociales*, 4:144.

42. Sumamente pobre, se procura la alimentación de mil diferentes maneras; ha sido pinche del Hotel Miranda, obrero del Municipio en las carreteras, albañil, etc. etc ; cuando el trabajo falta y las necesidades de él y su familia son apremiantes, va al monte y hurta haces de leña que vende después en el pueblo. Veces ha habido que ha andado seis y siete leguas para coger un montón de setas para las que algunas ocasiones no encontraba comprador."

43. *Reformas sociales*, 4:138.

44. *Reformas sociales*, 4:151. "La memoria del fiscal del Tribunal Supremo" for 1894, excerpted in the *Revista de los Tribunales y de Legislación Universal*, contained a plea for changes in the *Código Penal* with regard to misdemeanors (*simples faltas*) which had been converted to crimes (*delitos*) in 1876. The author of the *Memoria*, Juan de Aldana, wrote: "Above all, regarding the removal of wood from uncultivated lands whether public or private, the disproportion between the transgression and the criminal procedure and penalty goes beyond anything one can imagine. On winter days, a poor man seeing his family stiff with cold, goes to the woods and gathers a bundle of firewood. Moral concepts and the doctrine of moralists with respect to cases of extreme necessity aside, in the eyes of the law that individual has executed an act of transgression against the right of property, an act which falls under the jurisdiction of the person charged with overseeing the integrity of legally owned property. But it cannot be said that the man who acts thus in such circumstances is a delinquent, nor is any principle or need served by submitting him to the Calvary of a trial, or to the infamy consequent on a sentence which, even if it does not go beyond jail, perhaps deprives a family of the support and help it counted on, and engraves forever the name of the defendant in the register of criminals. The High Court is constantly intervening in matters like this in which the value of the stolen wood is set at ten and even five *céntimos* {...}" ("Sobre todo, en la sustracción de leñas de los montes, ya públicos ya particulares, la desproporción entre la transgresión y el procedimiento y la pena supera a cuanto se pudiera imaginar. En días de invierno, un pobre que ve a su familia aterida de frío, se va al monte y coge un haz de leña. Aparte el concepto moral y la doctrina de los moralistas para el caso de extrema necesidad, a los ojos de la Ley ese individuo ejecuta una transgresión contra el derecho de propiedad, que cae bajo la potestad del que tiene el encargo de velar por la integridad de lo que cada uno legítimamente posee; pero ni se puede afirmar que el que en tales condiciones obra sea un delincuente, ni obedece a ningún principio ni a ninguna necesidad que se le someta al calvario de un proceso ni a la infamia que imprime una condena que, si no pasa de la cárcel, priva tal vez a una familia del apoyo y sustento con que contaba, y graba para siempre el nombre de aquél en los registros de los criminales. De continuo tiene que estar interviniendo el Tribunal Supremo en asuntos de esta

clase, en que el valor de la leña sustraída estaba tasado en diéz y aun en cinco céntimos {...}" (28 [22 de septiembre de 1894]:564).

45. Acabo de ser autorizado para publicar el nombre del espada en cuya cuadrilla trabajaba el *Chato*. Llámase el maestro José García, y está a la disposición de las empresas. No tiene apoderado.

He hablado largamente con él acerca de las aptitudes taurinas del *Chato*.

—Nunca hubiera sido nada—me dijo—porque tenía las patas en forma de *violín* y siempre rodaba por el suelo."

46. "Con motivo de las fiestas que se celebraron hace tres años en El Escorial de Abajo para celebrar la inauguración del mercado, había colocado en el centro de la plaza una cucaña, cuya elevación era tan respetable, que ninguno de los mozos se atrevía tocar a su fin, no obstante consistir su premio en un jamón y un bolsillo con algunas pesetas, que en el extremo estaban colocados.

Entonces Julián García les dijo:

'No valéis *pa na*, yo subiré'; [sic] y sin pérdida de tiempo, con asombro de todos, trepó por el palo escurridizo, apoderándose del obsequio.

El entusiasmo fue extraordinario, y los presentes le obsequiaron con cigarros y vino."

47. "Éste bajó al pozo por ellos, mediante una soga, y cuando el *Chato* estaba en el fondo y se disponía a subir con los zapatos, los mozos tiraron de la cuerda y él exclamó:

'No importa que os hayáis burlado de mí, aunque me mate he de subir sin la cuerda.'

Al poco tiempo, con asombro de todos, logró salir del pozo gateando de una manera pasmosa."

48. "Su pasión favorita es la glotonería.

Según dijo, cuando estuvo en San Lorenzo de El Escorial de pinche en la fonda de Miranda, única época en su vida en que se nutría hasta hartarse, padecía cólicos diarios por efecto de la gula. No se cansa de deglutir ni adquiere repugnancia a ninguna clase de alimento, por fuerte que sea."

49. "La española es una raza que no come, y, en cambio, su desgaste orgánico por el trabajo, es rudísimo. Hay comarcas donde, si alguno cae enfermo, le llevan tres cosas a un tiempo: el chocolate, el médico y el cura. El cura, porque en la mayor parte de los casos, ya no hay tiempo para otra cosa; el médico, para que certifique la defunción; el chocolate para que el enfermo *no se vaya de este mundo sin probarlo*." For information on the wide-spread poverty in the Castilian countryside, see *Miseria y conciencia del campesino castellano* ["Memoria acerca de la información agraria en ambas Castillas."] Introducción, notas y comentario de textos por Julio Aróstegui (Madrid:Narcea, 1977), a reprint and commentary on an investigation into the agrarian crisis in Castile in 1904, conducted by Adolfo A. Buylla and G. Alegre for the *Instituto de Reformas Sociales*.

50. Martin W. Barr, M.D., "Mental Defectives: Their Classification And Training," in *Third International Congress For The Welfare And Protection Of Children* (London: P.S. King and Son, 1902), 257.

51. "Cual si las horas de soledad pasadas en su encierro hubiéranle permitido recapacitar acerca de la gravísima situación en que se encuentra y la constante meditación hubiera aguzado sus facultades intelectuales, el *Chato* da pruebas de una perspicacia que asombra discutiendo con argumentos de fuerza y sofismas sorprendentes todo cuanto se pone al alcance de su observación. Ya no es el hombre rudo que inclina la cabeza confundido por el cúmulo de cargos que le hacen, sino el ser que piensa y se ha penetrado de la importancia que su actitud puede tener en la marcha del proceso."

52. "En el *Chato* se ha observado hoy un cambio radical en la manera de expresarse.

Ha negado, no con monosílabos o frases cortas, sino contestando a las acusaciones con relativa verbosidad.

Parece que desde que su cuñado Crisanto lanzó sobre él la terrible acusación, ha sufrido una completa metamorfosis."

53. "El acusador Sr. Pico pregunta: ¿Es posible que la influencia de la epilepsia se conserve en un criminal durante cuarenta días que dura la comisión de su delito?

Calatraveño.—Hay períodos de descargo, pero sin llegar a la normalidad: el cerebro de un epiléptico es como una bomba de dinamita; siempre es peligrosa, y cuando se la toca estalla.

Presidente.—Sr. Calatraveño: en el histerismo debe haber grados, porque apenas se conoce una familia que no tenga histéricos.

Calatraveño.—Indudablemente ésa, como todas las enfermedades, tiene sus grados: desde la señorita caprichosa que repugna los alimentos y la que raspa las paredes y se come con delicia el yeso, hasta el que sufre convulsiones, hay muchos grados.

Presidente.—Lo que nos importa averiguar es si en ese período de tregua los epilépticos pueden cometer un crimen con perfecto conocimiento.

Calatraveño.—Es posible que en la calma, tengan voluntad propia, pero siempre atenuada."

54. In a review essay entitled "Gender, Class and Madness in Nineteenth-Century France," *French Historical Studies* 17/4 (1992):1059, Jill Harsin noted that both Joëlle Guillais in *La Chair de l'autre*, and Ruth Harris in *Murder and Madness*, recorded a reaction against deterministic explanations of criminal behavior and a return to ideas of individual responsibility in criminal cases tried in French courts in the late nineteenth century. Criminal responsibility in individuals suffering from epilepsy was difficult to determine among other reasons because a diagnosis of epilepsy was itself often problematic. See Ellen Dwyer, "Stories of Epilepsy, 1880–1930," *Framing Disease: Studies in Cultural History (Health and Medicine in American Society.)*, eds. Charles E. Rosenberg and Janet Golden (New Brunswick, N.J.: University Press, 1992), 248–272. Dwyer discusses the connection made between epilepsy, madness and crime, noting on page 256 that "Such claims of epileptics' predilection for violent behavior were lent credence by highly charged descriptions of incidents of homicidal epilepsy in medical and legal journals, as well as in the popular press." The lecture referred to above by Vicente Ots y Esquerdo was published as *La locura ante los Tribunales: Estudio médico-legal de la irresponsabilidad del loco* (Madrid: Góngora, 1894). The study also appeared in the *Revista de los Tribunales y de Legislación Universal* where the relevant sections on epilepsy appear in 28 (1894):273–282; 351–357. See also *Comentarios científicos-prácticos al Código penal de 1870,* vol.2 *Tratado de responsabilidad* por Federico Castejón (Madrid: Editorial Reus, 1926), 258–260. Judging by Castejón's essay, there had been no significant changes in the legal assessment of responsibility in epileptics since Ots y Esquerdo's study of 1894. Indeed, as late as 1926 Castejón wrote that epilepsy was important in penal law because Lombroso and his school had identified the delinquent epileptic with the "loco moral" and the born criminal, and found "la epilepsia psíquica" even in the man of genius. Still difficult to define in 1926, epilepsy could only qualify as an attenuating factor when the criminal act in question was committed under the direct influence of a seizure (260).

LOS LUNES DE EL IMPARCIAL

MADRID 7 DE MAYO DE 1894

No se devuelven los originales.

LA ACTUALIDAD

El niño de El Escorial.

UN GRABADO

Figure 2.1. "Current news: The Child at El Escorial," *Los Lunes de El Imparcial*, May 7, 1894.

Figure 2.2. "The most censorious are the first to demand all the facts." "—Bad, it's very bad for the press to cover certain immoral trials…but dammit! It's not right for a trial to be held behind closed doors so that reporters can't give us all the details." From *La Correspondencia de España,* May 9, 1894.

Figure 2.3. "Cultivated People". Left panel: "…just out, excerpts from a speech by Castelar, a novel by Galdós, a play by Echegaray, an article by Salmerón, verses by Campoamor and Nuñez de Arce… (No one is buying.)". Right panel: "…latest on the crime at El Escorial!!... (Delirium!!")". From *La Correspondencia de España,* May 7, 1894.

Chapter Three

The Escorial Case as Rural Gothic

Reporters for *El Imparcial*, *La Correspondencia de España*, and *El País* most notably, were adept in supplying the details (invented on occasion), recreated dialogue and scenes which invested the actions, individuals, and themes of this crime with the heightened emotion typical of melodrama. Within the bounds of this kind of fiction, allusions to the conventions of the terrorific or Gothic mode proved particularly successful in reporting the Escorial case.

On February 25, using language that nicely evoked the moral atmosphere of the Gothic novel, Eduardo Rosón wrote: "The horrendous crime committed at El Escorial reveals an instance of moral monstrousness almost without precedent in Europe. It is a phenomenon that stands out even among other criminal phenomena; it is the prime example of a crime that oozes vice and reeks of odors from the bordello and the cemetery" ("El crimen horrendo del Escorial revela caso de teratología moral de que hay pocos ejemplos en Europa. Es un fenómeno dentro de los fenómenos criminales; es la flor del crimen que trasuda vicio y huele a esencias de burdel y de cementerio"). Rosón—the most sceptical of the reporters who covered the Escorial case, and the only one to urge that other leads be followed, given the lack of evidence against Julián—turned out to be one of the most successful in capturing a *feuilletonesque* tone particularly well-suited for conveying the drama of a family crushed by unspeakable evil.

THE FAMILY CONFRONTED BY MONSTROUS EVIL

The nature of the victim, the crime, and of the alleged killer tempted journalists to intensify the horror of the known facts by appropriating a theme pervasive in the fiction of the nineteenth century. The theme of family decency beset from without by some version of obscene monstrosity had proved to be compelling in popular fiction—not only in Gothic tales, but also in the widely-read subgenre of vampire stories. A tale by Hugo von Hofmannsthal, translated as *La vampiresa*, was popular at this time (1893) in Spain. E.T.A. Hoffmann's tale, *Der vampyr*, in Spanish *La mujer vampiro*, was advertised two years later in *La Vanguardia.*[1]

"Terrorific" and Gothic novels published as *folletines* in newspapers, along with ballads recounting crimes which were sung in market places and published and sold as *literatura de cordel*, had prepared readers of the press for the melodramatic opposition set up by reporters from the beginning between the forces of good, incarnate in the humble but honorable family of the dead child, and the forces of evil, incarnate in the family (anomalous to begin with since the parents were absent) composed of the accused man, his three sisters, and one half-sister, fruit of an illicit union entered into by his mother after his father's death.[2]

Shortly before the Escorial trial began, a regular feature entitled "Trial News" ("Crónicas judiciales") in *El Día* on March 5, 1894 expressed the view that people had not only been prepared to accept reality filtered through certain types of fiction, but that they had an active wish to have it so. The desire for life to imitate popular fiction was related to attendance at criminal trials. And, in the opinion of some critics, the same desire explained why people read crime reports. The author of the "Crónicas" wrote:

> The people absent from shops, offices and halls of learning, abound in the various criminal sections of our courthouse [*Audiencia*]. There, wherever there is a trace of blood, or a whiff of gun powder wafting through the air, one inevitably finds a swarm of people from all social classes avid to witness in real life something of what awakened their interest in the literary sphere as narrated by the pen of Gaboriau or Montepin.[3]

From a different vantage point—that of a "respectable" woman, for example—attendance at court trials was one of the few accepted forays out and into a world where the kinds of information and emotions prohibited at home could be acquired and experienced. Joëlle Guillais, in *La Chair de l'autre*, described Frenchwomen of the same period who seem to have been in search of direct experience and information in the real world at least as much as they hoped to be gratified by reality mediated by popular fiction. Guillais wrote: "Whatever her social position may be, she is not afraid to show herself at a trial; it is almost like going to the theatre. While it is not proper for a young woman to attend a ball at the Opéra, she can, on the other hand, in complete tranquility, attend trials where she sometimes hears exchanges which in other contexts would be considered scandalous."[4]

MALE AUTHORITY, WORK, SEXUALITY

Whatever the motivations of readers, reporters clearly believed that superimposing certain themes familiar in popular fiction onto the Escorial case would increase the story's effectiveness. Those themes included that of the good, decent family beset by evil. Reporters opposed the Bravo family—which represented good—to the evil García family, primarily with respect to habits of work, sexuality, and their understanding and acceptance of the principle of authority. That principle, reporters made clear, was properly embodied and made manifest in a male member of the family.

Pedrín's father, Eugenio Bravo y Bravo, lived with his four brothers, his wife, Gumersinda, and their three children. On February 14, Hernández y Bermúdez, of *El Imparcial*, went to the Bravo's house, situated on Calvary Street (*calle del Calvario*), where he interviewed the only family member present at the time, an uncle of the dead child:

"Sr. Román, as they call Pedrín's uncle here, is the head of the whole family, a kind of patriarch whose decisions are respected by the other four brothers.

Román is a quarry worker. He contracts for the work and oversees his brothers, who also work at the quarries and obey him in everything" ("El Sr. Roman, como llaman aquí al tío de Pedrín, es además jefe de toda la familia, una especie de patriarca, cuyas disposiciones se acatan por los otros cuatro hermanos. Román es cantero, y él contrata las obras y ejerce de maestro director de sus hermanos, que trabajan en el mismo oficio y le obedecen en cuanto ordena").

When Hernández y Bermúdez asked whether the family had any reason to suspect that someone had killed Pedrín out of rancor or a desire for revenge, the uncle replied: "No, sir. We live peacefully. All we care about is earning our living honorably, and we do not have any enemies" ("No, señor. Nosotros vivimos tranquilos, preocupándonos sólo de ganar honradamente la vida y no tenemos enemigos"). Four days later, Rosón confirmed the preceding account of the family's rectitude: "Extremely hard-working and honorable, they are well-respected in the whole area despite the fact that they don't come from there" ("En extremo trabajadores y honrados, son por esto muy apreciados en toda la comarca, a pesar de que no son oriundos de ella").

On February 26, after an interview with some of the members of the García family, Rosón wrote a long article about them. One section of the piece, sarcastically headed "Modelo de familias," was designed to provide an explanation of the family's misfortunes and missteps based on Julián's incapacity for his assigned role: "The *Chato* was, by virtue of his age and sex, the one who should have figured as the head of the family, its counselor and advisor. That was not at all the case. Julián, a brusque, reserved, *unsociable* type, avoided his sisters, admonishing them harshly if they attempted to talk back to him. And his friendships with the young men in the town were quite limited—only three or four youths enjoyed this *favor*" ("El *Chato* era, por razón de su edad y sexo, el que debía figurar como cabeza de familia y consultor y consejero de ésta. Nada de esto ocurría; Julián, de genio brusco, reservado, *insociable*, huía de sus hermanas, dirigíalas duros calificativos si trataban de hacerle alguna reconvención, y su amistad con los mozos de pueblo era limitidísima; sólo tres o cuatro disfrutaban de este *favor*").

The reporters suggested that Julián's incapacity for assuming authority over his sisters had led to grave economic, moral, and social consequences. Julián's pattern of work and unemployment was summarized by Rosón on February 26: "He neither looked for work, nor did he turn it down. If it was offered to him, he took it willingly, and faithfully complied with the task at hand. But, if no one made him an offer, rather than borrow money, he would go off for fagots, or rabbits, or whatever he could, as his sisters so graphically put it." The two older sisters who lived in the house, Concha and Francisca, exhibited the same insouciance regarding work for:

> they get up at eleven in the morning in order to go to the monastery for the soup which is distributed every day to the poor. They have petitioned for it ever since the friars refused to let them do their laundry any more, for reasons having to do with cleanliness.
>
> After that, they go walking with their friends, eating wherever they are invited, or sometimes buying some trifle or other, and then home to sleep at an hour that is not the usual one for the majority of their neighbors.

Rosón framed and moralized the preceding information on the occupations and work habits of the family by concluding his remarks in this way:

> I include the following exchange as something that graphically conveys this family's mode of life:
>
> When we asked Francisca and Concha what their occupation was, they answered;
>
> "At the moment, it's well-known that we are quite impoverished..."
>
> And yet—Concha and Francisca had dressing gowns. Every morning they made their *toilette* before going to the monastery for the dole.[5]

Julián, his two sisters and half-sister, were owners of the house they lived in. Reporters did not explain how they had acquired it, but they did indicate that it was not inherited, having been built after their father's death. Ownership of a small house like theirs was a principal goal for poor *jornaleros* like Julián and his sisters.[6] Payment of house rent would have been a heavy burden for Julián, who probably earned no more than 1.50 *pesetas* per day when he worked—a bare subsistence wage. His sisters' wages as washerwomen for the monastery probably amounted to half that sum. According to *El Imparcial* of February 19, Julián, in jail, told four reporters that his savings amounted to 25 *reales* (about 6 *pesetas*)—an amount too small to have covered the purchase of his coffin. (Pedrín's child-sized coffin cost 15 *pesetas*.)

In contrast, and as further testimony to their hard work and thrift, the Bravo family savings (accumulated, to be sure, by several male bread-winners) according to *La Correspondencia de España* on February 26, amounted to 150 pesetas—all of which was spent in searching for their missing son. Mestre Martínez noted that Pedrín's father and uncle, Román, travelled to Madrid five times to look for the boy. They spent two nights at the León de Oro inn (*posada* del León de Oro, located in the Cava Baja), hoping to find Pedrín there. They suspected that he may have been kidnapped to be put to work as a street beggar. This was not an idle fear. *El Ideal* of May 17, 1894, printed statistics for 1891 which revealed that 165,492 boys and girls were living as beggars or prostitutes in Spain "vilely exploited, one must suppose, by a corresponding number of families sunk in misery and vice" ("vilmente explotadas, y debe suponerse, por otras tantas familias sumidas en la miseria y en el vicio"). Not finding Pedrín at the León de Oro, the two men in desperation had paid a fortune-teller three *pesetas* for some hint as to Pedrín's whereabouts. The subscription money which arrived from all over Spain, to their great relief, eventually recompensed them for the loss of their savings.

María, Julián's older married sister provided further clues concerning the García family's economic situation. Rosón interviewed her on February 25, quoting her remarks on the financial consequences of her estrangement from Julián and her sisters: "So you see that because I don't get along with them, I'm paying forty *reales* annually for a house even though I'm part owner of a house that could be worth three or four thousand to me ... and now we're going to lose everything" ("Ya ve usted, por no *congeniar* con ellos, estoy pagando cuarenta reales de casa al año, teniendo como tengo parte de propiedad que podía valerme tres o cuatro mil ... y ahora vamos a perder todo ..."). Despite the fact that their house represented an important asset, Julián and his sisters lived the hand-to-mouth existence typical of *jornaleros* throughout Spain, a life brightened occasionally by the dances, festivals, gambling and wine of which reporters intimated they were overly fond.

On February 19, Rosón noted that Francisca was unhappy because she wanted to go to a masked ball—the "baile del domingo de Piñata"—that was being held the following day in the theatre. Then, on February 21, Martínez of *La Correspondencia de España* revealed that the sisters had gone to a wedding party the day after Pedrín's body was found. On February 24, he again referred to their attendance at dances and other social occasions: "According to general opinion, the *Chato* family's capacity for dissimulation—its attendance at dances and other gatherings—over such a long period of time, reveals uncommon depths of moral corruption" ("El disimulo que por espacio de tantos días la familia del *Chato* ha guardado, asistiendo a bailes y otras reuniones, es indudable que acusa en los encubridores según opinión general, un fondo de corrupción moral poco común"). *El Imparcial* seemed to allude to the sisters' vanity and self-indulgence on February 26, when it reported that they had bought "goat hair for making toques and they have arranged to buy food from outside so they won't have to eat jail fare" ("pelo de cabra para hacerse toquillas y han dispuesto comprar la comida para no tomar el rancho del cárcel"). Where did they get the money? Two days later, according to *La Correspondencia de España*, the sisters were visited by ladies from Madrid. Perhaps visitors such as these curious women provided the sisters with pocket money.

Their supposed vanity—and certainly their patience at being subjected to so much unwanted publicity—had limits: all the sisters but Juana refused to be photographed. *El País* reported them as saying on March 2: "We don't want our faces coming out on matchboxes, the other sisters exclaimed—María above all. You newspaper people have us coming and going enough as it is, and for no good reason" ("—Nosotros no queremos salir en *las cajas de cerillas*—exclaman las otras hermanas, y sobre todo María; bastante nos traen y nos llevan ustedes los de los papeles...sin necesidad ninguna"). But, according to *La Correspondencia de España*, they changed their minds three days later.

Eleven year-old Juana, it should be added, also worked, as many poor children her age did—provided work could be found. At the trial, on May 8, 1894 Julián testified, as reported in *El Imparcial*, that Juana had worked as a servant in the house of a friend of the examining magistrate. She had been let go, he claimed, for being a gossip and for talking back. She did not attend school. Everyone—reporters, and the teachers and doctors who examined her—found her to be extremely bright; although, as was reported in *El Imparcial* on March 3, when she was examined on Christian doctrine, she proved to be quite ignorant on the subject.

In contrast to Julián and his sisters, who reportedly worked at a variety of jobs, but at the same time were said to have worked as little as possible, the Bravo family was represented as being commendably industrious. No member of the family was reported to have had to resort to poaching in order to provide food for the table.

The hard-working sobriety of the Bravo household presented yet another striking contrast to reporters' depiction of the disorderly household formed by Julián and his slothful sisters Concha, Francisca, and Juana. Pedrín's parents had suffered the loss of a son, but they had three other children, and Gumersinda was pregnant with her fifth child. Their legitimate fecundity won approbation from the reporters while the sexual irregularities of Julián and his sisters were recorded with unconcealed distaste and disapproval.

Julián himself testified before the examining magistrate that he masturbated often. Other witnesses charged him with a variety of sexual offenses. First of all, in his statement of February 20—according to Rosón, reporting two days later—Crisanto Jorge claimed that Julián had kept Pedrín tied up hand and foot in the loft where he abused him every day until his death. On February 24, *El Imparcial* reported the following:

"According to previous statements which I have been able to obtain and which depict the nature of this savage with a single stroke of the brush, not long ago, the *Chato* proposed to several friends of his who were with him on the outskirts of the town, that they snatch a little boy who was passing by and perform brutal acts on him. The companions of this man-monkey indignantly rejected such a proposal" ("Según antecedentes que he logrado obtener y que pintan de un solo rasgo el carácter de este salvaje, el *Chato*, en ocasión reciente, propuso a otro u otros amigos suyos que con él se encontraban en las afueras del pueblo, coger a un niño que por allí andaba y realizar actos brutales. Los confidentes de este hombre mono rechazaron indignados semejantes proposiciones"). And, the reporter continued, ominously: "There are other rumors circulating about Julián which, because of their enormity and until I can get confirmation from a trustworthy source, I shall not consign to newsprint" ("También circulan acerca de Julián otros rumores que por su enormidad y hasta tanto que no se confirmen de un modo fehaciente no consigno en esta carta"). *La Correspondencia de España* reported a similar story on February 25 after an interview with the altar boy who apparently originated the story. These rumors did not reappear. During the trial in May 1894, Julián was accused of having sexually assaulted a boy in 1884. Assuming that reporters were correct about the date, Julián would have been eleven years old at the time. He was also accused of having made improper advances to a young girl. Neither charge was substantiated.

Julián's sisters, Francisca and Concha, also suffered from epilepsy and under questioning experienced seizures which were at times thought to have been feigned. Reporters were at first ambivalent about the two young women, pitying them at one moment, accusing them of hypocrisy and deception the next. Their sexual purity was questioned shortly after Crisanto made his accusation against Julián. During the trial, over a year later, *El Nacional* reported (May 9) that according to the testimony of Drs. Leirado and Peña, Francisca was "honrada," but that there were doubts concerning Concha and Juanita. Pressed hard by the examining magistrate to confess knowledge of Pedrín's presence in the loft, Francisca finally did so, implicating as well, a young friend of Julián—Isidoro Muñoz. She claimed that he had helped her brother remove the boy's body from the house. Reporters at El Escorial immediately printed the rumor that Isidoro was Francisca's lover. For his part, Isidoro Muñoz was quoted on February 24 in *El Imparcial* as saying that the two girls "flirted shamelessly with everyone" ("retozaban con todo el mundo"). And Julián told the examining magistrate, according to the same paper on February 28, that without intending to attribute criminal tendencies to his family, he had observed that his sisters were fond of parties (*jaleos*) and liked to flirt (*retozar*) with his friends more than was seemly. More sensationally, Rosón had written three days earlier: "A rumor circulating in the town and considered to be true, has it that Francisca gave birth to two babies and buried each one shortly after birth in the patio" ("Por el pueblo corre como muy verídico el rumor de que Francisca ha tenido dos hijos que a poco de nacer enterró en el patio de su casa"). The patio was excavated but no bodies were discovered.

Several journalists suggested that the two sisters' sexual promiscuity lay behind their indifference to Pedrín's suffering. That indifference was clearly perceived as an unnatural feminine condition. Luis Bonafoux conjured up Pedrín's groans from the loft, lost, he wrote, amidst "the lubricious laughter of a family of whores and sodomites" ("las risotadas lúbricas de una familia de meretrices y sodomitas"). Though he had no proof for the following statement, Hernández y Bermúdez wrote on February 26: "The sisters of that savage climbed up to the loft from time to time in order to see the new spectacle offered to them. The suffering of that poor child could not rouse them from their criminal indifference by awakening the pity that every woman preserves eternally in the depths of her heart, nor could it move them to overcome their fear of the *Chato*'s threats" ("Las hermanas de aquel salvaje subían de vez en cuando, curiosas por ver el espectáculo nuevo que se les ofrecía, sin que el sufrimiento del pobre niño las arrancara de su criminal indiferencia despertando la piedad que toda mujer conserva eternamente en el fondo de su corazón, o dominara su miedo a las amenazas del *Chato*"). The sisters' "criminal indiferencia" toward Pedrín transformed them into monsters.[7]

"Little Monster" ("Pequeño monstruo") was, in fact, the heading for a section devoted to Juana on March 4 in *El País*. Rosón wrote:

> She is ten years old [sic], with an agreeable face and black, lively eyes. She is slight of build, with the peculiarity that her breasts are the most developed part of her body. She tries to make them even more prominent, by making them more visible [...].
>
> The natural child of the *Chato*'s mother when she was already a widow and of an advanced age, this young girl exhibits all the refined malice and precocious cunning which typifies the *offspring of senility* [...].
>
> Born in abject circumstances, raised and educated in a place of immense corruption, she leaves an impression of profound sadness on the minds of those who observe her. She is meat inevitably destined for the prison for women.[8]

Rosón read signs of Juana's moral defects in her body, whose precocious sexual development clearly attracted his attention. On February 25, 1893 he wrote: "The fruit of a lapse on the part of her mother when she was already a widow, Juana was disliked by her half-brother and sisters. Thus it is that despite her tender age, she manifests that perspicacity which one acquires with suffering, and that malice derived from early acquaintance with vice—all of which is painted in her weary features and in the contours of her not yet fully-developed body" ("Fruto de un desliz de la madre ya viuda, era malquista de sus hermanastras; de aquí que, no obstante sus pocos años, Juanilla tenga esa perspicacia que se adquiere con el sufrimiento, y esa malicia del vicio precoz, bien retratada en sus facciones fatigadas, y en las formas de su cuerpo aun no del todo desarrolladas"). Later, at the trial, as reported by *El Nacional* on May 10, 1894, Dr. Calatraveño, the expert witness on epilepsy, testified that Juana "is an hysteric, and when she enters puberty she will also become an epileptic" ("es ya una histérica, y cuando cambie su naturaleza será también una epiléptica").

The slothfulness and sexual irregularities that reporters attributed to the García family acquired increasingly sinister overtones after Crisanto's confession. By February 24, Mestre Martínez wrote in *La Correspondencia de España* that neighbors were referring to Julián and his sisters as "the accursed family" ("la familia maldita"). From then on, the reporter used the term routinely to suggest their dark and unspeakable viciousness. At the trial's end in May 1894, Crisanto Jorge's lawyer protested the prejudicial use of the term by the newspaper which, according to Mestre Martínez, sent out half of the words dedicated to the crime through the Escorial telegraph station.

THE VICTIM'S MOTHER

The contrast between the two families was thus clearly established within a few days of Crisanto's statement: on one hand "La familia maldita," and on the other, the bereaved, honorable family of the dead child. The February 24th edition of *El País* featured an interview with Pedrín's mother, Gumersinda, in which Rosón's mastery of the rhetoric of melodrama underscored the contrast: "I departed that house—yesterday the dwelling of domestic felicity, today the mansion of infinite regret—moved to the deepest recesses of my soul. I swear never to return, because it is impossible not to weep, transfixed with pain, in the presence of grief that is so profound, so terrible, and so justified" ("Salí de aquella casa, ayer morada de la felicidad doméstica, hoy mansión del dolor más infinito, emocionado hasta lo más íntimo de mi alma. Juro no volver, porque es imposible no llorar y sentirse transido de pena ante el espectáculo de dolor tan hondo, tan terrible y tan justificado").

Mestre Martínez had paid a visit to the Bravo household on February 21, finding only Gumersinda at home commiserating with a neighbor woman. The reporter offered this account of Gumersinda's state of mind and of her exemplary Christian character:

> I told her who I was and why I was there, and she indicated that she was not surprised by my visit, since she understood that people want to read in the newspapers about everything related to the crime that has made her forever unhappy.
>
> In response to my questions, she replied that she has three other children, named Eustacio, Carlos y Valentina, of 7, 5 and 2 years of age respectively—and that she is about to give birth to another baby.
>
> Sobbing and sighing, she showed me the places in the house where Pedrín used to play.
>
> She told me about the days of anguish they had endured and efforts they had made to find their beloved son.
>
> I told her that the perpetrator of the crime was now known, to which she replied, weeping, "Nothing matters to me now, after losing my son, but I do want justice to take its course" [...].
>
> She indicated that the family lived a hard life, and begged me to make their hardships public in case the good souls in Madrid should wish to help them.
>
> Pedrín's mother repeatedly embraced her neighbors as if to mitigate and share the grief that overwhelms her.[9]

Over a year later, when she was called to testify at the trial, Gumersinda's appearance made a strong impression. The scene, as described by Domingo Blanco for *El Imparcial* on May 10, again presented a sharp contrast between the sacred state of motherhood and its sorrows, and the unmarried, allegedly licentious way of life of Julián's two middle sisters:

> It is impossible to describe the painful scene which followed upon the entrance into the courtroom of Gumersinda Bravo, the child's mother. Who can describe the grief of a mother in the face of such a horrible misfortune!
>
> Her tears and great affliction touched the hearts of all those present in the chamber.
>
> "My own heart's child!," cried out the anguished mother.
>
> And the jurors wept, and those outside who heard her lamentations also wept. The poor, unfortunate mother!
>
> Her grief does not subside; overcome with emotion, she is supported on the arm of the porter and the prosecutor. The latter, who is the attorney for the private prosecution—the man who, in the name of the parents, has come to seek punishment for the most horrendous of crimes—informs the presiding judge that he does not want to question the mother in consideration of her anguished state of mind.
>
> The mother quits the courtroom, leaving behind an impression that time will never erase.[10]

Of all the figures involved in the dramatic scenes and events chronicled by the press—among them the innocent child and the accused epileptic, i.e., degenerate, killer—Gumersinda was meant to embody the ultimate significance of the Escorial case. When the trial was over, *El Liberal* on May 15, 1894, pinpointed what was at stake—the purity of what is natural, manifest above all in maternity, as opposed to the unnatural and the perverted: "Sounding an alarm for society was never as well justified as in the case of the crime at El Escorial. Everywhere—wherever a mother was to be found—this crime which constitutes an abomination of human nature, an unprecedented example of the perversion of all instincts, including even those which are most vile and ferocious, caused fear and horror" ("En ningún caso como en el crimen de El Escorial, estaba justificado invocar la alarma social. En todas partes, donde quiera que hubiese una madre, causó espanto y horror la comisión de este crimen, abominación de la naturaleza humana, perversión sin ejemplo de todos los instintos, aún de los más ruines y de los más feroces").

It was not necessary for reporters to spell out the general perception of mothers as the very incarnation of the values threatened by degenerates such as Julián. There was considerable public defining of motherhood in Spain in the mid-nineties. On April 15, 1889, in *La Ilustración Artística* Emilio Castelar had voiced a typical official view of motherhood. He wrote that all mothers, by nature and through the designs of Providence, share the sorrows of the Virgin Mary as well as her capacity to bear up under them. In motherhood, he wrote, "God has placed an invincible propensity for sacrifice which gives the appearance of being a slow form of suicide, and which constitutes a perpetual holocaust" ("ha puesto Dios invencibles propensiones al sacrificio que parecen como un suicidio lento y que son un holocausto perpetuo"). At the very least, mothers were thought to live out in their daily lives the values of self-sacrifice and renunciation. The journalist E. Alonso y Orera went even further. In an article of November 17, 1894 in *La Ilustración Ibérica*, he wrote that analytic reason [functioning rather like a gigantic wrecking ball], had levelled the edifice in which nineteenth-century Spain had been safely housed, protected by religion, morality and tradition, leaving nothing in place but the figure of the mother, bestower of selfless love, symbol of disinterest ("A la acción de la crítica analítica han caído destrozadas la religión, la moral de nuestros abuelos y la tradición, y sólo la madre nos queda, recordándonos su amor y su desinterés." In the same journal, about one month later (December 29, 1894), Alonso y Orera wrote that mothers were the sole bulwark against despair: "In the midst of the doubts that currently befuddle us, of the systematic indifference that leads us to despoil the heavens of their divine legends, and of the fatigue which obliges us to deliver ourselves over to pessimistic despair, the mother is the port of hope, a consoling source of belief, and of an almost mystic love which promises forgetfulness and pardon" ("En medio de las dudas que hoy nos conturbian, del indiferantismo que nos hace dejar despoblado el cielo de sus leyendas divinas y del desaliento que nos obliga a entregarnos a la desesperación pesimista, la madre es puerto de esperanza, creencia consoladora, amor casi místico que promete el olvido y el perdón"). The publicly-sanctioned view of mothers conveyed in Alonso y Orera's remarks was the one journalists implicitly adopted when they assessed the gravity of the crime committed at El Escorial. No mother in all of Spain could find rest or security in light of what had happened there. And mothers represented the best of what Spain was—or had left.[11]

Peter Brooks has called the principles of contrast and polarization of values typical of the melodramatic imagination's highly dramatized productions.[12] Those principles were clearly at work in the foregoing conceptualization of Spanish motherhood as well as in reporters' representation of Gumersinda Bravo. The values reporters endorsed and the techniques they employed to purvey them in this part of the Escorial story clearly shored up conservative assumptions about the mother as moral touchstone and bulwark of the family. On the other hand, the access to a large and heterogeneous public presumably made possible by the appeal of melodramatic elements injected into the story, undoubtedly fostered a genuinely popular, national interest in the criminal justice system and judicial issues. In that sense, Peter Brooks' idea that melodrama in the theater, in the novel—and it may be added, in crime reporting—serves to democratize cultural life by making its "representations clear and legible to everyone," seems especially apt.[13]

A HOUSE BUILT OF COFFIN BOARDS

Reporters' interest in setting an emotionally evocative scene naturally led them to describe the dwellings of the two families. The depiction of the house in which the crime had allegedly been committed necessarily became an important element in the story. At first, reporters who visited it limited themselves to describing its floor plan. But in the aftermath of Crisanto's confession, Mestre Martínez, transformed it into "the accursed house" ("la casa maldita"). This transformation is the clearest example in the coverage of the Escorial case of how a journalist might aim to fulfill the expectations of readers of popular fiction. Mestre Martínez was undoubtedly aware of the eery impact that mysterious and malevolent-seeming dwellings had in Gothic and terrorific fiction. Accordingly, on February 24 he broke the extraordinary story that the suspected murderer's house was constructed out of old coffin boards to which bits and tatters of funerary decoration still adhered. Under the epigraph "Coffin Boards" ("Las cajas de muertos"), Mestre Martínez explained: "It seems that the father made use of these boards. It has not yet been proven that the father dug up the dead. It is believed that when the cemetery ground was cleared years ago, the coffin boards were sold at public auction, and that he took some of them" ("Parece que el padre se utilizaba de estas maderas. No está probado aun que el padre desenterrase los muertos. Créese que, al ser removida la tierra de este cementerio, hace años, se vendieron en pública subasta los tablones y que se quedó con ellos"). He added that when the neighbors learned about this, terrified, they forbade their children to play outside. Later, on the same day, Mestre Martínez telegraphed it was "inexact" that Julián's father had dug up bodies in order to obtain the coffin boards; rather, they had indeed been sold at public auction. His conversations with neighbors revealed further that Julián's father, known as the "little Grandfather" (*Abuelito*), was highly regarded: "The neighbors all comment on the difference between the conduct of the father and that of the accursed family" ("El vecindario hace comentarios sobre la diferencia de conducta del padre y la de la 'familia maldita'"). Two days later, Mestre Martínez informed his readers that there had been no "profanation": "It is not true, as has been claimed, that the planks which formed a kind of loft in the *Chato*'s house came from coffin boards" ("No es exacto, como se ha dicho, que las tablas que formaban la especie de desván en la habitación de los *Chatos* procediesen de cajas de muertos").

On February 26, Rosón offered an explanation for his colleague's invention of the sensational coffin-board story: "It is appropriate for me to clarify some inaccuracies perpetuated by the correspondent for another paper. This man wishing, no doubt, to distinguish himself by putting out sensational news, forges a novel every day, complete with details, exactly as if it were copied from real life, when, in fact, it is nothing but a bag of tricks reporters employ to maintain suspense which flags at those moments when there is absolutely no information to give out."[14] Rosón then said that Julián's father did not steal the coffin boards with which to build the house for the simple reason that the house was built after his death. Finally, Rosón—perhaps at the request of residents of El Escorial—stated that coffin boards had never been dug up and sold at public auction in that town.

THE HOUSES OF THE RURAL POOR

Did the García house resemble those of other poor people in small towns like El Escorial? The inadequacy of both urban and rural dwellings in Spain was a frequent topic for newspaper articles during this period. Family life and moral values were often said to be threatened by the close, cramped, unsanitary conditions in which many people lived. Nine years earlier, the informant for *Reformas sociales* from the town of Piedrahita—not far from El Escorial and, like that town, located in the mountains—described workers' houses: "Workers here, as a general rule, own their own houses. That this is so, despite the precarious situation of the worker, is easily explained, for their dwellings, particularly in rural areas, are miserable. Built with no attention whatsoever to adequate ventilation, they are dark, humid, and flimsily constructed. In a word, there is nothing good about them at all."[15]

Rosón himself first visited the García house on February 25. His description of it appeared the next day:

> It is an exceedingly humble house, and one notices right off the neglect and uncleanliness of those who inhabit it. The few pieces of furniture are covered with a thick coat of dust, and a multitude of spider webs hang in ragged festoons from its blackened walls.
>
> It is impossible to stay in the house for even a short time without feeling nauseous, and the close air drives one into the street in order to breathe the pure oxygen from the nearby mountains.[16]

Mestre Martínez visited the house on March 1 and provided more details about its layout and furnishings:

> I have just visited the Accursed House. It has a living room, a kitchen, a very dark bedroom where the *Chato* used to sleep, another bedroom for the sisters, a room with a loft (*desván*), a covered feeding trough and corral.
>
> There are several secular pictures in the living room, along with devotional ones which include an *Ecce-Homo* and figures from Holy Scripture.
>
> The *Chato*'s room has a wooden bed. There is not a single chair in the house.
>
> There are unwashed pots and pans, as well as dirty clothes everywhere.
>
> The ladder leading to the loft is pitted by insects.
>
> All the rooms present a thoroughly disgusting appearance.[17]

DWELLINGS AS EMBLEMS OF MORAL CHARACTER

On March 2, both *El País* and *La Correspondencia de España* came out with reproductions of drawings and photographs of the people and places connected with the Escorial crime. The following is a complete transcription of the text accompanying the drawings of the two houses in *La Correspondencia de España*:

> The other drawing represents a corner of the accursed house: the ascent to the loft where Pedrín endured his captivity. The window in the background is the one from which the criminal lowered the body of his victim. It opens onto the house's small corral. The corral is protected by an easily-scaled dilapidated wall built up against the sides of the mountain which slope gently at this spot. The ladder leaning against the wall leads to the loft. That is the only means of access to the loft and that is how the *Chato* went up to take food to Pedrín. The loft is an immense garret with a tile roof. The only light there is filters in through cracks in the tiles. Through those cracks one can see fragments of a

very blue and very beautiful sky whose color and beauty are even more desirable when viewed from amidst the nauseating gloom of that dark mansion of crime.

The entire house is a veritable pigsty whose very recollection induces nausea. There are prints of saints everywhere, even in the executioner's room. On top of a chest in the living room there is a good-sized statuette of the Child Jesus (*Niño de la bola*)—all clean and shiny, as if it had just come from a booth at a fair. All through the house there are rags and more rags. The kitchen has no other source of light than what comes down through the chimney. On the floor there are large pools of dark and pestilential water.

The Bravo house constitutes the reverse of the medal. Located on Calvary street—as if to prophesy what its inhabitants are now suffering—it is cheerful, well-lit, clean and carefully kept-up. It has a microscopic garden, and elegant wrought iron grating guards on windows hung with bright curtains depicting lions and large birds. From the outside it looks like a small house. The Bravo family, however, lives in just one of the most modest rooms of that pleasant dwelling. Pedrín's little sister plays in the diminutive garden. Vines now withered, entwined in the iron grating, have climbed the walls of the house. There, it seems, one breathes in the pure atmosphere of an honorable family.[18]

El País presented a drawing of the García house from the exterior, as well as a floor plan. It did not publish a picture of the Bravo house. The caption under the García house reads thus: "A miserable, squalid little house, with a rotted door sill, and narrow windows, it exudes vice and external uncleanliness—a reflection of the soul of the house and of its inhabitants. There the crime was consummated, and there the sinister family council was held which condemned the unfortunate Pedrín to death" ("Casucha miserable, sórdida, de infecto umbral, de estrechas ventanucas, trasuda el vicio y el desaseo exterior, reflejo del alma de la casa y de los habitantes. Allí se consumó el crimen y allí se reunió el consejo de familia siniestro, que condenó muerte [sic] al infeliz Pedrín").

El Día, *El Heraldo de Madrid* and *El Imparcial* avoided the use of the terms "familia maldita" and "casa maldita." All referred to the unclean condition of the house, and of the loft, in particular—"a nest of disgusting rodents and insects and a storage place for dirty rags, the rejected cast-offs of poverty" ("nido de asquerosas alimañas y depósito de sucios guiñapos, restos despreciados por la miseria")—according to *El Imparcial* on February 26; but they did not, like Rosón and Mestre Martínez, make the house emblematic of the moral corruption of its inhabitants.

One of the most suggestive details Mestre Martínez provided was his reference to the few pieces of furniture the García house contained in contrast to the large number of prints (*estampas*) on the walls. His remark permitted readers to reflect on the rather unexpected fact that in the dwelling of this poor and illiterate family, a "wealth of imaginative literature [...] looked down [...]" from those walls.[19] While the presence of the pictures may have lightened somewhat the dire impression made on readers by the description of the rest of the house, the sinister image conjured up of Julián contemplating the figurine of the *Niño de la bola* must have gone far to revive it.

EL ESCORIAL DISHONORED BY CRIME

All the journalists covering the case at El Escorial were mindful of how jealously its nearly 2,000 inhabitants (there were about 5,000 in the parish) guarded its reputation. In a genial gesture meant to counter widespread sentiment that the town had been dishonored by the crime, reporters often extolled its honest neighbors. On February 13, Hernández y Bermúdez wrote that no one in that civilized place believed that an act of such barbarism could have occurred there: "The worker of El Escorial is honorable, hardworking, with an unusual sense of morality, an enemy of vice, incapable of committing reprehensible acts" ("El obrero de El Escorial es honrado, trabajador, de una moralidad poco común, enemigo del vicio, incapaz de cometer acciones reprensibles"). Nine days later, underlining the people's solidarity in the face of imputations of wrong-doing by someone among them, he wrote that until Crisanto made his confession, everyone in El Escorial denied that Julián García had killed the child. For his part, Pedrín's father told *La Correspondencia de España* on February 27, that Julián "had spread a stain over the people of El Escorial, which has always been notable for its love of children" ("había echado un borrón sobre el pueblo de El Escorial, que se ha distinguido siempre por su amor hacia los niños").

The monastery, as the reporter for *El Día* noted, seemed to cast a sheltering shadow of sanctity over the town, making the crime far more horrible by virtue of the contrast. The adjacent mountain heights, where Pedrín's body had been found, darkened with their shadows both monastery and town. Hernández y Bermúdez described the scene for his readers on February 13, emphasizing the steepness and barren terrain in the heights:

> In front of the Monastery's principal facade looms the mountain chain whose highest peak is called the Abantos summit. It is crossed by the 'Malagón Pass' which, counting from the monastery door, rises 1,919 feet. Lower down—seemingly an outgrowth of the mountain—is the Risco del Despeñadero, which one climbs with great difficulty, like a cat, since its nearly vertical slope falls at what must be a 70-degree angle.
>
> Midway down the Risco, one sees an outgrowth, and then, much lower down, a road.
>
> On the left and right extends the bare mountain range, divested of vegetation.

> It was at the midway point on the Risco—where the outgrowth is—that at a quarter past three on the afternoon of the tenth, Pedrín's purplish corpse appeared.[20]

Mestre Martínez, whose flair for sensational detail had earlier led him to promote the story about the coffin boards used to construct "la casa maldita," published a story on February 25 suggesting that the history of the monastery contained some dark episodes in its long tradition of piety and service. In a history of El Escorial, the reporter found the following account of the cross located in the park, southeast of the monastery between the Calle Larga and the railway station, known as the Prince's Garden (*jardín del Príncipe*):

> In the year 1577, on the 7th of November, a young fellow who was the son of Queen Ana's baker—a youth of 26 like the sadly celebrated *Chato*—having concealed himself in a dense thicket beneath the King's kitchen window where he devoted himself every day to brutal excesses whose victims were innocent young boys, killed one of them so that his secret would not later be revealed.
>
> The crime was discovered and, in accord with the law of the time, the *Chato* from three hundred years ago was condemned to be burned alive—a sentence that was read and executed on the spot where the cross now stands. Fray Juan de Quemada and Fray Juan de Santa María aided him in his last moments. Today that cross is known as the "The Cross of Villainy" in order to recall the horrible crime perpetrated there, so reminiscent of the one which has elicited the wrath of the honorable people of this royal site.
>
> A curious coincidence...[21]

Apart from the suggestive parallel this anecdote presents, reporters did not exploit the unusual possibilities which El Escorial offered as the scenario for the crime. But, despite their relatively few remarks on the setting, the Royal Site comprising Philip II's great palace, church, monastery, and mausoleum was certain to conjure up a variety of associations in the minds of readers.

In the early 1890s El Escorial was a popular summer resort for people from Madrid. Its altitude (3,432 ft.) and fresh air provided relief from the hot, dusty city streets. At fifty-one kilometers from the capital, the journey by rail took about two hours. The train stopped at the station in the old village of El Escorial de Abajo (below). Travellers then walked or took a horse-drawn omnibus up to San Lorenzo de El Escorial, less than a kilometer distant. Quarries still provided work for some of the townspeople, including the male relatives of Pedrín Bravo. Most of the town's activity centered around the Monastery and the seasonal tourism it attracted, the School of Forestry (*Escuela de Ingenieros de Montes*), located on the Calle de la Parada bordering the Royal Monastery on the north side, and the boys' school housed in the northwest corner of the monastery which had been established by the Augustinians in 1885. During the school year students mingled with the townspeople and visitors who strolled along the Paseo de los Pinos, or walked past the western facade of the Monastery along the Paseo de las Arenitas, over soft grass-land, and then for a mile or so through a stand of oaks to the King's Seat (*Silla del Rey*)—the vantage point from which Philip II had monitored the Monastery's construction.

There was a market and, in the lower town, a bullring. Of the hotels and inns—all located in the upper town—the Hotel Miranda was considered the best, even into the early years of the twentieth century, and was often mentioned in press coverage of Pedrín's murder. In the 1890s tourists and journalists favored the Miranda, located as it was on the Plaza del Ayuntamiento, one block from the north side of the Monastery. The García family's small house was in the Romeral neighborhood, not far from the Monastery, on a steep street lined by other small, one story dwellings. The Bravo family lived on the Calle del Calvario, also fairly close to the Monastery, in a house inhabited by several families.

Many tourists and visitors remarked on the gaiety of summer nights spent at El Escorial. Pedrín's murder thus became a source of great consternation to those who enjoyed its pastoral attractions and, in particular, to families from Madrid worried about their children's safety during the annual summer holiday.

But El Escorial was far more than a pleasant summer resort. As a reporter for *El Heraldo de Madrid* (14 March 1893) put it, the town lay in the "sacred shadow of an historic Monastery" ("la sagrada sombra de un Monasterio histórico"). For the Spaniards and foreign travellers who went primarily to visit the Monastery, El Escorial evoked vivid images of Spain's imperial past under Philip II, and of the uncompromising Catholic faith that animated him. Even visitors sympathetic to Philip II and his policies were taken aback by the barrenness and isolation of the site he chose for his austere memorial. The mausoleum's sombre gloom, above all, greatly impressed visitors. In 1885 when José María Quadrado and Vicente de la Fuente contributed an essay for a series of volumes on the artistic treasures of Spain, they wrote that El Escorial was now nothing but the dwelling place of memories, and of the dead.[22]

Those unsympathetic to Philip II and his monument effortlessly transformed the monastery into a Gothic fortress of death whose many staircases, underground passages, cells, unexpected courtyards, and dark mausoleum disoriented and frightened the sensitive visitor: "the Escurial surrounds, holds, and crushes you; the chill of its walls penetrates to your marrow; the gloom of its sepulchral labyrinthine passages invades your soul [...]." The author of these words, Edmondo de Amicis, who visited Spain in the early 1870s, nearly fainted with fright in the mausoleum when his guide extinguished the light. He found the scene outside equally forbidding: "Everywhere one sees that sombre, dead color; there is not a living soul stirring, and the silence of an abandoned fortress broods over it; beyond the black roofs rises the black mountain, which seems to hang over the edifice and give it an air of mysterious solitude. The place, the lines, the colors, everything, seems to have been chosen by the founder for the purpose of offering to the eyes of man a sad and solemn spectacle."[23]

Several visitors to El Escorial added to the terrorific aspect of the place evoked so effectively by De Amicis, with the claim that Charles V's coffin—the first one to be placed in the mausoleum which his son, Philip II, ordered built for that purpose—had been opened in the early 1870s. Henry M. Field's macabre description was published in 1888: "A few years since, when the Emperor of Brazil visited the Escorial, the coffin was opened and the face uncovered. They even permitted photographs to be taken, which are sold today in the shops of Madrid. It is a ghastly figure. The lower jaw has fallen down so that the mouth is wide open, like that of an idiot. And this is all that is left of that Imperial countenance 'whose bend did awe the world'!"[24]

The mausoleum was a disquieting place even without the added *frisson* stories such as this lent to it. Like other visitors to the mausoleum, Field recalled that Alfonso XII's young first wife, Mercedes de Orleans, had been horrified at the prospect of burial in the Escorial mausoleum. Upon her death in 1878, she was instead buried in one of the side chapels in the church above.[25]

All that was lacking in depictions of El Escorial as a gloomy, death-haunted, Gothic mountain fastness was a vampire to frequent it. There were foreign Protestant visitors—and undoubtedly, some Spanish visitors as well—in whose view Philip II had bled the country white, and who found it entirely appropriate on that account to call him a vampire. His memory thus invoked completed the dismal picture.[26]

Reporters who covered Pedrín's murder did not directly exploit the terrorific possibilities to be found in a Gothicized Escorial; much less did they suggest a connection between Philip II and vampirism. The reference to the pederast of 1577 did, however, explicitly relate sexual transgression in the religious context of Philip II's Monastery to Julián's crime which had also had its point of origin in a holy place. And the crime in this setting resonated with terrorific possibilities. The last reliable witness to have seen Pedrín saw him in the Patio de los Reyes, the principal entrance to the Royal Monastery. An abduction of a three-year-old boy from the courtyard facing the church could not help but recall the circumstances of tales of ritual murder preserved in law and legend. Awful as the murder of an innocent child was, it could further be associated in this case with well-remembered stories of Christian children abducted by Jews from the very portals of churches so that they might be killed and their blood mixed with stolen hosts for the preparation of unleavened bread. From such a perspective it was plausible to refer to Pedrín as a sacrificial victim—martyr to a modern counterpart of the child-stealing

Jew, i.e., to Julián, a criminal with all the marks of an atavistic beast. Perhaps this is why, on May 15, 1894 in *El Globo*, Luis Bonafoux called the crime against Pedrín a crime against humanity and apostrophized the dead child thus: " Poor Pedrín, with your crown of thorns, alone in the barren desert!" ("¡Pobre niño Pedrín, con tu corona de espinas sobre el campo yermo...!").

THE TRANSGRESSION: PROFANATION OF THE MASKS OF BOTARGA AND BOTARGUILLA AT THE FEAST OF THE MAGI

The accumulation of coincidences was one of the tasks Mestre Martínez, more than the other reporters, set for himself. He was the first to report an episode which, unlike the coffin-board rumor, was true and did constitute the act of profanation or transgression which the reporter appears to have thought important to the story he wanted to tell. On February 22, *La Correspondencia de España* printed the following, under the epigraph "Botarga y Botarguilla":

> In this town, the Brotherhood of God has established a tradition for celebrating the Arrival of the Magi. It is a celebration in which two individuals don masks in order to perform the roles of *Botarga* and *Botarguilla*, and stick in hand, collect money and food for the feast to be held later.
>
> This year those parts were taken by Julián and Crisanto.
>
> That is to say, that when this celebration was in progress, the horrible crime had been committed, or at least, the child's abduction had taken place.
>
> It is horrifying to imagine the sangfroid with which Julián took part in this celebration, if—as is believed—he was the author of this terrible crime.
>
> The people have recalled this circumstance, calling it an abomination.
>
> Julián and Crisanto spent a pleasant afternoon, leaving the innocent Pedrín to weep at their ferocity.

Mestre Martínez added later that his disclosure of Julián's and Crisanto's part in the festival was taken very seriously by the examining magistrate for it demonstrated the strength of the bonds between the two men precisely at the time when the child was undergoing his "martyrdom." Finally, on February 24, Mestre Martínez was able to inform readers that a certain D. José López, a former municipal judge, had begun to collect signatures for a petition "so that next year at the celebration of the Magi organized by the Brotherhood of God, no one would be permitted to wear the disguise of Botarga and Botarguilla, since those costumes recalled the time of Pedrín's terrible martyrdom, and because the *Chato* and Crisanto had profaned the ancient disguises."[27]

Julián García's participation in the festivities of Epiphany helps explain the initial reluctance of the townspeople to believe that he was guilty of the abduction, abuse and murder of Pedro Bravo. He had—at least on one occasion—filled a position of public trust. The outraged reaction of the former municipal judge and the signers of his position may have been somewhat opportunistic; it did provide a convenient pretext for a public assertion of their uprightness and civic virtue. Even so, their response indicates the importance officially ascribed to the conduct of men given the roles of *Botarga* and *Botarguilla*. Julián's participation in the Festival of the Epiphany is significant since it indicates his previous standing in the town and reveals the extent to which even the poorest day laborer might take part in public celebrations and festivities. But above all, the profanation of the mask provided further evidence of the extent to which Julián had desecrated religion. For Catholic readers this act unquestionably made his demonization by reporters more convincing.

CRISANTO JORGE

During the pre-trial investigation, reporters tried to cast Julián's brother-in-law, Crisanto Jorge, in the role of foil to the villain. There were inescapable indications, however, that he was not a suitable candidate to represent a poor, but honest *jornalero*. On February 18, Rosón described him: "a man of some thirty years [sic] of age, he has a very hard life; he takes on whatever *turns up*, and on more than one occasion the Civil Guard and the municipal court have had to impose penalties for his misconduct" ('hombre de unos treinta [sic] años de edad, es de vida en extremo acuitada; dedícase a *todo lo que sale*, y en más de una ocasión la guardia civil y el Juzgado municipal han tenido que imponerle correctivos"). The next day *El Imparcial* reported that Crisanto seemed intelligent though calculating, and on February 25, Hernández y Bermúdez wrote: "This man inspires more sympathy than Julián. There is a note of sincerity in what he says, something that predisposes people in his favor" ("Este hombre es más simpático que Julián. En su acento hay sinceridad, algo que predispone en favor suyo").

After Crisanto accused Julián on February 20, Rosón indulged his taste for *feuilleton*-like analyses of motivation and character in which potential nobility is shown to be present in every man's breast: "Despite Crisanto's background [...], he possesses noble sentiments, born of remorse. During the time he was not able to communicate with anyone, he must have suffered a great deal as he reflected on the horrible nature of the crime. His tremendous secret weighed so on his heart, he cast it from him and thus revealed the truth" ("A pesar de los malos antecedentes de Crisanto [...], nótanse en él sentimientos nobles, nacidos del remordimiento. Durante su incomunicación ha debido sufrir mucho reflexionando sobre lo horrible del delito, cuyo tremendo secreto pesaba en su corazón con inmensa pesadumbre, que arrojó de sí revelando la verdad").

On March 2, Rosón interpreted Crisanto's character as revealed in his physiognomy—just as he had done with Juana. The reporter then delved into Crisanto's thought processes, rendering their working in free indirect discourse: "In his visage, which is not at all common-looking, one observes indications of shrewdness and foresight. If the body had been buried, their plan would have worked. The smart one did not take into account the fear and the cowardice of his accomplices. Ah, if he had only carried out the whole business as he had planned it!... But genius is not always accompanied by ability and zeal" ("En su fisonomía nada vulgar se notan los rasgos de la astucia y de la previsión. Si se hubiera sepultado el cadáver, su plan habría triunfado. Ese sabio no contó con el miedo, con la cobardía de sus cómplices. Ah, si él hubiera ejecutado como concibió el asunto... Pero el genio no siempre es secundado por la habilidad y el celo"). Finally, on March 4, Rosón speculated that Crisanto might possess some paternal feeling, but he was not certain even of that.

Crisanto seems to have been a secretive, scowling figure—"the dour Crisanto" ("el sombrío Crisanto"), one of the reporters called him. His role in the story was perhaps less remarkable to the reporters trying somehow to dramatize it than it is to a modern reader. As the only person in the two families who could read and write, he signed the *acta del juicio* every day. More important, he read *El Imparcial* from the very beginning of its coverage of the case. His avid interest in following the accounts of the crime did not go unnoticed, and on February 24, *El Imparcial* speculated that Crisanto's demeanor at the newsstand may have led someone to tip off the authorities about his possible involvement in the crime. Crisanto's motive in reading about the crime was later attributed by Julián's lawyer to his desire to master everything known about the case, the better to incriminate Julián.

Unsympathetic as he was, the public was appalled when in 1895 the jury's 1894 verdict was appealed, and Julián drew a sentence of *cadena perpetua* while Crisanto's penalty was changed from imprisonment to death. His prior conviction for assault with injury made the death penalty mandatory—an absurdity the public found intolerable in view of Julián's sentence.

If Julián's lawyer was right and Crisanto used newspaper reports to frame his brother-in-law, journalists who suspected as much from his depositions could have represented him as an ironic example of the dangers of literacy—a tack Rosón may have been taking when he referred to Crisanto's masterminding of the removal of Pedrín from the García house. But, in the rural context of this case, connections between literacy, diabolical intelligence, and criminality were not as compelling or convincing as those between illiteracy, animal craftiness, and criminality. The story being told was not about a fiendishly clever and manipulative criminal, but rather, about an atavistic throwback to the ape.

THE DEFENDANTS IN JAIL

It is likely that for some readers this story was modified by the intermittent glimpses reporters provided of the accused in their jail cells. Julián and his sisters, imagined by reporters drinking and carousing in their miserable dwelling while Pedrín was slowly dying in the loft was one thing: their depiction as helpless prisoners in the cold, bare Escorial jail was another. When the reporters referred to visits to the jail, they dedicated considerable copy to praise of the admirable administration of its director. Nonetheless, the physical and mental suffering of the family was described—though without noticeable compassion for they were still presumed guilty—in such a way as to suggest their pitiable powerlessness. Whether that weakened the representation of the family as evil and monstrous may have depended, to some extent, on the politics of the individual newspaper reader. *El Socialista*, at any rate—in a rare comment on a criminal case—took the position on May 25, 1894 after the verdict came down, that this family of unfortunates deserved compassion: "instead of jail they should go to an insane asylum, and instead of gross curses and insults, what is needed is a bit more commiseration and compensation, in so far as is possible, for the grave crime committed against this family by society—this society that is hypocritically scandalized by crime yet does nothing to foresee and avoid it by helping those who need physical direction and intellectual nourishment."[28] Catarineu, the reporter for *El Nacional*, went further, writing on May 15, 1894 that the García family had been selected from the dregs of society so that the accusation made against them would seem more plausible. The very baseness of their origins served as incriminating evidence ("Las [víctimas, i.e., los García] recogieron entre la hez para que la acusación fuera verosímil, dieron por datos sus malos antecedentes [...]").

The popular columnist, Kasabal, considered the access reporters had to María and Crisanto Jorge, Julián, Francisca, Concha and Juana in their jail cells to be an invasion of privacy. Some of the reporters assumed prosecutorial roles, interrogating and often bullying the prisoners. On February 27, for example, after Julián had faced a morning of questioning and confrontations, Hernández y Bermúdez and several other reporters questioned him in his cell, "without obtaining any results whatsoever since he systematically persists in denying everything" ("sin obtener resultado alguno, pues persiste en su sistema de negarlo todo"). But, provided the examining magistrate or the director of the jail had no objections, journalists were free to appear at any time and request an interview.

In addition to providing an account of the interviews, reporters included a good deal of information about the jail, its regimen, and how prisoners were treated. Hernández y Bermúdez described the exterior appearance of the jail on February 19:

"The El Escorial jail is a magnificent building which holds two hundred people.

Large windows with iron rails provide light to the cells. One sees evidence everywhere of the care taken by Sres. López and Vergara to ensure that no needed service is neglected, despite the fact that the jail personnel is limited to these two individuals."[29] Rosón, who was accompanied by the reporter for *El Imparcial* on their first visit to the jail, described it on February 18: "it is solidly built, well-fitted out, and extremely clean" ("es de sólida construcción, muy bien acondicionada y sumamente limpia"). He turned then to the prisoners: "At the moment there are twenty-six prisoners, among them a *counterfeit friar* who was going through the towns roundabout begging money for the *order*, wearing a Franciscan habit, and underneath it garments that were both clean and elegant. He passes himself off as an engineer, a lawyer, a newspaperman, and as Sr. Serrano Fatigati's law clerk. He is an individual we have often spotted in the Puerta del Sol selling books and offering...other things.

Sr. López Merelo, helped by Sr. Vergara, gives them all reading and writing lessons."[30]

The last sentence informed readers throughout Spain of a significant feature of the administrators' regimen at the Escorial jail. Measures taken to eradicate illiteracy in jails and prisons seemed forward-looking not simply because they were seen as humanitarian, but because illiteracy was customarily associated with criminal behavior. A decree of 1873 had mandated the establishment of a library in places of incarceration. In accord with the provisions of the decree: "Instruction must be the first element of penal reform. The teacher and not the rod must correct the convicts; books and not chains must restrain their passions. Therefore, there must be a school in every house of correction; and for this reason also, there must be a Library."[31]

The medical care provided by Dr. Peña was another feature of life in the jail which the journalists praised. Julián and his sisters had to be attended during and after their epileptic seizures. María's two-year-old daughter, who was with her mother, fell into the *brasero* one day and had to have her burns treated by the doctor.

Less impressive were the cells themselves. Prisoners were responsible for cleaning them; they also had to provide their own pallets and blankets. They sat on straw-stuffed mats. When the accused were not incommunicado by order of the examining magistrate, the sisters were allowed to be together. Julián was, at times, allowed to share a cell with other male prisoners. The sisters were able to withstand the rigors of the winter cold in jail: so long as they could be together they did not complain to reporters about the conditions of their confinement. They spent the time sewing and talking.

Julián was not so fortunate. On February 24, Rosón reported that Julián had been moved to a cell alone:

"The place he is in now is at some distance from the other cells and is extremely cold.

Julián shouts for them to return him to the jail cell where he was before. He begs the jailers to show pity because he is freezing" ("El local donde ahora se encuentra está muy retirado y es sumamente frío.

Julián pide a voces que le vuelvan al calabozo en que estaba, implorando de la piedad de sus carceleros, porque en el que está se hiela)."

Not long after, Julián became ill with pneumonia. Hernández y Bermúdez reported on March 1:

"The *Chato* is spitting up blood. It is thought that this is a symptom of pneumonia. He has had pneumonia twice before.

When they speak to him about anything that has to do with the crime, he gets so frightened he acts as if he were crazy and has an attack.

The magistrate has given an order that he not be disturbed and that he be given an iron bed with a mattress, blankets and pillows.

Dr. Peña visits him frequently."[32]

Reporters who had written about the cold temperatures which Pedrín allegedly suffered in the loft where he was thought to have been confined, did not describe the suffering Julián was undergoing in his cold cell. As he recovered, they did note that his appetite returned and that he was once again consuming great quantities of food.

GRAPHIC REPRESENTATIONS OF THE CRIME

Several days before the trial began at El Escorial, a number of leading dailies, including *El País*, *El Heraldo de Madrid*, *La Correspondencia de España*, and *El Liberal*, ran front-page stories with illustrations on the history of the crime along with speculation concerning the trial's outcome. The one image found in all the papers was a reproduction of a photograph of Julián García's house. The cross erected in the child's memory, photos of his family, of the García family, and of the representatives of justice who figured in the case were also present in one or another paper.

On May 7, 1894, the day before the trial began, the prestigious, widely-circulated *Los Lunes de El Imparcial* dedicated most of its first page to a succinct account of "El niño de El Escorial." Spanning the top of the page was a reproduction of a drawing which represented the place where Pedrín was found. On the right, on an elevated flat shelf of land, outlined against barren hills and a lowering sky is a stone cross. Two eagles hover in the near distance. At the foot of the cross, boulders lie scattered over the bare ground, and there among the stones, lying on his side, naked except for a cloth thrown over his loins, lies a child.

A precipice drops to the left of the height on which the cross and the boy are placed. Down below, partially hidden by an escarpment of stone carved out by time and weather into monstrous rounded shapes creased with deep folds, stands the monastery. Clouds cover much of the expanse of sky above the monastery, and behind and below it, the distant plains stretch out to the horizon.

Under the drawing, on the left hand side of the page, taking up the space of what would have been the first column, is a reproduction of a photograph of Julián García. He looks steadily out at a point to the right of the viewer, a beret on his tilted head, a checkered, loose-fitting jacket on his slightly slumped frame. Below his photograph is a reproduction of a shot of what *El Imparcial* always referred to as "La casa del crimen"—Julián's house seen from the rear with the loft window visible.

The similarity between the illustrations heading the article on the Escorial crime in *El Imparcial* (as well as the other papers mentioned above) and the woodcuts (*xilografías*) that headed nineteenth-century ballads is apparent. As Isabel Segura wrote in her prologue to a collection entitled *Romances horrorosos*, the woodcut which appeared at the top of the sheet containing the ballad offered a visual synthesis of the verses or prose that followed: "For that reason, considerable importance is given to their forcefulness and impact; and it is also for that reason that in many of them, the morbid sensibilities of the potential buyer of ballads are exploited. The more macabre and violent the scenes represented, the more heads rolling on the ground, the more knives there are and bodies slit open, the more certain that sales will be good."[33]

The illustrations in *El Imparcial* would have recalled to readers familiar with the Escorial crime the fortuitous encounter which preserved the child's body from being devoured by animals and birds of prey—such as the eagles circling near the cross. They would also undoubtedly have remembered that when his corpse was turned over, the onlookers drew back, for his empty eye sockets swarmed with "nests of worms" ("nidos de gusanos").

The contrast between what appears to be a sleeping child's soft naked flesh and the hard bare boulders, barren hills and stone monastery is skillfully evoked. The barely visible legend inscribed on the cross is printed below in the article: "On the 10th of February 1893, the Body of the Unfortunate Child, Pedrín Bravo y Bravo, a Victim of Brutal Savagery was Found on this Site" ("El 10 de febrero de 1893, fue hallado en este sitio el cadáver del desgraciado niño Pedrín Bravo y Bravo, víctima de brutal salvajismo"). The drawing represents human vulnerability in the midst of an awesome expanse of stone and sky. Depending on the viewer, the presence of the monastery in the scene may have seemed ominous, or it may have served as a comforting reminder of the Christian context in which the story unfolded. The photograph of Julián and of his house, not in themselves horrifying or morbid, nonetheless recalled the theme of degeneracy, as well as the accursed, filthy site of the crime.

THE CRIME AND TERRORIFIC LITERATURE

The article accompanying the graphics summed up the story as the three correspondents based in El Escorial had presented it to the public a year earlier. First of all, it was uniquely horrible: "There has never been recorded in all the history of crime any more horrible than that attributed to the *Chato* at El Escorial" ("No se registra en toda la historia de los crímenes un delito más horrendo que el atribuido al *Chato* del Escorial"). Second—also squarely in the tradition of popular terrorific literature—the motive for the crime was not normal in the sense that it was not understandably human: "Neither hatred, nor ambition, nor revenge—those passions that generally lead to violence—motivated this crime. It was the product of a disordered inclination toward vice. It was the satisfaction of a ferocity from which human nature is usually exempt" ("El delito no lo había engendrado el odio, la ambición o la venganza, esas pasiones que generalmente arrastran al crimen; era el producto de una inclinación desordenada hacia los vicios; era la satisfacción de una ferocidad de que generalmente se halla exenta la naturaleza humana"). Third, the innocent victim and his family—above all, his grieving mother—represented the good folk of El Escorial standing in stark contrast to the atavism and perversity of the García family—"la familia maldita." Of the latter, *El Imparcial* wrote: "It could be said that the whole family constitutes one single wretched, sombre personality, with the instincts of a wild beast and strangely cruel tastes" ("Pudiera decirse que toda esa familia constituye una sola personalidad triste, sombría, con instintos de fiera y gustos de crueldad extraña").

The story told by Hernández y Bermúdez, Mestre Martínez, and Eduardo Rosón followed familiar thematic patterns that depended for their effects on vivid contrasts, attention to detail, and facile, portentous language as typical of the *folletín* as of the *romances de ciego* (i.e., " The mother's grief, the strange disappearance of the child, the fear that a crime had been committed wounded everyone's imagination and moved their hearts; all but the hearts of the criminals" ("El dolor de la madre, la extraña desaparición del niño, el temor de un crimen herían todas las imaginaciones y conmovían todos los pechos; pero no llegaba al pecho de los criminales"). Critics and readers alike during the nineteenth century often expressed a desire for presumably unmediated reality in the form of memoirs, history and news reports. Certain journalists in their coverage of the Escorial case foiled that desire—with serious consequences for the defendants—by filing reports that were mediated by familiar fictional patterns and rhetorical techniques. Was that what the public really wanted?

Armando Palacio Valdés, who often alluded indirectly to contemporary events and issues in his fiction, offered an ironic observation on this question in his 1894 novel, *El origen del pensamiento*. In this work he illustrated the people's supposed preference for filtering reality through fiction, unmistakably relating it to the Escorial case. At the end of the novel, four-year-old Mario has been kidnapped and hidden in an attic by his deranged grandfather. The grandfather, obsessed with a mad design for a "scientific" experiment, intends to remove the top of the child's skull in order to observe the physical origin of thought in the last moments of the exposed brain's functioning.

No Spaniard reading about the abduction and confinement of little Mario could have failed to think of the fate of the real-life Pedrín. There were parallels beyond the circumstance of the kidnapping and confinement in an attic. On May 10, 1894 *El Imparcial* reported on testimony describing the elder Bravo's attempts to find his son. The gist of his remarks had already been printed during the pre-trial investigation in 1893. Pedrín's father declared: "it was said that the child had been taken off by a puppeteer and I searched for him from town to town until I caught up with him in Chinchón. He didn't have the child. Then I went to Madrid twice and I managed to find the people who were said to have seen the child. But I got the same result from my long search through the city."[34]

Just as Pedrín's father set out from El Escorial several times in search of his son, so Mario's father sets out from Madrid in search of his little boy. In Palacio Valdés's novel, Mario's father hears that a blind man, probably in cahoots with a woman, has abducted his child and fled on a train to Arganda. He hires a coach and sets out for Arganda at midnight, accompanied by a police agent. The agent falls asleep. The wakeful father's musings forcefully recall the thoughts that reporters attributed to Pedrín's mother—even her cry of anguish at the trial is echoed here: "His imagination, tormented by grief turned first in one direction, then another, presenting him with a thousand terrifying pictures. His son kidnapped, his son mistreated, his son hungry and thirsty in some cave, his son calling him with piercing lamentations while a pair of brutal hands covered his mouth... My heart's child!" ("Su imaginación se revolvía atormentada por el dolor, presentándole mil cuadros aterradores. Su hijo secuestrado, su hijo maltratado, su hijo pasando hambre y frío en culquiera cueva, su hijo llamándole con acerbo llanto, mientras unas manos brutales le tapaban la boca...¡ Hijo de mi alma!").

When they arrive at Arganda at three o'clock in the morning they find the blind man, but he does not have the child. They cannot find the woman who supposedly had accompanied him. The distraught father rouses everyone:

> The town was in a state of commotion, and many neighbors came out into the streets to find out what was going on even though it was still dark. When dawn broke, the streets filled with people and everyone turned into detectives in order to find out where the kidnapped child was hidden. This matter above all preoccupied the women, whose speculations were endless. So it was that in less than an hour two or three novels were making the rounds of the town. The child was the son of an important man who was offering ten million for his ransom. He was a foundling whose mother, unable to redeem him, had had him kidnapped. He was an orphan in the care of this man looking for him, whose disappearance had been arranged for by his uncles, etc., etc. Small groups savored with delight these bits of information with their novelesque flavor.[35]

That Palacio Valdés should have taken a real event—the 1892 abduction of Pedrín—and placed a version of it in a novel was no more than accepted practice for many nineteenth-century writers. But, in a curious development, his fictional characters, confronted with Mario's abduction, transform this "real" event within the novel into several fictionalized versions evidently designed to satisfy expectations formed by popular literature. Even within a fiction—the novelist appears to be saying—people want ever more fiction. His townspeople of Arganda (especially the women), like the newspaper-reading masses of the nineties as characterized by their critics, "savored with delight those pieces of news with their novelistic flavor"—in this case going so far as to concoct their own tasty dishes.

Ordinary people did not have a forum in which they could respond effectively to the implications of Palacio Valdés's anecdote any more than they could respond to the commentary on mass taste and ways of perceiving reality reviewed above in relation to crime reporting. It is also difficult to know how the public reacted to the reports from El Escorial filed in May 1894 by reporters who were not convinced of Julián's guilt—as the three reporters mentioned above had been—and who were not committed to the story those three had constructed. Despite that story's proven value in selling papers, there were reporters who began their coverage of the trial in May by duly noting the defense lawyers' allegations of procedural lapses and irregularities on the part of the examining magistrate. They also wrote about the supposedly improper formation of the *sumario*, and of improprieties and even brutality on the part of some members of the Civil Guard. Several journalists pointed to the lack of evidence or proof of Julián's guilt. The critical attention that some reporters applied to the facts of the case may have come too late for the reading public whose supposed predilection for the sensational had instead been fed by details describing "la casa maldita" and "la familia maldita" who inhabited it.

The pre-trial significance of the Escorial case lay in the fact that some members of the press—basing their choice on their assessment of what the public wanted—preferred retailing fictionalized accounts of the crime to reporting the facts available to them, and in so doing brought the case before a large number of people, including even non-readers. The trial and its aftermath shifted attention to another important facet of the case—its implications for Spain's six year-old jury system. In the discussions that followed, the ways in which the intellectual elite had defined the masses and mass taste in attempts to explain contemporary crime reporting could also be employed to explain the assumptions and behavior of the "mass" jurors selected from the census rolls.

NOTES

1. See *La Vanguardia*, 4 June 1896. Frank Schneider's "E.T.A. Hoffmann en España: apuntes bibliográficos e históricos," *Estudios eruditos in memoriam de Adolfo Bonilla y San Martín (1875–1926)* (Madrid: Jaime Bates, 1921), 1:286, notes a translation of Hoffmann's *Cuentos fantásticos* in Barcelona in 1887, but records no other translations of his work until 1898. I have not been able to identify the original Hofmannsthal story. As for vampirism in real life, Fernando Alvarez-Uría, *Miserables y locos*, 195, cites M. Barbastro, author of *El homicidio y la antropofagia* for the following: "At the end of the century draculism became more common and several children were killed by men with tuberculosis who believed in the regenerative power of children's blood to restore their health" ("A finales de siglo el draculismo se generalizó y fueron asesinados varios niños por tuberculosos que creían en el poder regenerador de la sangre infantil para devolverlos la salud").

2. My assumption is that the "melodramatic imagination" as Peter Brooks defines it in *The Melodramatic Imagination*, 17–20, informs the literature of terror which, for the late nineteenth century, includes the Gothic and the vampire tale. Specialized studies in these genres are noted in the course of this chapter. Three useful historical and bibliographical studies are: David Punter, *Literature of Terror: A History of Gothic Fictions from 1765 to the Present Day* (London: Longman, 1980); Frederick S. Frank, *Guide to the Gothic. An Annotated Bibliography of Criticism* (Metuchen: Scarecrow Press, 1984); Benjamin Franklin Fisher IV, *The Gothic's Gothic. Study Aids to The Tradition of the Tale of Terror* (New York: Garland Publishing Inc., 1988).

3. "La gente que falta en los talleres, oficinas y aulas, abunda en las secciones de lo criminal de nuestra Audiencia, y allí donde hay un rastro de sangre o vaga por la atmósfera el humo de un disparo, pulula indefectablemente un enjambre de personas de todas las clases sociales, ávidas de presenciar en la vida real algo de lo que despertó su interés en la esfera literaria, narrado por la pluma de Gaboriau o de Montepin."

4. "Quelle que soit sa position sociale, on ne craint pas de s'exhiber au tribunal; il s'agit presque d'une représentation mondaine. Alors qu'il n'est pas recommandable pour une jeune femme de se rendre au bal de l'Opéra, celle-ci peut en revanche assister en toute quiétude à des procès où l'on entend parfois des propos qui en toute autre occasion seraient qualifés de scandaleux." *La Chair de l'autre*, 313. In a piece entitled "Instantáneas. Feminismo," by Ovejero, in *El Globo* of August 25, 1896, the author complained that women were going out more than was seemly. They went to bull-fights, the theatre and into courtrooms where they even sought to express and have their opinions recorded: "And there isn't a trial that does not feature among the sealed documents amassed by the tribunal letters entered into the proceedings from some woman from among those who congregate at our *Lady of the Salesas*, as Mariano de Cavia termed it [the Palace of Justice] in one of his last articles" ("Y no se comprende proceso sin que entre los pliegos de papel sellado amontonados por la curia aparezcan en la causa las cartas de alguna mujer de *La dama de las Salesas*, como la denominaba gráficamente en uno de sus últimos artículos Mariano de Cavia).

5. "Ni solicitaba, ni rehusaba el trabajo: si se lo ofrecían, aceptábalo de buen grado y cumplía fielmente con su obligación: si nadie le hacía proposiciones, antes de pedir prestado, *iba a la carbonilla, o a los conejos, o a lo que se podía*, como gráficamente me dicen sus hermanas." The second passage quoted: "se levantan a las once de la mañana, para dirigirse *por la sopa de los pobres*, que a diario reparten en el convento, y que solicitan desde que, por razones de *limpieza*, les retiraron el lavado de la ropa los frailes de la comunidad.

Después íbanse de paseo con las amigas, cenaban donde las convidaban, o bien adquirían alguna *friolera*, y marchábanse a dormir, a una hora que no se acostumbraban hacerlo aquí la mayoría de los vecinos." And the last passage quoted here: "Como dato que pinta gráficamente el modo de ser de esta familia, allá va el siguiente:

Cuando nosotros preguntamos a Francisca y Concha su ocupación, nos respondieron:

'En la actualidad somos *pobres de solemnidad...*' [sic]

Pues bien, Concha y Francisca *tenían peinadora*; todas las mañanas se hacían la *toilette* antes de marchar al monasterio por la sopa de los pobres."

6. Referring to the *jornalero del campo*, the report on Avila in "Memoria de la Comisión Provincial de Avila," *Reformas sociales*, 4:137 noted that, "The day-worker never abandons the ideal of buying a house, a goal which he usually attains in the end; and in a few cases, if he did not have it before, he manages also to buy a piece of land to help him out in his old age. The dwelling, whether his own or one he has rented—in which case the rent ranges between 20 and 60 pesetas per year—is similar to that of permanent workers" ("El jornalero no abandona jamás el ideal de comprar casa, que al fin consigue por lo común, y en pocos casos, como antes de venir a este estado no lo tuviera, logra algún pedazo de terreno que le alivie en la vejez. La vivienda, propia o alquilada—y entonces la renta gira entre 20 y 60 pesetas anuales—es semejante a la del trabajador permanente." María's rent, reported to be 40 *reales* (see text below) is so low as to suggest that it may have been incorrectly recorded.

7. *El Globo*, 15 May 1894, quoted parts of Bonafoux's article which originally appeared in *La Época*.

8. "Tiene diez años, rostro agradable, ojos negros y vivaces, cuerpo enteco, con la particularidad de que la parte más desarrollada es el pecho, que ella procura exagerar, haciéndole más visible [...].

Hija natural de la madre de los *Chatos* cuando ésta era ya viuda y de avanzada edad, tiene esta chiquilla toda la refinada malicia y procoz astucia que caracteriza a los *productos seniles* [...]

Esta muchacha, nacida en la abyección y criada y educada en un foco de corrupción inmensa, deja en el ánimo del que la contempla una impresión tristísima.

Es carne infaliblemente destinada a la Galera."

9. "Díjele quién era, y a qué iba, y ella manifestó que no extrañaba la visita, pues comprendía que las gentes quieren leer en los periódicos todo cuanto ha ocurrido en el crimen que la hace desgraciada para siempre.

A las preguntas que le dirigí, contestó que tenía tres hijos más, llamados Eustacio, Carlos y Valentina, de 7, 5, y 2 años respectivamente, encontrándose muy próxima a dar a luz.

Entre sollozos y suspiros me indicó los sitios de la casa en donde jugaba Pedrín.

Refirióme los días angustiosos que pasaron y los esfuerzos que hicieron para encontrar a su hijo querido.

Díjele que ya se sabía quién había sido el autor del crimen, a lo cual me repuso llorando: 'Nada me importa ya, después de haber perdido a mi hijo, pero lo que quiero es que la justicia cumpla su deber' [...].

Manifestó que vivían con muchos apuros, y me suplicó que hiciera esto público por si las buenas almas de Madrid quieren socorrerla.

La madre de Pedrín se abraza constantemente a sus vecinas, como para mitigar y compartir la pena que la ahoga."

10. "Imposible describir la escena de dolor que ha producido al entrar en la sala Gumersinda Bravo, madre del niño. ¡Quién puede describir el dolor de una madre por tan horrible desgracia!

Sus lágrimas y sus congojas han llegado al corazón de todos los que estaban en la sala.

—¡Hijo mío de mis entrañas!—decía la angustiada madre.

Y los jurados lloraban, y los que desde lejos oían aquellas lamentaciones lloraban también. ¡Pobre madre!

Su dolor no cesa; está acongojada sobre los brazos del portero y el fiscal; el representante de la acusación privada, el que en nombre de los padres ha venido a pedir castigo para el más horrendo de los crímenes, dice al presidente que no quiere interrogar a la madre en consideración a su estado de angustia.

La madre abandona la sala, dejando en ella una impresión que no se borrará jamás."

11. By the early 1890s there were a number of literary representations of mothers that did not conform to the official view. Leopoldo Alas's Doña Paula, from *La regenta* (1884–85); Jacinto Octavio Picón's Susana, from *La honrada* (1890); Armando Palacio Valdés's Rosa Coote, from *La espuma* (1890); and the same author's Amalia, from *El Maestrante* (1893); Pérez Galdós's Doña Perfecta from the 1876 novel of the same name, presented in a stage version in 1896. This list of mothers includes adulteresses, child abusers, and manipulative and corrupt seekers after power. Conceptualization of the mother in the 1890s must be placed in the context of the feminist movement, the anarchist movement, and the Cuban War. It was clearly and frequently stated in the press that feminism was an important issue because it affected the family, "the essential and primary foundation of the State's vitality; hence the emergence of feminism presents four aspects, comprising political, economic, juridical and social elements" ("base esencial y primera de la vida del Estado; por eso [el feminismo] tiene un cuádruplo aspecto, abarcando caracteres políticos, económicos, jurídicos, sociales" ("El Congreso feminista de Berlín," *El Globo*, 11 October 1896). Women were active in the revived anarchist movement of the 1890s. Their demands, as feminists and anarchists, ran counter to most everything that shored up the official image of woman and mother. The press made note of the changes. Ovejero, for example, wrote an article in *El Globo* on August 25, 1896 in which he referred to the long list of women prisoners in Barcelona arrested for anarchist activities, and went on to discuss the disruptive consequences of female political action for Spanish society. As for the war, numbers of poor mothers—unlike their grandmothers—were willing to demonstrate against it rather than submissively accede to the prospect of losing a means of support (a son) in old age. Naked concern for self, rather than acquiescence to the demands of the fatherland, decidedly did not conform to the official version of the essential nature of motherhood. Such deviations made it the more necessary to insist on the official model.

12. Peter Brooks, *The Melodramatic Imagination*, 11–12.

13. Peter Brooks, *The Melodramatic Imagination*, 15. See Julia Przybos, *L'Entreprise mélodramatique* (Paris: Librairie José Corti, 1987), 194, for the tendency of melodrama's productions to support the status quo.

14. "Conviéneme hacer algunas aclaraciones repecto a inexactitudes cometidas por el corresponsal de un colega, que, sin duda por el afán de distinguirse comunicando noticias de sensación, forja una novela cada día, contada con sus pelos y señales, ni más ni menos que si copiase de la realidad, y no fuera todo recurso *reporteril*, empeñado en mantener viva una expectación que en determinados momentos decrece, por falta absoluta de noticias."

15. "Las habitaciones de los obreros son aquí, por regla general, de su propiedad. Esta adquisición se explica fácilmente, por precaria que sea la situación del obrero, pues las viviendas, particularmente en los pueblos rurales, son miserables, construidas sin tener para nada en cuenta la cubificación atmosférica, sombrías, húmedas y faltas de solidez. No tienen, en una palabra, ninguna condición buena." From "Piedrahita," Informe de D. Marcelino Rivera, vol.4, *Reformas sociales*, 308–309. See also L. Torres Balbás, "La vivienda popular en España," vol.3, *Folklore y costumbres de España* (Barcelona: Casa Editorial Alberto Martín, 1946), 419–423. Torres Balbás quotes several paragraphs from an article by Constancio Bernaldo de Quirós, "La casa rural del Guadarrama," which had originally appeared in *Arquitectura* I (1918):86. The poor in this region, according to the author, inhabited stone dwellings whose dark, cold, and smoky interiors had little or no furniture.

16. "La casa es de humildísimo aspecto, notándose el descuido y falta de aseo de las que la ocupaban. Los escasos muebles están revestidos de gruesa capa de polvo, y de sus ennegrcidas paredes cuelgan, formando festones de pingajos, multitud de telas de araña.

Es imposible estar durante algún tiempo encerrado en la casa sin sentir náuseas, y la rarificación del aire le impulsa a uno a salir a la calle para aspirar el oxígeno puro que nos envían las cercanas montañas."

17. "Acabo de visitar la Casa maldita. Se compone de sala, cocina, una alcoba oscurísima, en donde dormía el *Chato*, otra alcoba de las hermanas, un cuarto con desván y la cuadra y corral.

En la sala hay varios cuadros profanos y de devoción con la efigie del *Ecce-Homo* y personajes de la Historia Sagrada. La alcoba del *Chato* tiene una cama de madera, no existiendo en toda la casa ni una silla.

Por todos lados se ven cacharros si [sic] fregar y ropas sucias.

La escalera del desván está apolillada.

Todas las habitaciones presentan aspecto repugnante."

18. "Representa el otro dibujo un rincón de la casa maldita: la subida al desván donde sufrió Pedrín su cautiverio. La ventana que aparece en el fondo fue por la que descolgó el criminal el cuerpo de su víctima. Da al corralillo de la casa protegido por un muro ruinoso, fácilmente escalable y apoyado en las estribaciones del monte, muy suaves en aquel punto. La escalera apoyada en la pared conduce al desván. Es la única subida que éste tiene y por allí iba el *Chato* a dar los alimentos a Pedrín. El desván es inmenso, aguardillado y cubierto a teja vana. No hay allí más luz que la que se filtra por los requicios de la techumbre, por donde se descubren trocitos de cielo muy azul y muy hermoso, cuyo color y hermosura resultan más apetecibles al ser contemplados entre la nauseabunda lobreguez de aquella tenebrosa mansión del crimen.

Toda la casa del *Chato* es una verdadera zahurda, cuyo recuerdo solo produce náuseas. Abundan las estampitas de santos por todas partes, hasta en el mismo cuarto del verdugo. Encima de la cómoda que hay en la sala se ve un *Niño de la bola*, de regular tamaño, limpio y reluciente de color, como si acabara de salir de la barraca de un feriante. Por toda la casa trapos y más trapos; la cocina no tiene más luz que la que penetra por el cañon de la chimenea; en el suelo hay grandes charcos de agua oscura y pestilente.

La casa de los padres de Pedrín es el reverso de la medalla. Está situada en la calle del Calvario, como queriendo profetizar el que ahora sufren. Es alegre, bien soleada, limpia y jabelgada con esmero; tiene un jardín microscópico, una verja elegante y unas ventanas con unos visillos de color con leones y pajarracos. Desde fuera parece un hotelito; ellos habitan uno de los cuartos más modestos de aquella alegre vivienda. La hermanita de Pedrín juega en el jardincillo, en cuyas verjas se enlazan y suben las paredes unas enredederas mustias. Allí parece respirarse la atmósfera pura de un hogar honrado."

19. The phrases in quotation marks are from David Vincent's *Literacy and Popular Culture*, 198, where he discusses the kinds of imaginative narratives in the form of cheap illustrations found on the walls of the poor and illiterate in England, and how those narratives helped to shape the imaginations of those who looked at them each day.

20. "Frente a la fachada principal del Monasterio elévese la cordillera cuyo pico más elevado llámase cerro de loa Abantos y hállase cortado por el `Puerto de Malagón,' que tiene 1.919 pies de altura a contar desde la puerta del Monasterio. Más abajo, y como una excrecencia de la montaña, se encuentra el Risco del Despeñadero, para subir al cual se necesita caminar gateando dificultosamente por tener un declive casi vertical que seguramente llega a 70 grados.

En la parte media del Risco, siempre descendiendo, se ve una excrecencia del terreno, y luego, mucho más abajo, un camino.

A diestro y siniestro prolóngase la cordillera pelada, desprovista de vegetación.

Pues bien, en esa parte media del Risco, donde se halla la excrecencia del terreno, aparecía a las tres y cuarto de la tarde del día 10 el cadáver amoratado del niño Pedro Bravo."

Like the reporters who described El Escorial, visitors such as the French painter, Pierre Paris, were struck by its barrenness. In 1895 he approached it by bicycle from Madrid: "It is a desert; everywhere the same desolate, slightly hilly landscape; not a house, not a field, not a flock to be seen. One interminable stretch of 5 to 6 kilometers is picturesque as it leads through the rocky heights with a view below of a somewhat greener and more fertile valley—a valley which is not, however, put to use. At last, one sees the Guadarrama range ahead in the distance, white at the top, completely gray and treeless, with a spot on it—the town of the Escorial and the Escorial" ("C'est le désert; toujours le même paysage désolé, un peu accidenté; on ne voit pas une maison, pas un champ, pas un troupeau. Une côte interminable, de 5 à 6 kilomètres, est pittoresque, à travers les rochers, avec vue sur une vallée un peu plus verte et fertile, mais dont on ne profite pas. Enfin, en face, on aperçoit la sierra de Guadarrama, blanche à la cime, complètement grise et sans arbres, avec une tache, la ville d'Escorial et l'Escorial"). *L'Espagne de 1895 et 1897. Journal de voyage* (Paris: E. De Boccard, 1979), 49.

21. "En el año 1577, el 7 de noviembre, un joven, hijo del panadero de la reina doña Ana, de la misma edad que hoy tiene el tristemente célebre *Chato* (26 años) [sic], ocultándose en un jarel que había muy espeso, debajo de la cocina del rey, se entregaba diariamente a brutales excesos, haciendo víctimas a inocentes jóvenes, a uno de los cuales asesinó para que no le delatara después.

El crimen fue descubierto, y según la ley de aquellos tiempos fue condenado el *Chato* de hace tres siglos a ser quemado vivo, sentencia que le fue leída y ejecutada en el sitio donde la cruz se levanta, auxiliándole en sus últimos momentos Fray Juan de Quemada y Fray Juan de Santa María. Aquella cruz en el día se llama la `Cruz nefanda' en recuerdo del horrendo crimen perpetrado y parecido al que hoy tanto indigna al honrado pueblo de este real sitio.'

Extraña coincidencia."

22. José María Quadrado and Vicente de la Fuente, "Castilla la nueva," vol.1, *España. Sus monumentos y artes—Su naturaleza e historia* (Barcelona: Daniel Cortezo y Cia., 1885), 256.

23. *Spain and the Spaniards* (Philadelphia: Henry T. Coates & Co., 1895), 271;259. De Amicis visited Spain during the reign of the Italian-born Amadeo I (1870–73). A Spanish translation of his *Spagna* (Firenze: G. Barbera, 1873) was available by 1877. H. Giner de los Ríos published a translation in 1884. Other editions followed in the 1890s.

24. *Old Spain and New Spain* (New York: Scribner's Sons, 1888), 188. See also Augustus J. C. Hare, *Wanderings in Spain* (New York: G. Routledge, 1872), who claimed that "in 1871, during the visit of the Emperor of Brazil [...] hundreds of people flocked forth from Madrid to look upon the awful face of the dead [Charles V] which was entire even to the hair and eyebrows, though perfectly black" (149). John Hay's version of the story on p. 236 of *Castilian Days* (London: William Heineman, 1903), orig. publ. 1871, is somewhat different. He wrote that the coffin lid was opened by the Ministers of State and *Fomento* in the spring of 1870, disclosing "the grim face of the Burgess of Ghent, just as Titian painted him—the keen, bold face of a world-stealer."

25. Henry M. Field, *Old Spain and New Spain*, 187.

26. John Hay in *Castilian Days*, wrote, for example, that "All that was human died out of him [Philip II] years before his actual demise, and death seemed not to consider it worth while to carry off a vampire" (236).

27. "En esta población hay la tradicional costumbre de celebrar el día de Reyes, por la hermandad titulada de Dios, una fiesta en la cual se visten dos individuos de máscara para desempeñar los papeles de *Botarga y Botarguilla*, y recabar por medio de éstos, que llevan una porra en la mano, fondos y comestibles para llevar a efecto la fiesta.

Dichos papeles los desempeñaron este año, Julián y Crisanto.

Es decir, que cuando esto ocurría habíase perpetrado el horroroso crimen, o por lo menos el secuestro del niño.

Horroriza el pensar, la sangre fría con que Julián tomó parte en esta fiesta, si como se cree éste ha sido autor del horrible delito.

Esta circumstancia se recuerda y comenta con execración por el vecindario. Julián y Crisanto pasaron la tarde alegremente, mientras que el inocente Pedrín lloraba las consecuencias de su ferocidad." And the final quoted passage: "Para que el año próximo no se permita en la fiesta de la Hermandad de Dios que se celebra el día de Reyes, se vista nadie con el disfraz de Botarga y Botarguilla por recordar dichos trajes la época del martirio del niño Pedrín y por haber profanado así antiquísimos disfraces el *Chato* y Crisanto." For information on the figures in question, see Joan Corominas, *Diccionario crítico etimológico castellano e hispánico* A-CA (Madrid: Editorial Gredos, 1980), s.v. "Botarga"; S. García Sanz, "Botargas y enmascarados alcarreños (Notas de etnografía y folklore)," *Revista de Dialectología y Tradiciones Populares* 9 (1953):467–492. On pp. 476–477 the author describes a *botarga* from Tortuero who was appointed by the Ayuntamiento to collect alms on January 6, but that *botarga* was not masked. María Elisa Sánchez Sanz in "La censura popular en Aragón," *Les productions populaires en*

Espagne 1850–1920, 94, referring to instances of mute censure wrote: "The other example is the `botargas' who covered their faces with false faces or a leather mask in towns near Aliga (Teruel), such as Hinojasa de Jarque, Jarque de la Val and even Mirambel. If these individuals talked, they were unmasked. On occasion they acted in completion of a promise. Recently the *botargas* have received some compensation from the city hall. They also used to frighten girls by cornering them and trying to lift up their skirts in order to soil them with excrement. ("El otro ejemplo, es el de las `botargas' que cubrían sus rostros con caretas o máscaras de cuero en los pueblos próximos a Aliga (Teruel), tales como Hinojosa de Jarque, Jarque de la Val e incluso en Mirambel. Si estos personajes hablaban eran descubiertos y en varias ocasiones han salido cumpliendo una promesa y las botargas, en los últimos años, han recibido algún donativo del Ayuntamiento. Además, asustaban a las chicas, las 'encorrían' y trataban de levantarles las faldas y mancharlas con excrementos."

28. "en vez de la cárcel reclama el manicomio, y en lugar de los anatemas y epítetos gruesos, exige un poco más de conmiseración y reparar en parte y en lo que sea posible el delito grave cometido con ella por la sociedad, esa sociedad que se escandaliza hipocríticamente ante el crimen y no le prevé y le evita acorriendo en auxilio de los que necesitan dirección física y alimento intelectual."

29. "La cárcel de El Escorial es un magnífico edificio, todo de piedra, donde caben doscientas personas.

Las prisiones reciben luz por grandes ventanas provistas de rejas, y en todas partes se advierte el cuidado que los Sres. López y Vergara ponen en que los servicios no se vean desatendidos, a pesar de que el personal del establecimiento se limita a ambos señores."

30. "En la actualidad hay veintiséis reclusos, entre ellos un *fraile falsificado* que recorría estos pueblos pidiendo para la *comunidad*, con hábito de franciscano por fuera, y vestido interiormente con gran pulcritud. Se finje [sic] ingeniero, abogado, periodista, y pasante del Sr. Serrano Fatigati, y es un individuo a quien muchas veces hemos visto en la Puerta del Sol vendiendo libros y ofreciendo...otras cosas.

A todos ellos da lecciones de lectura y escritura el Sr. López Merelo, ayudado por el Sr. Vergara."

31. "La instrucción debía ser...el primer elemento de la reforma penal. El Maestro, no el cabo de vara, ha de ser el que corrija los penados; el libro, y no el grillete, el que enfrene sus pasiones. Por esto en toda casa de corrección debe haber una Escuela; por esto también y como necesario complemento, ha de haber en aquélla una Biblioteca." From Antonio Viñao Frago, "A la cultura por la lectura. Las Bibliotecas populares" (1869–1885):311. See Enrique Ferri, "Educación, ambiente y criminalidad," *La España Moderna* 49 (1893):118–134. For discussions of perceived connections between illiteracy and criminality in the nineteenth century, see Harvey J. Graff, *The Legacies of Literacy*, p. 337 and the same author's *The Literacy Myth. Literacy and Social Structure in the Nineteenth-Century City (New York: Academic Press, 1979)*, especially Chapter 6, "Literacy and Criminality," 235-267. In 1893 Fernando Cadalso described the dismal state of the library in the prison of which he was director in Madrid. The few books there were—which were of no interest or value in any case—lay piled on the floor as there was no money for bookcases. Nor was there money for a librarian. From "Memoria de la prisión celular de Madrid, presentada al Excmo. Señor Ministro de Gracia y Justicia por el Director de dicho establecimiento, Dr. Fernando Cadalso." *Revista de los Tribunales* 27 (1893):120.

32. "El *Chato* arroja esputos de sangre. Se cree que esto es síntoma de pulmonía. Ya había padecido dos pulmonías.

Cuando le hablan algo referente al crimen, se asusta de tal manera, que se vuelve como loco y le da el accidente.

El juez ha dispuesto que no le moleste nadie y que se le facilite una cama de hierro con colchones, mantas y almohadas.

El doctor Peña le visita con frecuencia."

33. "Por ello se concede a su fuerza e impacto una importancia considerable; y de ahí que en muchas de ellas, para captar la atención del posible comprador de romances, cuanto más macabras y violentas sean las escenas representadas, cuantas más cabezas haya por el suelo, aberturas en canal y puñales, más se asegura la venta, explotando la morbosidad del compra-

dor." *Romances horrorosos*. Selección de romances de ciego que dan cuenta de crímenes verídicos, atrocidades y otras miserias humanas, ed. Isabel Segura (Barcelona: Editorial Alta Fulla, 1984), xiii.

34. "se dijo que el niño había sido llevado por un titiritero y de pueblo en pueblo corrí tras él hasta encontrarle en Chinchón; no tenía el niño. Luego fui a Madrid dos veces y conseguí encontrar las personas que se decía habían visto al niño; igual resultado me dió aquella larga peregrinación por la corte."

35. "El pueblo se había puesto en conmoción, y muchos vecinos, aunque todavía era noche, salieron a la calle para enterarse. Cuando amaneció las calles se llenaron de gente y todos se convirtieron en agentes de policía para averiguar el paradero del niño secuestrado. El asunto preocupaba sobre todo a las mujeres, que no cesaban en sus comentarios. De tal suerte, que en menos de una hora corrieron tres o cuatro novelas por el pueblo. El niño fue hijo de un gran señor que daba diez millones por su rescate; fue un expósito a quien su madre, no pudiendo reclamarlo, hacía secuestrar; fue un huérfano al cuidado de aquel señor que allí estaba y que unos tíos quisieron hacer desaparecer, etc., etc. En los corrillos se saboreaban con deleite estas noticias de gusto romancesco." "El origen del pensamiento," vol. 2, *Obras completas* (Madrid: Aguilar, 1959), 562a-563b.

Chapter Four

The Case of the "Niño de El Escorial" and the Attack on the Jury

SPANISH PRIDE IN THE JURY REINSTITUTED IN 1888

One of the stanzas from a ballad (*romance*) entitled "The Horrible Parricide Committed on the Person of María Anguera Cavallé by Her Son, Domingo Amorós on July 1, 1897 in the town of Alforja" ("Horroroso parricidio cometido en la persona de María Anguera Cavallé por su hijo Domingo Amorós el día 1 de julio de 1897 en el pueblo de Alforja"), expressed the hope and pride that many Spaniards had in the jury system reinstituted in 1888:

> The Amorós trial
> was heard by jurors.
> The justice-dealing court
> that lets the people judge,
> is the court that
> by its independent action
> will make justice shine
> in the Spanish nation. [1]

Spaniards holding a variety of liberal political views believed that national honor and pride had been vindicated by recent adaptations to contemporary continental judicial practices. In 1882 secrecy in preliminary criminal investigations and in subsequent trials was ended, followed six years later by the reinstitution of the jury. (Earlier, from 1872 to 1875, juries had been empanelled to sit on criminal cases.)[2] The establishment in 1888 of the open, accusatorial trial by jury appeared to ensure that the opportunity thus afforded qualified prospective jurors to exercise civic responsibility would enhance the people's sense of dignity.

Not everyone was pleased or convinced that these changes would be effected successfully. The inadequate financing of the judicial system led many people initially in favor of the jury to express skepticism. In 1893 the budget and level of personnel for the Ministry of Justice were below those of 1850, causing Pedro Calvo Camina to remark: "If we continue along this path, it will soon be necessary to resort to a public subscription in order to support the judicial system in Spain" ("Si continuamos por este camino, dentro de poco será necesario acudir a una suscripción pública para mantener el poder judicial en España").[3] For his part, the lawyer, legal correspondent for *El Día*, and trial reporter for the *Revista de Tribunales y de Legislación Universal*, Angel Ossorio y Gallardo, in referring specifically to the scandalous plight of jurors unable to collect their stipends (*dietas*), sarcastically implied in *El Día* on June 3, 1894 that a misguided wish to emulate more progressive countries had led Spain to adopt the jury system before it was ready to support it: "The thing is to be able to say to the civilized countries: —We're as good as anyone else. We also have this business of the jury or something like it. Of course we're liberals!" ("El caso es poder decir a los países cultos: —Nosotros no somos menos que nadie. Aquí tenemos también *eso* del Jurado o algo parecido. ¡Si seremos liberales!").

In addition to questions concerning inadequate funding of the judicial system, there were calls to revise the Penal Code, and there were doubts about the competency of the judiciary. The large number of cases that had to be dismissed because of judicial errors in 1891 and 1892—25,195 out of 41,137 in the latter year—led *El Nuevo Régimen* on September 17, 1892 to declare that: "The number of dismissals is the symptom that most clearly reveals the deficiency in the organization of our judicial system" ("La cantidad de sobreseimientos es el síntoma que más claramente revela la deficiencia de la organización de nuestra justicia").

THE ESCORIAL VERDICT

Throughout the 1890s there were attacks on the jury system, some public and others covert. The Escorial case is important in this connection because it received extraordinary publicity. The press's coverage aroused strong emotions and the reaction to the unexpected verdict led publicists and the general public to discuss and reflect on the criminal justice system. The jury, a notably vulnerable part of that system, took the brunt of the criticism generated by that and subsequent discussions on the topic, finally disappearing two decades later, in 1923.

In the days that followed the jury's May 14, 1894 verdict in the Escorial case, more than a dozen Madrid dailies alone featured front-page editorials, letters, or articles attacking, defending or trying to explain the jury's action.

On May 16 a debate in the Senate on the outcome of the trial led the Minister of Justice to draw the attention of the prosecutor (*fiscal*) of the *Tribunal Supremo* to the "*enormidad legal*" occasioned by the verdict, the questions that had led to it, and the sentence. The *fiscal* of the court in which the case had been tried was ordered to appeal the decision. The journalist for *El Nacional* who reported this development on May 17, 1894, ended by asserting—undoubtedly with some justification—that "this triumph of justice (i.e., the appeal to the high court) must be ascribed to the efforts of the press which has identified itself with public opinion" ("este triunfo de la justicia se deberá a los esfuerzos de la prensa identificada con la opinión pública").

The prospect of an annulment defused some of the popular outrage, permitting public discussion to focus more closely on what had gone wrong and why. This discussion eventually included not only specific problems concerning the jury brought to light in the aftermath of the trial, but also problems thought to be inseparable from the jury system as constituted in 1894.

When the jury was asked whether Julián García was guilty of strangling the child, Pedro Bravo, it answered "Yes." Public indignation focused on the answer given to a later question as to whether the accused had committed the crime with the qualifying circumstance of *alevosía*, i.e., whether the child's weakened condition and physical traumas had enabled the killing to take place without risk to the aggressor or aggressors from any defense which might have been mounted by the victim. The jury answered "No" to that question, as it did also to the question as to whether the killing was premeditated. The first answer made the killing a homicide rather than murder (*asesinato*). The second, by eliminating any aggravating circumstance, saved Julián from the garrote.

Press exegesis of this inexplicable response—inexplicable because a three-year-old child was not thought capable of defense against a grown man—included the following interpretations: 1) the jury was too obtuse to understand what it was responding to; 2) the jury was not convinced of Julián's guilt, but responded as it did in order to satisfy the public's desire for vengeance and, at the same time, spare the life of the accused; 3) question number 20, which was phrased confusingly, was for that reason improperly posed by the *Tribunal de derecho* to jurors disarmed by legal inexperience in order to discredit the jury system in general by discrediting this jury in particular. Any one of the three explanations led to the conclusion that the jurors were incapable of fulfilling their duties.

Supporters of the jury system defended the Escorial jury first on the grounds that it had been handed a poorly constructed case, devoid of real proof. *El Nacional*, for example, in its May 15, 1894 comment on the verdict wrote: "We have been given a decision by the jury without proof of any kind [...]" ("Y hemos llegado al juicio por jurados sin prueba ninguna, ni grande ni chica [...]"). And later, "And the jury, when it delivered its verdict in the case against the *Chato* and his co-defendants, did not overlook the proof because none was put forward by a *sumario* whose flimsiness subsequently weakened the verdict. But the jury did not follow its own criteria strictly. By condemning the *Chato* to *reclusion temporal*, it is astonishingly inconsistent, because the crime is so horrendous it admits of no intermediary punishment." The reporter ended: "And there are those who believe they can explain the real reason for the legal inconsistency by thinking that *reclusion temporal* is not, in this case, a penalty, but rather a compromise the jury made between the extravagant demands of the public and their own consciences. They reconcile the two by sending the *Chato* to prison."[4]

Jury supporters argued also that the ineffectiveness and apparent internal division amongst the attorneys and magistrates constituting the *Tribunal de derecho* had led to a failure to provide proper guidance to the jurors. Long before the trial began, there were indications of disagreements between different representatives of the judiciary involved in the case. On February 16 and 26 of 1893, at a time when the pre-trial investigation was in progress, *La Correspondencia de España* had reported that the *fiscal* of the *Audiencia* in Madrid was displeased with the preparation of the *sumario*. The specific source of his displeasure was not revealed. Between those two dates the *Guardia Civil* telegraphed the *gobernador civil*, Aguilera, notifying him that one of their members had taken a statement from Crisanto Jorge that accused Julián García of the crime. The communication assured the liberal governor that Crisanto's sworn statement effectively settled the case. Meanwhile, the press had more than once noted the anxious desire on the part of the authorities to conclude the case by securing a suspect. It was surely not coincidental that there was no further reference in the press to reservations about the *sumario* on the part of the Madrid *fiscal*.

Several days after the trial ended, *El Heraldo de Madrid* on May 18, 1894 carried an editorial apology for attributing error to the jury for its verdict. Upon reflection it was clear, wrote the editorialist, that the defective formulation of questions and the sentencing tribunal's determination of responsibility derived from the answers to those questions were at fault—both errors devolving on the judges of law, the *Tribunal de derecho*, not on the *Tribunal de hecho*, the judges of fact, i.e., the jury.

The question concerning *alevosía* was, in fact, a difficult one. Preceding jurisprudence was inconsistent as to whether it was always a factor in homicides perpetrated by adults whose victims were children. The question on premeditation was less thorny from a legal point of view. It appeared likely to some contemporary observers that the jurors were not aware of the consequences of answering "No" to this question. Nonetheless, in so doing, they had eliminated a possible aggravating circumstance that could lead to the imposition of the death penalty rather than *reclusion temporal* or *cadena perpetua* in the event that a later ruling converted the crime from one of homicide to murder (*asesinato*). In any case, the point made by *El Heraldo de Madrid* was that the responsibility for formulation of the questions and instruction to the jurors had not been conscientiously fulfilled. On May 17, 1894, *El Nacional* also drew attention to the evident disagreements between the *fiscal*, Córdoba, and the other magistrates at the end of the trial. Those disagreements hinged on the propriety of the questions asked of the jury and whether any errors in their formulation could be immediately remedied.[5]

On May 16, 1894 a reporter for *El Ideal*, whose political orientation was "revolutionary Republican," charged that the Escorial jury had been deliberately discredited by the *Tribunal de derecho*. Behind this body, as the reporter put it, looms the monarchy which like the *manzanillo* tree is so poisonous the very shadow it casts is deadly. The reporter did not deny the absurdity of the jury's verdict: "And since the Escorial verdict is truly absurd, they [the monarchists] have the way cleared to create an atmosphere which is inimical to this essentially democratic institution." He then listed the tactics used by its enemies to undermine the jury:

> Fines, inconveniences, endless annoyances—everything possible is done so that the people—who asked for the jury system as a guaranty of justice—will tire of it. But there is still more. In this entrenched dual system consisting of two courts which function at the same time—the popular court [of fact] and the court of law—the latter directs and controls the proceedings and is able to present the questions which the former must resolve in a confused and involuted form.[6]

The reporter's analysis reflected a widespread belief among opponents of the ruling Monarchist parties that the latter had reinstituted the jury only because the times demanded it, while behind the scenes, as enemies of the jury, they did everything in their power to undermine it. Similarly, opponents charged that the current Prime Minister, Práxedes Sagasta—active in the September coalition that replaced the deposed Isabel II—paid empty lip service to another of the fundamental goals of the 1868 revolution, universal suffrage. The political history of the last twenty five years distilled the bitterness and frustration felt by such opponents. In exchange for the Provisional Government's acceptance in 1869 of the Democrat program (universal suffrage, religious freedom, the jury, and freedom of the press and association), the Democrats had relinquished power in office and accepted a so-called democratic monarchy. Subversion of Democrat goals followed. From the perspective of the Democrat opposition, accommodationists of the Restoration regime continued to look on in the 1890s while *caciques* made a mockery of universal suffrage and the jury.

Only *El Día* and *La Época*, both on May 16, 1894, ran pieces that took an unequivocally hostile stand against the popular tribunal. Enrique Sepúlveda wrote in *El Día* that the absurdity of the Escorial verdict had inscribed an

INRI on the institution of the jury. The author of the article in *La Época* called the verdict the most outrageous one yet to come from such a "wise and democratic institution" ("sabia y democrática institución"). He asserted that the fault lay in an institution that submitted the solution of questions involving life and honor to judges lacking the serenity and discernment necessary in order to exercise the most exalted of all human functions.

SELECTION AND COMPETENCE OF JURORS

The inadequate education and culture of jurors had been a principal argument against the reinstitution of the jury in Spain. It was commonly made in the nineties as well, not only by political conservatives, but also by politically conservative criminologists such as Garofalo, Lombroso, Ferri and others, who preferred that scientific experts should decide questions of responsibility and determine appropriate penalties.[7]

An opponent of the jury writing in 1893 in the *Revista de los Tribunales* made his case against the institution by drawing attention to poor, rural jurors whose dress, food, and manner of eating in themselves implied a kind of cultural incompetence further demonstrated by their near illiteracy, ignorance of the law and lack of civic sense. The author called upon the Minister of Justice to travel incognito to a small town in order to see for himself what rural jurors—such as those in Alforja—were like:

> You would have to observe them before and after their court duty, intermingling amicably as if they were on holiday, dressed in shirt-sleeves during the summer and wrapped in their coarse sleeveless overcoats in winter, seated before the door of a tavern with a plate of codfish on their laps, in their hands chunks of bread, and at their sides a jug of cheap wine. And then there is no doubt that you would exclaim: 'Is it to this man or to these men that the law entrusts the sacred office of administering justice?' You would have to see them at an inn eating with the families of the accused, or with the accused themselves; for they cannot refuse the company of people they know from their hometown or from the nearby areas. And if this happens now when they go to the provincial capitals, what will happen the day that they meet in the hometown itself, or in the one adjoining? There was a reason for writing into law the impediment to exercising the judiciary function—which does not govern these judges of fact who do not, for the most part, know how to do more than spell out words and draw marks—because we have already noted that Madrid is not the whole of Spain. The nation has a great many towns and villages that do not know the law and which do not consider serving on the jury as a right, but rather as a burden that everyone tries to shake off as best he can.[8]

The issue of how jurors were selected was not addressed specifically in the press with reference to the Escorial jurors.[9] Nonetheless, it was widely recognized in the early 1890s that government control over the judicial system—and, in particular, over the preparation of the primary lists of jurors—was all-pervasive. The perception was that in many regions *caciques* determined which potential jurors would be called and which would be excused. Indeed, the 1894 *Memoria del Fiscal del Tribunal Supremo* (the annual report compiled on the functioning of the justice system and read at the opening in September of the *Tribunal Supremo*) confirmed this perception with facts.

A sizeable section of the 1894 *Memoria* was dedicated to the jury. Juan de Aldana, the *Fiscal* of the *Tribunal Supremo* who made the presentation, began by noting that the impressions and opinions of the representatives of justice whose individual reports formed the foundation of the *Memoria*, were not only unfavorable to the jury, but were even more pessimistic than in previous reports. The jury, in general, was not functioning well. Why not? Because jurors were ignorant, they lacked independence of judgment, they resisted service on the jury, they were harsh with respect to crimes against property, and they were too lenient with respect to crimes against persons.[10] The problem, in the opinion of some of the informants, lay in the formation of first lists. Others believed that public opinion opposed the jury, that even its most ardent former supporters had lost confidence in it. All the informants believed that the time had come to suspend it.

Aldana denied that Spain was not ready for the jury system or that the jury as such posed a threat to the execution of justice. Instead, he enumerated the specific reasons why the jury was not functioning as it should. First, *caciques* located primarily in rural areas, motivated by political considerations, selected the names for the first lists. Jurors thus chosen were rightly assumed to lack independent judgment. Second, the people best qualified to serve evaded jury duty. Third, the stipend (*dietas*), which jurors were entitled to receive, was frequently not paid out. Aldana's recommendation was that the best-qualified people be selected from the first lists as far as was compatible with the popular nature of the institution.[11]

On September 16, 1894 *El Liberal* ran an editorial entitled "*Jurados y caciques*" in response to Aldana's presentation. The editorialist pointedly observed that the *Memoria* did not call for the suppression of jurors but rather of the *caciques* whose pernicious influence in the formation of first lists and of verdicts was what truly threatened the jury system. Yet, with no prospect of practical reform in sight, the editorial ended with a warning that the enemies of the jury were about to administer its death blow: "Here in Spain the jury died a violent death at the advent of the Restoration, and now that it has been resuscitated, it looks as though a mortal blow is again being prepared" ("Aquí en España murió [el jurado] a mano airada al advenimiento de la restauración, y al resucitar ahora, parece que se le prepara golpe mortal").

On February 10, 1893, *El Imparcial* ran a story that presented the problem of jury selection in clearly understandable class terms. The reporter noted that the jury hearing the case of the *crimen de Valverde* had returned three verdicts—all defective—which indicated "an intellectual level which is not very flattering or comforting" ("un nivel intelectual poco lisonjero y consolador"). Why, he asked, was this so often the case? The answer: "The well-off classes, whose level of intelligence should be higher, avoid the duties of a juror out of a desire for comfort, or because of egoism. Since the thousands of loop-holes which the law provides makes this easy to do, those duties like a heavy burden come to rest on the shoulders of men who cannot avoid it whether out of ignorance or out of fear." The result: verdicts decided by individuals unable even to understand the questions put to them by the magistrates. The reporter called, therefore, for a reform of the law that would ensure the selection of the people best qualified for the task. He ended with a warning: "These aptitudes are not acquired by customary use over a few years; but it is undeniable that if the absence of habitual practice is compounded by a lack of culture, then the results will necessarily be harmful."[12] The reporter did not develop his suggestive distinction between "*costumbres*" or "*hábitos*," and "*cultura*." Definitions of these terms and meaningful discussion of how customs and culture affected the conduct of civic affairs are difficult to find in the public forums, especially the press, of the nineties.

An article by a conservative, "El Hujier Domingo," in *El Día* on April 23, 1893, referred even more circumstantially than the *Imparcial* reporter had done to class conflict among jurors. He drew attention to the deep division between jurors caused by differences of birth, culture, education, habits, clothing. Those who wear frock coats, he wrote, vote one way; those who do not, vote in the opposite, presumably, wrong way. None of this was likely to change, the reporter concluded, until the liberal party addressed itself to the public, conceding that although their intentions had been good: "accommodation to the people has turned out to be a detestable mistake" ("lo popular ha sido cosa detestable").

Six years later, in 1899, Bellver de Oña, in a study of the criminal justice system, discussed the same problems reviewed here—the formation of the primary lists, the avoidance of jury duty by the most capable, the unacceptable verdicts returned by jurors unprepared for such service—terming them serious defects which were still awaiting resolution.[13]

In the course of the Escorial trial some of the issues that informed contemporary debate about the jury came to light. A reference, for example, to the financial problems besetting the criminal justice system appeared in the press in the aftermath of the trial. About two weeks after the Escorial trial ended, *La Época* on May 30, 1894, reported that a large number of jurors from the judicial district of San Lorenzo de El Escorial had appeared at the newspaper's office complaining that they had not received their *dietas*. The jurors in question may have included some or all of those empanelled at El Escorial up to May 14, 1894. If so, their request for *dietas* would have been an indication of real penury since the *dietas* were so meager to begin with and difficult to obtain.[14]

PRESS REPRESENTATION OF THE ESCORIAL JURY

Readers of the press, aware of the controversies revolving around these issues and, in particular, of unfavorable characterizations of jurors, naturally wanted information about jurors and their competence in specific cases. Who were the jurors in the Escorial case and how did they comport themselves?

The jurors who were finally sworn in at the tribunal set up in the *Ayuntamiento* at El Escorial came primarily from two towns within the jurisdiction of San Lorenzo de El Escorial; according to *El Nacional* on May 8, 1894, some were from nearby Robledo de Chavela, others from Villanueva del Pardillo. Most of the newspapers covering the trial provided their names. Domingo Blanco supplied such a list and described them as: "farmers [...] simple folk, what we call a rural jury—which generally turns out to have good sense and an undeviating concept of justice" ("labradores [...] gentes sencillas, lo que llamamos un jurado rural, que generalmente suele dar pruebas de un buen sentido y de un recto espíritu de justicia"). This characterization of the moral qualifications of the jurors was never questioned by reporters covering the case.

During the Escorial trial the jurors' comportment, as recorded especially by Domingo Blanco, bore out the journalist's initial favorable assessment of their rectitude. In particular, the *Imparcial*'s reporter singled out their commitment to the institution of the family and to motherhood. On May 9, the same reporter described the scene on the previous day when Pedrín's mother was unable to testify: "Who could describe a mother's grief in the face of such a terrible misfortune!" ("¡Quién puede describir el dolor de una madre por tan horrible desgracia!"). Everyone was moved: "And the jurors wept, and those who from a distance heard those lamentations also wept. Unfortunate mother!" ("Y los jurados lloraban, y los que desde lejos oían aquellas lamentaciones lloraban también. ¡Pobre madre!"). Jurors distinguished, however, between mothers. When one of the lawyers for the defense in an attempt, no doubt, to draw attention to the way in which reactions to the defendants were manipulated by the press and the prosecution, asked that the jurors show compassion for Crisanto's elderly and ailing mother as well, his plea apparently fell on deaf ears. At any rate no one recorded subsequently that she had received sympathy from any quarter. As the mother of a man who was universally considered to be loathsome and animalistic, neither jurors nor the public could place her in the category of good mothers alongside Gumersinda. The pollution resulting from the crime that Crisanto had allegedly helped Julián to commit, spread, moreover, to his wife as well as to his mother. María, whose two-year-old daughter lived with her in prison, had another baby while she was incarcerated. Reporters referred on occasion to the hardships the young woman endured, but they did not present her as a mother deserving of sympathy.

On May 9, Domingo Blanco telegraphed that the defense lawyers had approached the jurors, aware of their unfavorable attitude towards the accused: "They talk with them in the cafe—with complete propriety, to be sure—but they do discuss the evidence, reject the charges against their clients, and affirm their innocence. The jurors listen...until they finish their cup of coffee. Then they withdraw, as if such conversation was disagreeable to them." In view of the jurors' silence, Blanco resorted to speculation about their reactions to the crime. He suggested that they were thinking about the child's martyrdom and the mother's grief. But beyond that: "The impressions they have formed about the *Chato* family must also have a powerful influence on the jury. Their habits, the vices of those people gathered together in the shack near the Romeral—these people who have filed through the courtroom inspire such repugnance that more than once I have heard someone say: 'What a pity we can't destroy that house with all those people in it!'"[15] The reporter thus encouraged the jurors—as he did all those Spaniards following the Escorial case—to share consecrated sentiments of veneration for motherhood, and repugnance for the vice so notoriously exemplified in the defendants.

On the first day of the trial, Crisanto Jorge retracted his accusation against Julián García, claiming that it had been coerced by the Captain of the Civil Guard with the knowledge and complicity of the examining magistrate.[16] Domingo Blanco of *El Imparcial*, along with most of the press, discounted the retraction as a familiar ploy. The jury, Blanco informed his readers, did not believe the retraction, according to conversations overheard in the inn where many jurors congregated for coffee.

At the end of the second day of the trial, as the accused were being escorted on foot to the jail, Crisanto Jorge tried to run away, according to *El País*, which reported the incident on May 9. The paper added that the attempted escape had a noticeable effect on the jury, prejudicing them against Crisanto. On May 10, Blanco also noted the incident and remarked that, "The jurors' impressions are unfavorable to the criminals" ("Las impresiones que hay respecto al jurado son desfavorables a los reos"). The report, however, was false. *El Nacional* corrected the record on May 10, noting that the director of the jail, Merelo, explained that Crisanto had merely loosened his handcuffs to alleviate the pain they caused him. Merelo noted that on a previous occasion Crisanto had received permission to loosen them when they made his hands bleed. Hardened as readers' attitudes were toward the accused men, such references to their physical suffering were undoubtedly met with indifference.

On May 12, there were two other pieces of information concerning the jurors' opinions and perceptions. Blanco reported that they were impressed with the *fiscal*, Sr. Córdoba, because of his impartiality. One juror was said to have spoken up in order to refute the statement of a defense lawyer that was contrary to a previous statement given by a doctor. On May 12, Domingo Blanco wrote with disapproval of the defense lawyers' "siege" of the jurors, and this time—no longer resorting to speculation—assured readers that the jurors were in accord with public opinion:

> In the cafe and on the street those who are apparently so convinced of the *Chato*'s innocence and of how favorable the evidence is to his case have repeated the spectacle of their "siege of the jurors."
>
> I believe that these attempts are useless because the jury—in agreement with public opinion—continues to believe that "it's all in the family." And this belief has become even firmer following the statements made by the defense lawyers ("En el café y en la calle se ha repetido el espectáculo del `asedio de los jurados' por aquellos que tan convencidos parecen de la inocencia de los Chatos y de lo favorable de la prueba.
>
> Creo que son inútiles esas gestiones, porque el jurado como la opinión sigue creyendo que `la cosa está en la familia.' Y esta creencia se ha arraigado aún más después de los informes de los defensores.")

Although the jury had been represented as favorable to Córdoba, on May 13 *El Nacional* wrote that when he characterized Crisanto's retraction during his summing up statement as a "poorly-rehearsed play" ("mal ensayada comedia"), his words caused "astonishment in the jury which has seen a tragedy where the public prosecutor claims to see nothing but a farce" ("asombro en en el Jurado que ha visto tragedia donde el ministerio público pretende no hallar más que un sainete"). If the jury reacted as the journalist claimed it did, it was a singular instance of reported sympathy on their part with the plight of the defendants.

On May 16 in *El Día*, Enrique Sepúlveda tried to make sense of the verdict inexplicably handed down by jurors thought to be in accord with public opinion on Julián's guilt. He tried to imagine what the Escorial jurors had experienced in the course of the trial by imagining what rural jurors in general might have experienced: "An honorable farm-worker arrives from the nearby countryside, a person deserving of all respect." The honest farmer who can barely read, or even understand the oral testimony very well is confused by the conflicting claims of individuals representing opposing sides, clothed in their impressive togas. What is the result?: "And the jury, which has not learned anything about the facts of the case except for what it has just now observed in court; the farmer suddenly transformed into a judge, abruptly separated from his `normal surroundings,' from his `usual pursuits,' from `what he knows,' from everything, comes up panting and deserving of pity to a finale in which he knows not what to think, in which he longs for the moment when the questions will be formulated in order to resolve the situation `through his impressions' and in good conscience."[17]

The reporters' characterization of the jurors during the trial was inconclusive in the end as far as confirming or denying their competence measured by education and culture. Much of what was reported about them—as in the cases of Domingo Blanco and Enrique Sepúlveda—amounted to speculation. It is true that that speculation tended to reinforce generally-held notions about the moral conservatism and intellectual limitations of jurors from the country. The usual characterization of rural jurors as poorly-educated rustics, unused to thinking rationally, and too often inclined to leniency in crimes against persons, was generally thought to be confirmed by the Escorial jury, and undeniably served the purposes of conservative campaigns designed to undermine confidence in the jury system. In fact, the principal argument of conservative editorials and articles was that the jury simply was not a viable institution in Spain given the uneducated, uncultivated condition of most jurors—an argument many people unquestionably found persuasive.[18]

THE PRE-TRIAL INVESTIGATION AND JURORS' ACCESS TO THE *SUMARIO*

The reference Enrique Sepúlveda made in *El Día* to the jurors' probable lack of acquaintance with the *sumario* was an important consideration in this case, as it undoubtedly was in many others. In fact, the *sumario* (the word refers both to the conduct of the pre-trial investigation and to its written record), was singled out as problematic before the Escorial trial began. There were two principal reasons for this; the first revolved upon the sense that the measure of secrecy which was needed as pre-trial investigations were being carried out had not, in this instance, been properly observed; the other had to do with the actual conduct of the investigation.

The Minister of Justice, Manuel Alonso Martínez, in the "*Exposición de motivos*" which prefaced the "*Ley de Enjuiciamiento Criminal*" presented to the King on September 14, 1882 and approved by him on that same date, noted that the law did not open up the *sumario* to publicity from the moment of its initiation. Alonso Martínez averred that such was the aim of "certain radical schools of thought [...]" ("ciertas escuelas radicales [...]"), but that while this aim was indeed the ideal, "it is necessary for the State to have some advantage during the first moments, if only in order to be able to collect the traces of the crime and the clues which point to the guilt of its author."[19]

Aggressive and persistent reporters found ways to circumvent the letter of the law and inform their readers about the *instrucción* of certain cases almost from the outset of given investigations. In the Escorial case, reporters sent to the scene as soon as the body was found followed the activities of the examining magistrate as closely as possible from that time forward. Two weeks after the discovery of the child's corpse, on February 25, 1893, Rosón of *El País* wrote: "Señor del Río has ordered great precautions to be taken in order to prevent us newspapermen from finding out what is going on in the courtroom, none of which hinders us from trying to keep our readers informed—perhaps with even more details than before the arrival of said 'señor.' And for the record—we have not tried to poke into the secrets of the summation, nor has any functionary revealed anything of any kind to us."[20] In fact, reporters—Rosón among them—printed information about the clues found near Pedrín's body. They had also printed conclusions reached by the doctors who performed the autopsy, notably the speculation that Pedrín had been given milk. Julián García's lawyer, Cuevas, believed—as noted earlier—that Crisanto Jorge had constructed his accusation against his brother-in-law with details such as those he read in the press.

On May 2, 1894, five days before the Escorial trial began, Angel Ossorio y Gallardo in *El Día* criticized journalists for their reporting of pre-trial investigations: "From the documenting of testimony up to the handing over of the summation to the Court, newspapermen have been providing mountains of news items, especially sensational ones. They have characterized events and people, put attention-grabbing titles to their articles, and have guided public opinion along the path of truth on occasion, but more often than not, they have led it down the road of error." He concluded his editorial (entitled "The Press and the Courts" ["*La prensa y los tribunales*"]) by noting that publicity and openness were legitimate conquests of liberty, "But, woe to those who forget that freedom when it is poorly understood is worse than the blindest absolutism!"[21]

The defense in the Escorial case—as has been pointed out above—believed that the press had wrongly informed public opinion while the prosecution raised no complaints at all on that score. A possible corrective lay at hand in the form of the *sumario*, the written record of the pre-trial investigation. But, although the jurors had the right to ask for the *sumario* and review it at their leisure, there is no indication that they did so.

In his commentary on the *Ley del jurado*, Pacheco devoted several pages to the shocking way in which the *sumario* was typically prepared in Spain, arguing that the institution of the jury, which realizes the principle of "the oral nature of a trial" ("la oralidad del juicio"), could alone compensate for its inadequacies. Yet despite the right which jurors had to acquaint themselves thoroughly with the *sumario*, Pacheco, in effect counselled ignorance:

"Jurors will not take the summation into consideration, they will judge strictly on the basis of what they see in the courtroom."[22]

Other commentators disagreed with Pacheco's position on the primacy of the *juicio oral*. Barcáiztegui y Orfila, for example, insisted on the jury's right to read and study the *sumario*.[23] In the discussion concerning the Escorial case, however, no one suggested that the jurors should have perused the *sumario*. Since there is no indication that any one of them asked to examine the dossier, it is most likely that what they read in the press and what they saw and heard at the trial formed the sole basis of their evaluation of the crimes and of the accused. Julián García's lawyer, José de las Cuevas, as was noted earlier, complained, according to *El Imparcial* on May 12, 1894, that it was the press which has "conducted the pre-trial investigation, has directed the oral trial, and wants to dictate the sentence" ("Ha sido la que instruyó el sumario, la que ha hecho el juicio oral y la que quiere dictar el fallo").

Several books appeared in the late 1880s and the 1890s that instructed the public and prospective jurors, in particular, on correct judicial procedures, including the proper formation of the *sumario*. Among reporters, Rosón was the first covering the Escorial case to point out an apparent lapse on the part of the examining magistrate. He noted that there was no investigation at the monastery despite the fact that the only reliable witnesses to have seen Pedrín before he vanished, saw him there, leaving the Patio de los Reyes. Other infringements of procedure could have been singled out by anyone who had perused a handbook for jurors. *El Día* pointed out on May 9, 1894, for example, that the examining magistrate had not personally searched the house of Julián García, much less had he done so in the owner's presence, as was required by law. The same reporter, nonetheless, wrote that the "informalities" and "incorrect procedures" which characterized the pre-trial investigation mattered little since the motive force behind them was the noble one of uncovering a horrible crime.

Aside from certain other defects in the formation of the *sumario* pointed out by the defense lawyers at the trial—such as the examining magistrate's failure to expunge an incriminating "Yes" response, made in a moment of distraction by a witness giving a deposition when a "No" was the intended answer—there was an important incident in the pre-trial examination that was available to the jurors through the press's coverage in 1893, and which was also cursorily alluded to in the 1894 trial. Eleven-year-old Juana del Valle, Julián García's half-sister, was the first—and for several days following the discovery of the child's corpse on February 10—the only person to implicate her half-brother in the crime. On February 16, 1893, *El Día* reported that she had been lodged in the barracks of the *Guardia Civil* for two days. While she was there, not only was she fed, but she also slept in the same bed with a member of the *Guardia Civil*. By February 17, 1893, as a result of Juana's statements to the examining magistrate, Julián García had become the prime suspect in Pedrín's murder. On May 8, 1894, at the beginning of the trial, *El Imparcial* also wrote in regard to Juana's testimony: "Next she recounted in detail that when they took her to the Civil Guard barracks, they treated her well, gave her supper, and that she slept by the side of a guard" ("En seguida refiere minuciosamente que cuando la llevaron al cuartel de la Guardia civil la trataron con mimo, la dieron de cenar, y durmió junto a un guardia"). There is no report of any subsequent questioning of Juana by the jurors regarding her stay at the barracks. Nor was it reported that Cuevas used this information to foment doubt in the jurors' minds concerning the role of the *Guardia Civil* and Juana's reliability as a witness. It is unlikely, however, that Cuevas and Juana's lawyer, Dionisio Díez Enríquez—who in 1903 published a book entitled *El derecho positivo de la mujer*—failed to emphasize Juana's two nights in the barracks and to draw conclusions damaging to her credibility.[24]

THE POWER OF RHETORIC AND CIRCUMSTANTIAL EVIDENCE

Three theories had been advanced in the press to account for the jury's verdict. The first, the notion that the jurors were too obtuse to understand the questions put to them was not confirmed by reporters on the scene at El Escorial, although they did not clearly refute generally accepted ideas of rural jurors' incapacity. The second theory, according to which key questions were improperly formulated, was voiced most notably by *El Heraldo de Madrid*, and was backed up subsequently (as is noted below) by the *Tribunal Supremo*, which ruled that *alevosía* was indeed a qualifying factor. The third theory in explanation of the verdict was that the jury was not convinced of Julián's guilt, but wished to satisfy the public's desire for vengeance, and, at the same time, spare the life of the accused man. In order to accept this explanation, it was necessary to conclude that despite their alleged rectitude and good sense, the jurors consciously and deliberately answered the questions regarding *alevosía* and premeditation as they did in order to save Julián's life. What might have convinced them to do so?

Enrique Sepúlveda believed that the jurors had been swayed by the eloquence and rhetorical skills of Julián's lawyer, José de las Cuevas. Since the trial was not public, Sepúlveda had to rely on those present in an official capacity to convey information to him about the proceedings. And, as a man certain from the outset of Julián's guilt, Sepúlveda was hardly an unbiased listener to what his informants had to tell him. In any case, his theory concerning the jurors' susceptibility to Cuevas' persuasive power ignores the fact that—as several reporters pointed out—there was no conclusive evidence against Julián García. Cuevas, according to newspaper coverage of the trial, emphasized that point above all else.

In *Strong Representations: Narrative and Circumstantial Evidence in England*, Alexander Welsh traces the development in legal thought which gave priority no longer to direct evidence provided by witnesses, but rather to circumstances. Jurists in the eighteenth century, he writes, developed the maxim that unlike human witnesses, "circumstances cannot lie," particularly if woven into a persuasive narrative.[25] While skepticism on this point increased in the course of the following century, it is clear that the narrative woven from the circumstances divulged by the investigation conducted in the Escorial case and presented to the public by reporters—notably by Eduardo Rosón of *El País*, Hernández Bermúdez and Domingo Blanco of *El Imparcial*, and Mestre Martínez of *La Correspondencia de España*—proved to be highly persuasive. Indeed, Cuevas argued that the case against his client—a case built on the weakest of circumstantial evidence—appeared plausible because the press had, in effect, fictionalized it. As a story enhanced by familiar thematic material and narrative devices borrowed from fiction it succeeded in entertaining many readers and, at the same time, convincing them of the *Chato*'s guilt. In short, circumstances could be manipulated and thus made to lie. The conviction of an innocent defendant was the possible outcome. This was the message, in effect, of the immensely popular novel, published in 1887 by Jules Mary, *Roger-la-Honte*.

Instructional books for prospective jurors such as Barcaíztegui's 1894 manual (*Estudio teórico-práctico*), stressed the great importance of conclusive evidence in capital cases. It would be difficult, however, to demonstrate that this and similar manuals were read by the people for whom they were intended. And such advice, in connection with the Escorial trial, had to be balanced against the sensational case made against the defendants. Their representation in the press and by the prosecution as monstrously vicious made it easier for the public and jurors to yield to the attraction of circumstantial evidence, however weak it was. When the examining magistrate, for example, on the basis of depositions taken from doctors made it known that, in their opinion, Pedrín had been strangled with one hand and that that hand was a left hand, it was immediately obvious to many readers and to some reporters that the case against Julián was clinched, for he was left-handed. Cuevas failed to get a report from the *Real Academia de Medicina* entered into the record even though it dealt with the possibility, first, of strangling a child with one hand, and, second, of determining whether the hand in question was a left or a right hand. (According to *El Nacional* on February 7, 1895, the Academy's report claimed that it was impossible to state which hand, the left or the right, had strangled Pedro Bravo.) Cuevas' request was further denied on appeal to the *Tribunal Supremo*. Yet it was this "evidence" along with the proximity of Julián's house to the site where Pedrín's body was discovered that constituted the principal *circumstantial* evidence against Julián. There was no other evidence or proof of any kind. The testimony of his brother-in-law and of his sisters, although accepted, no doubt, by some members of the public, was demonstrably unreliable.

On November 23, 1895 Angel Ossorio y Gallardo, instead of filing his customary report, "*Crónica de tribunales*," for the *Revista de los Tribunales y de Legislación Universal*, devoted seven pages (744–751) to the High Court's November 15, 1895 appeal filed in the Escorial case. He did so, he explained, because of the case's intrinsic importance, and because of interest expressed by subscribers to the journal. Jury supporters who read these pages setting out the High Court's decision would have found limited confirmation of the criticisms directed against the *Tribunal de derecho* in the Escorial case. The *Tribunal Supremo* found that the actions of the two men in question constituted *asesinato* with no attenuating circumstances, but in the case of Crisanto Jorge it found that there was an aggravating circumstance, that of a prior conviction. It noted further that it was not within the jury's competence to answer the question concerning *alevosía*, and that it should not have been asked to do so. It was a question for judges of law, not for judges of fact. The abusive use of superior strength, *abuso de superioridad*, had also been advanced as an aggravating circumstance, but was rejected as being, in effect, equivalent to *alevosía*. The Court did not reconsider the circumstance of premeditation. It ruled that because Crisanto Jorge had a prior conviction for assault, in accord with article 418 of the Penal Code, he was to receive the maximum penalty—death. He was sentenced to be garroted at El Escorial. Julián García, in accord with the same article, was sentenced to the lesser penalty of *cadena perpetua*.

Public outrage which in 1894 was directed at the jury for its answer to the question on *alevosía* was directed one year later against the ruling of the *Tribunal Supremo* and its strict construction of the penalties provided for by the Penal Code. The Court had condemned Crisanto Jorge to death as a recidivist whose previous offense was relatively minor, and had spared the life of Julián García for lack of an aggravating circumstance. In connection with the Court's ruling, Ossorio drew the attention of "lovers of the Penal Code" and "detractors of the jury" to two sentences handed down in the previous week. A woman found guilty of infanticide had smashed the head of her infant, placed it on the fire, put it in a pot, and then thrown it into a well. She was condemned to four years and six months. The following day a poor wretch appeared on the bench who had tried to pay off a debt with counterfeit *pesetas* and had subsequently tried to pass two more. The public prosecutor asked that he be sentenced to eight and one-half years. Ossorio commented:

> These monstrous inequities are not designed to ensure the nation's tranquility.
>
> The jury erased the scandalous disparity in these two cases as well as it could, handing down a guilty verdict for the infanticide and a verdict of inno-

> cent for the trafficker in counterfeit money. But in any case, the example should not be forgotten since it highlights the question of which is more worthy of censure, the jury—which is always scorned—or the Code—which is always exalted.[26]

In three subsequent numbers of the same journal, members of the editorial staff analyzed the High Court's ruling on the Escorial verdict. Their conclusion was that the sentences handed down were an affront to justice and a blow to the conscience, but that they was, unfortunately, completely legal. In what appears to have been a corporate show of solidarity with the court of law, they stated that the primary fault lay with the jury for answering as it did, although they did fault the judges of law for the improper formulation of the questions—especially the infamous number 20.[27]

The press claiming, as always, to reflect public opinion, expressed dismay. Domingo Blanco traveled to El Escorial with other reporters in order to sound out the reactions of the inhabitants. As in Madrid, people in El Escorial were indignant at the lesser sentence given to Julián García. And also, like people elsewhere in Spain, they wanted a pardon for Crisanto: "as a means of avoiding what appears to be an injustice, no matter how much in harmony with the law it may be" ("como medio de evitar lo que parece una injusticia por muy en harmonía que esté con las leyes"), as Domingo put it in *El Imparcial* on November 17, 1895.

On December 7, 1895 the following brief notice appeared in the Madrid papers: "The High Court has ruled favorably on the request for a pardon for Crisanto, brother-in-law of the *Chato* of El Escorial, who had been condemned to death by the Madrid court" ("El Tribunal Supremo ha informado ayer tarde favorablemente al expediente para el indulto de Crisanto, el cuñado de *Chato* de El Escorial, condenado a muerte por la Audiencia de Madrid"). Thus the High Court averted the perceived injustice of condemning Crisanto to death, even though he had been found less responsible for Pedro Bravo's death than Julián García, solely because he had been found guilty previously of a minor assault.

There is no reason to believe that the public was mollified by the sentence of *reclusion temporal* Crisanto and Julián were to serve. The bitterness of the following comment was probably widely shared. In *La Época* of December 1, 1895, "A Letter from the Old Man" ("*Una carta de `El* Cano' [Lucanor])" satirized various contemporary events. He had this to say about the Escorial crime:

> It's like I say. You rob someone or kill somebody—or maybe both. You go to jail and then prison...then if you serve your time and you get out, what more do they want? You paid for what you did and that's it. Take the *Chato* from El Escorial—when he's served his time, why shouldn't he set up a school for

boys? Believe me, only reactionaries go around saying that it's right to stigmatize people...[...][28]

Once the sentences for the two men were handed down and announced in the press, there was no further newspaper coverage describing their fates, the fate of the families they left behind, their transport to Ceuta, or the conditions that shaped their lives in the North African Penal Colony. Readers who might have wanted to follow their trail in order to learn about prison life and how the two men fared there had to wait until Domingo Blanco alluded to Julián García and Crisanto in a dispatch from Ceuta in 1897 that centered primarily on the anarchists imprisoned there following a wave of terrorist attacks. In effect, Domingo Blanco's report basically reiterated the demonization of the two men that had characterized their depiction throughout the coverage of the crime from 1893 to 1895.

By early 1895 news of the Cuban insurrection began to dominate the newspapers, while anarchism, terrorism, and new horrible crimes made further claims on readers' attention. But while the Escorial crime eventually faded from people's memories, the recollection of the jury's unpopular verdict undoubtedly remained alongside recollections of other unpopular verdicts handed down by men so often characterized as unsuited for the charge of sitting in judgment on their fellow men.

NOTES

1. "El juicio de Amorós
fue la causa por jurados,
el Tribunal justiciero
que al pueblo sienta en estrados,
tribunal que al funcionar
con su libertad de acción
hará brillar la justicia
en la española nación."

From *Romances horrorosos*, 100. A versifier of a different political stripe wrote the following sonnet, we are told, at the time of the jury's reinstitution:

Sonnet
A crucifix and a missal; for candelabra
magistrates who shed little light
and who would function at home the same
as in that court, where they are ciphers.
At their side fourteen gentlemen who
not knowing what is happening to them there,
will make countless blunders
and then ask for their separate payments.
Justice determined by a flip of the coin;
law that is changeable, statutes that vary,
ignorance instead of expert opinion;

the door opened wide to fraud and bribes,
everyone abominating justice,
and the people themselves, as Judge, dissatisfied.
(Soneto
Un cristo y un misal; por candeleros
Magistrados que prestan luz escasa
y que lo mismo harían en su casa
que en ese Tribunal, donde son ceros.
A su lado catorce caballeros
que no sabiendo allí lo que les pasa,
palos de ciego pegarán sin tasa
y pedirán después sendos dineros.
A cara o cruz jugada la justicia;
tornadiza la ley, vario el derecho,
la ignorancia en lugar de la pericia;
la puerta franca al dolo y al cohecho,
todos abominando la justicia
y el mismo pueblo, Juez, no satisfecho)

Qtd. from L.M. "*Juzgadores de Alforja,*" *Revista de los Tribunales* 26 (1 y 8 de abril de 1893):106–107.

2. For the short-lived jury system of 1872–1875, see the *Enciclopedia Universal Ilustrada Europeo-Americana*, 1907, 30, s.v. "Jurado." Written soon after the suspension of the jury in 1923, the section entitled "*Crítica,*" which offers commentary on the institution, presents only one opinion in favor of the jury and five against. See also Juan Antonio Alejandre, *La justicia popular en España. Análisis de una experiencia histórica: Los tribunales de jurados* (Madrid: Editorial de la Universidad Complutense, 1981) for the history of the jury and an extensive bibliography of the institution in Spain. Pages 111–146 cover the jury from 1868–1875. For a comparative view, see *The Trial Jury in England, France, Germany 1700–1900*, ed. Antonio Padoa Schioppa (Berlin: Duncker & Humblot, 1987); *Comparative Studies in Continental and Anglo-American Legal History*, eds. Helmut Coing and Knut Norr. Vol.4. For France, see Emile Yvernès, *Le Crime et le criminel devant le jury* (Paris: n.p., 1894); André Cambréal, *Le Jury criminel: comment se forme, délibère, et statue le jury de cour d'assises* (Paris: Rousseau & cie., 1937); James Donovan, "Justice Unblind: The Criminal Classes in France, 1825–1914," *Journal of Social History* 15 (Autumn 1981):89–107.

3. *La instancia única en lo civil y la organización de tribunales. Proyecto de bases para la reforma de la ley del Jurado de 20 de abril de 1888* (Pontevedra: José Eiras García, 1894), 11.

4. "Y el jurado, al emitir su veredicto en la causa formada al *Chato* y consortes, no prescindió de la prueba porque el sumario no supo traerla y el juicio se resintió después de la ligereza del sumario; pero tampoco siguió inflexible las leyes de su criterio. Condenando al *Chato* a la reclusión temporal se incurre en una falta de lógica asombrosa, porque el crimen es tan horrendo, que no admite término medio de apreciación." And lastly; " Y hay quien cree adivinar el fundamento verdadero de esta incongruencia legal, pensando que la reclusión temporal, en este caso, no es una condena, es una transacción entre los extravíos de la muchedumbre y la propia conciencia de los jurados, y lo armonizan mandando al *Chato* al presidio."

5. The reporter for *El Nacional* pointed out that apparent disagreements led the magistrate Loayza, who had presided throughout the trial, to absent himself at the moment of judgment. The reporter asked: "Did he disagree with his colleagues about the formulation of the questions? Did it seem to him that that way of formulating them was not appropriate, judging in advance that they were otiose or that they might prove to be counter-productive? Did he assess the evidence differently than his colleagues and, as a consequence, arrive at different legal conclusions?" ("¿Es que disintió de sus compañeros en la redacción de las preguntas? ¿Es que le pareció que aquel modo de formularlos no era el indicado, estimando de antemano que eran ociosas o que pudieran ser contraproducentes? ¿Es que opinó de modo diverso en la apreciación y deducciones legales que de los hechos hacían sus compañeros?").

6. "Y como realmente el veredicto de El Escorial es absurdo, encuentran el camino fácil para crear atmósfera en contra de esta institución esencialmente democrática." And, the follow-

ing passage: "Multas, molestias, vejaciones sin cuento, todo se emplea para que el pueblo, que pedía el jurado como garantía de justicia, llegue a cansarse de él. Pero hay más. En ese dualismo constante de los dos tribunales que a un tiempo funcionan, el popular y el de derecho, está de parte de éste las funciones directivas, y en ellas puede presentar las cuestiones que aquél ha de resolver, confusas e involucradas." Many witnesses to Restoration equivocation made the point which the reporter for *El Ideal* made in the article cited above, i.e ,: "The jury system in Spain, imposed by the needs of the times we live in, has been accepted *a fortiori* by the monarchical parties, and today its functions are managed by its enemies. And these enemies do everything in their power to discredit it" ("El Jurado en España, impuesto por las necesidades de la época, ha sido aceptado *á fortiori* por los partidos monárquicos, y hoy funciona manejado por sus enemigos. Y éstos extreman toda su habilidad para desacreditarlo"). In *Fin de Siglo*, Iris Zavala, for example, quotes the anarchist and bohemian of Russian origin, Ernesto Bark, who in 1900 characterized the Restoration as follows: "It compromised on universal suffrage [...] in order to prostitute it, with the jury in order to ridicule it, with freedom of association and the press in order to mystify them" ("Transigió con el sufragio universal [...] para prostituirlo, con el jurado para ridiculizarlo, con las libertades de reunión y de imprenta para mistificarlas"), 9. The passage quoted is from p.24 of Bark's *El Internacionalismo*. (Madrid: Biblioteca Germinal, 1900).

7. See César Lombroso, "*Aplicaciones judiciales y médicas de la antropología criminal*" *La España Moderna* (Mayo 1893): 83–84; 94–95, in which Lombroso cited with approval Tarde's rejection of the jury on grounds of its incompetence and ignorance. Pedro Dorado Montero also favored evaluation and penalization of criminals by experts. See his *"A propósito de la causa de Varela," La España Moderna* (Mayo 1894):91–93.

8. "Era preciso verles antes y después de sus funciones, a estilo de ferial, compartiendo entre sí amigablemente, en mangas de camisa en verano, y envueltos en sus anguarinas en invierno, sentados a la puerta de un figón, con un plato de bacalao entre las piernas, en las manos un pan dividido en zoquetes y al lado el jarro del negro peleón, y entonces de seguro exclamaría; ¿es ése o es a ésos a los que la ley confía el sagrado sacerdocio de administrar justicia? Era preciso que le vieran en un mesón cenando con las familias de los procesados o con los procesados mismos, a los que, por conocerlos del pueblo o de los inmediatos, no puede rechazar su trato. Y si esto sucede hoy concurriendo a las capitales de provincia, ¿qué sucedería el día que se reunieran en su mismo pueblo o en el inmediato? Para algo se han escrito en las leyes la incompatibilidad de los funcionarios de la judicatura, que no rige para esos Jueces de hecho que no saben, en su mayor parte, más que deletrear y hacer palotes, porque ya hemos dicho que Madrid solo no compone la nación; que ésta tiene muchísimos pueblos y aldeas que no conocen los derechos y que no tienen como un derecho el ser Jurado, sino como una carga de justicia que el que más y el que menos procura sacudir como puede." M. L. "*Juzgadores de Alforja," Revista de los Tribunales 26 (1 abril; 8 abril 1893):105.*

9. In 1878 William Forsyth had referred to the extent of government control over the judiciary desired by European states: "hence, in all the continental nations where it [the jury] has been introduced, the governments have endeavored to retain some influence over its decisions by entrusting the formation of the primary lists of the jurors, out of whom the particular twelve are to be selected, to their own officers." *History of Trial by Jury*, 2nd edition (New York: Burt Franklin, 1971), orig. publ. 1878, p. 361. In Spain ten years later, i.e., at the time when the jury was reinstituted, Francisco de Asís Pacheco drew attention to the crucial importance of the primary lists and the difficulties involved in their formation so long as the census (*censo electoral*) was unreliable, and so long as the selection of jurors from those lists was likely to be arbitrary. *La Ley del Jurado*, comentada por D. Francisco de Asís Pacheco (Madrid: Imprenta de la Revista de Legislación, 1888), 398–399.

10. James M. Donovan in "Justice Unblind: The Juries and the Criminal Classes in France, 1825–1914," 90–94, quotes several contemporary French observers on the class composition of the jury in France. All confirmed Jean Cruppi's statement (in *La Cour d'assises* [Paris, 1898], 256) that "This system [...] has established, without thought and against its own principle, a true class jury [...] the jury of the middle classes" (94). As in Spain, juries were lenient when judging crimes against people, severe with crimes against property. Donovan speculates that this bias may have been partly due to an increase in property crimes. Michelle Perrot's explana-

tion—which Donovan accepts—is that bourgeois juries quite naturally protected bourgeois interests. This theory seemed to be borne out by the fact that after 1908 when juries were democratized, admitting workers, the "new non-property owning jurors evidently did not feel as threatened by property crimes as their bourgeois predecessors did, and were therefore more likely to place equal value on both life and property" (94). I know of no statistical studies on the class composition of jurors in Spain in the 1890s, although contemporaries—including José de Aldana in 1894—often referred to jurors as uneducated and unqualified for such service, implying non-middle class status. The tendency of Spanish jurors to judge crimes against property as their French bourgeois counterparts did, may be an index of their loyalty to the wishes and instructions of *caciques*, at least in rural areas. The 1888 *Ley del Jurado* listed the requirements for serving on the jury in Articles 8 and 9. Art. 8 specified that only secular persons could serve. Art. 9 read as follows: "In order to serve on a jury it is necessary : 1. To be at least thirty years old. 2. To be eligible fully to exercise civil and political rights. 3. To know how to read and write. 4. To be the head of a family and resident in the municipal jurisdiction in question for at least four years" ("Para ser Jurado se requiere: 1. Ser mayor de treinta años. 2. Estar en pleno goce de los derechos civiles y políticos. 3. Saber leer y escribir. 4. Ser cabeza de familia y vecino en el término municipal respectivo, con cuatro o más años de residencia en el mismo"). Art. 9 also stipulated that those in possession of an academic or professional title, or those who had served in a public office or had been "Concejales, Diputados provinciales, Diputados a Cortes o Senadores, y los retirados del Ejército o la Armada," could serve even if they did not head a family.

11. "*La Memoria del Fiscal del Tribunal Supremo*" [excerpts], *Revista de los Tribunales y de Legislación Universal* 28 (22 de Septiembre de 1894):575–579.

12. "Las clases acomodadas, aquellas en las cuales tal nivel debe ser de otra altura, por comodidad, por egoismo, rehuyen las funciones del Jurado, y como esto es fácil merced a las mil salidas que facilita la ley, vienen a quedar aquellas funciones como pesada carga sobre quienes no pueden apartar el hombro o por ignorancia o por temor." And finally: "No se adquieren esas aptitudes por costumbres de pocos años; pero es indudable que si a la falta de hábitos se une la de cultura, entonces los resultados necesariamente han de ser lastimosos."

13. Antonio Bellver de Oña, *El Juicio Criminal. Manual teórico-práctico. Con el texto de las Leyes de Enjuiciamiento y del Jurado, formularios y doctrina de la fiscalía del Tribunal Supremo* (Madrid: Ricardo Fé, 1899), 228–229.

14. On June 3, 1894 in *El Día*, Angel Ossorio y Gallardo devoted his column on the Law Courts to the problem of non-payment of *dietas*. *El Heraldo de Madrid* on July 12, 1894 ran an article "*Cosas de la justicia*," subtitled "*Cómo administra el Sr. Capdepón*," which also referred to the plight of poor jurors unable to collect their *dietas*. *El Heraldo* accused Capdepón, the new liberal Minister of Justice, of sharing his conservative predecessors' repugnance for the jury—hence his insensitivity to jurors' complaints. A story printed in *El Día* on April 14, 1894, entitled "¡*Pobres testigos*!" illustrated the plight of witnesses, who, like jurors, were frequently unable to collect their compensation and were treated with similar contempt:

"The witnesses made the journey from Navalagamella, a town twelve hours away from Madrid, on foot since they had absolutely no money for transport. When the trial was over and they requested the stipend they were entitled to, they were told that there was no money and they were handed a credit, which like the ones given out for Cuba, will be honored God knows when.

When they protested, they were told `to go tell it to the Minister of Justice.'

In the meantime, the unfortunate men would have gone without eating that day if a charitable soul had not given them money for that purpose"

("Desde Navalagamella, pueblo distante doce horas de Madrid, hicieron [los testigos] el viaje a pie, por carecer en absoluto de recursos, y cuando, terminado el juicio, reclamaron la indemnización a que tenían derecho, se les contestó que no había dinero, entregándoles un abonaré, que a semejanza de los de Cuba, cobrarán cuando Dios quiera.

Al protestar se les dijo que `se lo contaran al ministro de Gracia y Justicia.'

Entretanto, los infelices hubieran pasado el día sin comer si una persona caritativa no les hubiera facilitado dinero para ello").

15. "Hablan con ellos en el café—con toda corrección, eso sí—pero discutiendo las pruebas, rechazando los cargos contra sus defendidos, afirmando su inocencia. Los jurados escuchan...escuchan hasta consumir la taza del café. Llegado este momento, se retiran como si les fuera desagradable aquella conversación." Finally: "Las impresiones respecto a la familia de los Chatos también han de influir poderosamente en el ánimo de los jurados; las costumbres, los vicios de aquella gente que se reunía en la choza del Romeral que ha desfilado por la sala de la Audiencia inspiran tal repugnancia, que más de una vez he oído decir: — ¡Qué lástima que no se puede destruir aquella casa con toda esa gente dentro!"

16. See Adrian Shubert, *A Social History of Modern Spain* (London: Unwin Hyman, 1990), 179–182, for the role of the *Guardia Civil* in nineteenth-century Spain, especially its assumption of police functions in rural areas. See also Pedro Trinidad Fernández, *La defensa de la sociedad*, 92–94; 298–301 for relations between the Guardia Civil and local oligarchs.

17. "Llega del contorno un labrador honradísimo, persona merecedora de todos los respetos." Then: "Y el jurado, que no supo del hecho de autos sino lo que ahora ha visto desfilar por la sala del juicio; el labriego súbitamente transformado en juzgador, cambiado de repente de 'atmósfera,' de 'aficiones,' de 'conocimientos.' de todo, llega jadeante a un extremo digno de lástima, en que no sabe qué pensar, y ansia la hora a las preguntas, para resolver `por impresiones' y para resolver en conciencia."

18. Bellver de Oña referred to the question of leniency in his discussion of criticisms of the jury: "The worst of it is that the jury usually puts itself in conflict with the popular conscience which it incarnates and represents; because in its judgments it ignores facts which have been perfectly well demonstrated and are even obvious, facts which can only not be admitted by people who have some interest in ignoring them. Sometimes a jury pronounces a man innocent right after the accused declares himself to be guilty" ("Lo peor del caso es que el jurado suele ponerse en contradicción con la conciencia popular que encarna y representa; porque prescinde en sus fallos de hechos perfectamente demostrados y hasta evidentes, sólo recusables para quien tenga interés en desconocerlos; a veces pronuncia la inculpabilidad a renglón seguido de haberse declarado reo el procesado.") *El Juicio Criminal*:220.

In a piece entitled "*Juicio por jurados*," written in 1894 for *La Ilustración Artística*:311–314, Eduardo del Palacio described an experience, purportedly his own, while serving on a jury. His amusingly presented story, complete with dialogue, emphasized the ignorance, reluctance to condemn, even in the face of confessions, and general thoughtlessness of jurors. In addition to the type of the uneducated juror portrayed in sketches such as Palacio's, the popular theatre (*La Chula*, for example,) presented the type of the foolish, uneducated man who speaks in legal jargon and prides himself on the smattering of information he has picked up whiling away his time in the court room.

19. "menester es que el Estado tenga alguna ventaja en los primeros momentos, siquiera para reconocer los vestigios del crimen y los indicios de la culpabilidad de su autor." See pages 13–18, in particular, of the "*Exposición de motivos*" by the Minister of Justice, Manuel Alonso Martínez, which prefaced the *Ley de enjuiciamiento criminal de 14 de septiembre de 1882* (Barcelona: José María Bosch, 1956).

20. "El señor del Río ha dispuesto que se tomen grandes precauciones para evitar que los periodistas nos enteremos de lo que en el Juzgado pasa, lo cual no obsta para que nosotros procuremos tener enterados a nuestros lectores quizá con más detalles que antes de la llegada de dicho 'señor.' Y conste que ni siquiera hemos pretendido inmiscuirnos en el secreto del sumario, ni funcionario alguno nos ha hecho revelación de ninguna especie."

21. "Desde la formación del atestado hasta la remisión del sumario a la Audiencia, viene dando [el periodista] noticias a granel, sobre todo si son de las sensacionales, aplicando calificativos, poniendo a sus escritos títulos rimbombantes y guiando a la opinión pública por el camino de la verdad algunas veces, pero por el del error las más." And: "Pero, ¡mal hayan los que olvidan que la libertad mal entendida es más funesta que el más ciego absolutismo!" This admonition is as timely now in some quarters as it was in the mid-1890s.

22. "Los jurados no tendrán en cuenta el sumario, no juzgarán sino por lo que vean en el juicio." *La Ley del Jurado*, comentada por D. Francisco de Asís Pacheco. Con un Prólogo del Excmo. Sr. D. Manuel Alonso Martínez (Madrid: Revista General de Legislación y Jurisprudencia, 1888), 123.

23. Ventura Barcáiztegui y Orfila, *Estudio teórico-práctico del concepto de la culpabilidad*, 72–73.

24. *El derecho positivo de la mujer. Mujer soltera, casada, viuda y religiosa, según los códigos civil, penal y de comercio, los derechos forales y administrativos. Numerosa jurisprudencia, comentarios, algunas notas de legislación comparada, procedimientos y formularios* (Madrid: A. Pérez y Compañía, Impresores, 1903).

25. The first chapter, "Stories of Things Not Seen" (pp. 1–42), of Welsh's *Strong Representations. Narrative and Circumstantial Evidence in England* (Baltimore: Johns Hopkins University Press, 1992) chronicles the history and analyzes the development of the idea that "circumstances do not lie." Douglas Lane Patey's review essay in *Eighteenth-Century Studies* 26 (1992–93): 334–338 of Barbara J. Shapiro's *"Beyond Reasonable Doubt" and "Probable Cause"* includes discussion of Welsh's book within the larger context of proof and probability. The possibly dire consequences of relying on circumstantial evidence were driven home to ordinary people in works of fiction such as Jules Mary's extremely popular novel, *Roger-La Honte*, published in 1887. See "*Roger-La Honte. Le roman de l'erreur judiciaire*," by Claude Aziza in the special edition entitled "*Le crime. Juges et assassins depuis 5000 ans*" of *L'Histoire* 168 (Juillet/Août 1993): 90–91. Aziza considers Mary's novel the archetype of the novel of judicial error that flourished at the end of the nineteenth century.

26. "Estas desigualdades monstruosas no son apropósito para tener tranquilo a un pueblo.

El Jurado borró, en cuanto pudo, la escandalosa diferencia, dando un veredicto de culpabilidad a la infanticida y de inculpabilidad al expendedor. Pero de todos modos, el ejemplo no debe olvidarse para depurar qué es más digno de censura, si el Jurado, siempre menospreciado, o el Código, siempre enaltecido." From "Crónica de tribunales," *Revista de los Tribunales y de Legislación Universal* 29 (23 de noviembre de 1895):751.

27. *Revista de los Tribunales y de Legislación Universal* 29 (7 de diciembre de 1895):769–773; 30 (18 de enero de 1896):33–39; 30 (25 de enero de 1896):49-54. The rulings on the appeals made in the Escorial case handed down by the *Tribunal Supremo* on February 6, 1895 and on November 15, 1895 may be consulted in *Colección legislativa de España. Sentencias del Tribunal Supremo de Justicia* (Madrid: Revista de Legislación, 1895–1904).

28. In what was meant to be an amusing parody of sub-literate speech, the columnist wrote: "Porque es lo que yo digo. Que has robao o asesinao u ambas cosas; que vas a la cárcel y luego al presidio...pues si cumples tu condena y sales ¿qué más quieren? Ya pagaste lo que debías, y como tal cosa. Vamos a ver: ¿por qué el *Chato* de El Escorial, cuando remate su pena, no había de poder encargarse, por ejemplo de una escuela de niños? Créeme: eso de decir que son justos los estizmas, es propia de gentes reaccionarias...[...]."

Chapter Five

Missed Opportunities

Press coverage of the Escorial crime exemplifies the commercial press's opportunism in the 1890s and is remarkable, first of all, for its duration and broad dissemination. *El Imparcial* and *La Correspondencia de España*, most notably, but even *El País*, in the end, appealed to their mass readers by transforming a crime whose principal suspect was convicted in the absence of strong incriminating evidence into a convincing narrative of culpability. It was a narrative dark with suggestive themes that were further enhanced by techniques drawn from terrorific fiction.

The press's success in marketing its versions of the case alarmed critics who routinely voiced fears about the effects of such reporting on newly-literate mass readers, and who regretted (less vocally) the attraction it had for the cultured reader. Negative criticisms of crime reporting concentrated on the inappropriate knowledge it furnished to women, in particular, and on the corrupting influence it had on all readers—the contagion it spread leading inevitably to more crime. But further effects of crime reporting which critics did not address included incentives to tighten the defenses of the social body and to justify greater intervention by the forces charged with maintaining order and security. Reporters contributed to these and similar social agendas by effectively exploiting the detailed contrasts they established between the García and the Bravo families. The Bravo family emerged as a model for the virtues, values and beliefs considered essential to the maintenance of Restoration society.[1] None of the contemporary critics of crime reporting—or of the reporting, in particular, of the Escorial case—analyzed the political and social implications of the ways in which journalists depicted the accused, i.e., their lives as poor, rural laborers or their roles as men and women. Nor did contemporaries comment on their coverage of child sexual abuse.

Apart from urging the imposition of censorship or self-censorship, critics of the press complained but did not present alternatives to the kind of crime coverage they decried. Yet the Escorial case provided precisely the kind of opportunity for advocacy of child protection laws seized by reporters elsewhere—in the United States in the late 1870s following a child abuse scandal, and in Britain in the mid-eighties. W.T. Stead's series, the "Maiden Tribute of Modern Babylon," published in the *Pall Mall Gazette* in 1885, drew attention to the significant issues embedded in a sensational story—the abduction of young girls into the White Slave Traffic. His articles did much to fortify the London SPCC's efforts to win approval by the House of Commons for the Criminal Law Amendment Bill which contemporaries sometimes referred to as the Stead Bill.[2]

The press's power to influence public opinion was acknowledged in Spain as it was elsewhere. Its failure to use that influence in the public interest did not go unnoticed. In their brief discussion of the White Slave Traffic in Madrid, for example, Constancio Bernaldo de Quirós and J.M. Llanas Aguilaniedo pointed out that the police did not often publicize criminal acts related to this traffic, "nor do the newspapers lament the scandalous events connected with the infamous traffic except very occasionally, and even then they present it as something anomalous."[3] In the nineties *El Nuevo Régimen*—the weekly federalist organ with a relatively low circulation—undertook to persuade the public of the death penalty's anachronistic cruelty. Newspapers on the left typically opposed execution also, but the sporadic opposition of critics did not assume the proportions of the sustained campaign waged, for example, by Stead. In an article entitled "El siglo XIX," published in *El Nuevo Régimen* on July 25, 1896, A.M., the author, regretted that neither the press nor society agitated to end vivid coverage of public executions. Instead, the press enhanced the cruelty and horror of such events by printing detailed descriptions of the death agonies suffered by victims of the current legal system. Significantly, A.M. did not suggest any ideas on how the press could substitute its (and the public's) preoccupation with grisly descriptions of death by garroting with a serious publicity effort to abolish the death penalty.

Spanish reporters might themselves have tried to channel public outrage at Pedrín's violation into active support of beneficent organizations such as the recently-formed private philanthropic *Asociación de Padres de Familia* (discussed above in Chapter II), one of whose principal goals was the protection and rescue of children.[4] Newspapers often reported on the activities of the association. On January 27, 1894 *La Época* printed an account of the services performed by the *Asociación* in Cataluña during 1893:

> Girls rescued from vice and sent to charity asylums, 54.
> Girls rescued from vice and sent back to their families, 162.

Women denounced and jailed for causing public scandals and for corruption of minors, 42.
Houses of perdition closed, 9.
Pernicious bookstores closed, 2.
Immoral societies closed, 1.
Denunciations of pornographic or impious publications, 32.
Denunciations of other immoral publications, 6.
Denunciations of corruptors of minors, fortune-tellers,
quacks and other immoral types, 25.

[...] In addition it [the society] secured jobs and lodgings for young people of both sexes who were in danger of perdition; it gave financial aid to some families; it obtained information about the conduct of suitors contemplating marriage with honorable young women, thus avoiding their deception by dissolute men; and, in short, lent other services known to ecclesiastical, civil and judicial authorities, but which cannot be detailed here because of their nature.[5]

Despite what many Spaniards may have considered legitimate activity, the attempts (faithfully chronicled in the press) which the *Padres* made during 1893 and 1894 to prosecute the Liceo Ríus transvestites and the French dancer known in Spain as "La Bella Chiquita," evidently struck some members of the press and a significant part of the reading public as crabbed puritanism rather than genuine concern for moral reform.[6] A reporter for *El Imparcial* who signed his article "Zapatero," wrote on January 13, 1894—apparently in support of the *Padres*—that, "The general opinion is that spectacles offered by the likes of `La Bella Chiquita' should not be permitted as they are alien to Spanish culture" ("La opinión general censura que no se eviten espectáculos como el de la Bella Chiquita, como impropios de la cultura española"). Alien and inappropriate perhaps, but theaters were packed wherever the dancer performed in Spain. (The Asociación had threatened to take her to court in June of 1893 when she was playing at the Circo Price [frequented by families] in Madrid, but desisted when she agreed not to perform the "danse du ventre"—precisely what people clamored to see.)

The *Padres* were doubtless discredited in the eyes of many Spaniards for their excessive zeal in prosecuting people such as "La Bella Chiquita" and the Liceo Ríus transvestites, individuals who were, after all, doing little harm compared to the many exploiters and abusers of children who might have been prosecuted. In the event, while the activities of the association were duly reported in the commercial press, instead of inspiring anything approaching a moral crusade, reporters frequently made the *Padres* the butt of cynical jokes.[7] Closer study of the history of this organization and the reception it received from the press and the public would deepen understanding of attitudes toward crime and the legal system in the nineties. As it is, establishment of such a philanthropic organization during this period, together with the press coverage of crime referred to in the present study, go far toward demonstrating public awareness in Spain, as elsewhere, of widespread child abuse. The time was ripe for reform in child protection laws, for rethinking penalties for the abuse of children, and related matters. Nonetheless, publishers, editors and reporters did not incorporate such discussion into coverage of the Escorial crime or of other crimes involving children during this period.

Reporters for the papers mentioned above sensationalized what little information they had and demonized the defendants in the course of their coverage. Would it have been possible with different suspects for reporters to frame discussion of child sexual abuse in ways that could have avoided demonization of the perpetrators—ways that might have led to a more dispassionate assessment of the causes and consequences of such acts? Press coverage of child abuse cases suggests that readers were encouraged to think of most child abusers (perhaps excluding the clergy and the aristocracy, such as the exceedingly cruel Duquesa de Castro-Enríquez) as freakish monsters who were best dealt with summarily—by lynching, for example.

The sensationalized presentation of the Escorial case attracted readers who were subsequently led to think about various aspects of the Spanish criminal justice system—largely as a result of the unpopular verdict returned by the jury. But, here again, what might have been turned into a meaningful airing of difficult issues in the press was considerably undermined by criticism, indeed the denigration, of the masses by intellectuals and other authoritative figures. Their negative definitions of the masses helped to crystallize dissatisfaction with the jury. Readers of the commercial press who did not consider themselves to be the targets of those almost uniformly unfavorable remarks doubtless found it difficult to place confidence in the representatives of the people who served on juries, since those representatives were understood to be members of the masses. How could the deficient masses who thrived on sensationalized crime reports in newspapers discuss and analyze the criminal justice system? More particularly, how could rural jurors—the majority of Spain's masses—fulfill their exalted function? These and similar questions were posed in a society experiencing increasing class conflict and were answered in part by the decision made in 1920 to remove the jury in Catalonia from the prosecution of "social crimes," i.e., terrorist acts of violence. Three years later, under the dictatorship of Primo de Rivera, the jury was suspended throughout Spain. It would not be reinstated until 1995.

NOTES

1. See Pedro Trinidad Fernández, *La defensa de la sociedad*, 246–247 for the influence of press and *folletín* accounts of crime in encouraging and reinforcing mechanisms of social control.

2. For the child abuse scandal in America, see p. 265 of Ian Hacking's "The Making and Molding of Child Abuse." George K. Behlmer has an account of W.T. Stead's series in the *Pall Mall Gazette* and its connection to reform in England on pp. 73–77 of *Child Abuse and Moral Reform in England, 1870–1908*. Judith R. Walkowitz devotes two chapters (pp. 81–134) of

City of Dreadful Delight. Narratives of Sexual Danger in Late–Victorian London (Chicago: University of Chicago Press, 1992) to an analysis of Stead's articles and their cultural impact.

3. "ni los periódicos lamentan sino muy de tarde en tarde y como caso anómalo, sucesos escandalosos del infame tráfico" (*La mala vida en Madrid* (Madrid: B. Rodríguez Serra, 1901), 308.

4. Pedro Armengol y Cornet lauded the work of a like–minded philanthropic group in France in his 1895 article on the deficiencies of child protection legislation in Spain: "M. Brijean, founder and advocate of the Society for the protection of abandoned or vicious children, can never be sufficiently praised or recompensed. Assisted by men of worth and zeal including MM. Joly, Voissin, Riviere [sic], Arbous, Petit and others, the Society is saving hundreds of children of both sexes, who abandoned or perverted by their parents, would go on to swell the ranks of criminals and prostitutes if that Society, which is a genuine safe haven for their salvation, had not been created in Paris" ("Nunca será bastante elogiado ni recompensado M. Brijean fundador y propagador de la Sociedad para la protección de la infancia abandonada o viciosa, que asistido por hombres de la valía y el celo de MM. Joly, Voissin, Riviere, Arbous, Petit y otros, están salvando centenares de muchachos de uno y otro sexo, que abandonados o pervertidos por sus padres, irán a engrosar las filas de la criminalidad y las listas de la prostitución, si no hubiesen creado en París aquella Sociedad que es un verdadero puerto de salvación" See his "Una gran deficiencia del Código civil" in la *Revista de los Tribunales y de Legislación Universal* 29 (29 June 1895):410-412.

5. "Jóvenes sacadas del vicio y mandadas a Asilos benéficos, 54.

Jóvenes salvadas al ir a ser seducidas, 30.

Jóvenes sacadas del vicio y mandadas a sus familias, 162.

Mujeres denunciadas y encarceladas por escándalos públicos y corrupción de menores, 42.

Casas de perdición cerradas, 2.

Librerías perniciosas cerradas, 2.

Sociedades inmorales cerradas, 1.

Denuncias contra periódicos pornográficos o impíos, 32.

Idem contra otras publicaciones inmorales, 6.

Idem contra corruptores de menores, cartamanceros, curanderos y otras inmoralidades, 25.

Legitimación de matrimonios, 5.

Causas sobre legitimación de hijos, 3.

Separación de concubinarios y reconciliación de cónyuges separados, 15.

Blasfemos multados, 36.

Láminas, fotografías y libros obscenos recogidos con denuncia contra las expendedores, 3,728.

Además procuró colocación y asilo a jóvenes de ambos sexos, expuestos a perderse; socorrió a algunas familias; enteróse de la conducta de los que pretenden matrimonios con jóvenes honradas, precaviendo así el engaño de los disolutos, y prestó, en fin, otros servicios, de que tienen conocimiento las autoridades, eclesiásticos, civiles y judiciales, y que, por su índole, no pueden detallarse."

6. A reporter for *El Imparcial* wrote on February 26, 1893 that the "Padres" had lost the legal battle to put an end to the transvestites' balls. He proceeded to recount the scene at court with tongue firmly in cheek:

"This association had thought that it could oppose the flourishing of the foulest vice capable of degrading a people. Fat chance! The municipal court in the Hospital district, where the association had presented a complaint against the impresario of the Liceo Ríus because of the balls for *gentlemen* disguised as ladies, has condemned a member of the "Fathers of Families" who lodged the complaint to five days arrest and payment of court costs.

The celebration over the ruling could not have been more picturesque. Six of the individuals fond of changing sex externally, enthusiastic habitués of the above-mentioned balls, were in attendance [...]" ("Había esta sociedad pensado que podía oponerse al desarrollo del vicio más hediondo que puede envilecer a un pueblo. ¡Qué si quieres! El juzgado municipal del distrito del Hospital, donde la sociedad había presentado querella contra el empresario del Liceo Ríus por los bailes de *caballeros* disfrazados de *señoras* ha condenado al padre de familias querellante a cinco días de arresto y a pagar las costas del juicio.

La celebración de éste ha sido de lo más pintoresco. Han asistido seis de los individuos aficionados a cambiar exteriormente de sexo y entusiastas concurrentes de los consabidos bailes [...]").

7. José Muñiz de Quevedo lampooned the "Padres" in a pamphlet entitled *Besugos de la moral o los papás de familia*, advertised in *La Correspondencia de España* in early 1894. I have been unable to locate this pamphlet which is not listed in the catalog of the Biblioteca Nacional in Madrid. Its intent, if not its impact, may be divined by a report in *El Ideal* on May 19, 1894 according to which, "The Society of Fathers of Families has called before the court Sr. Muñiz de Quevedo, author of the pamphlet entitled 'Codfish of Morality or the Papas of Families'" ("La Sociedad de Padres de Familia ha demandado ante los Tribunales al Sr. Muñiz de Quevedo, autor del folleto titulado 'Besugos de la moral o los papás de familia.'"

Epilogue

IN CEUTA

In mid-August of 1897 Domingo Blanco, one of the reporters for *El Imparcial* who had covered the child murder case at El Escorial, was sent to the Spanish Penal Colony of Ceuta in North Africa to initiate a series of articles on Spanish prisons.[1] Seven prisons were located in Ceuta; the most notorious were the Hacho (formerly spelled Acho) and the General or Principal Barracks. The other five were Talleres, Barcas, Jadú, Serrallo and Hospital.[2] Blanco began his series by interviewing the four anarchists confined in Ceuta in connection with the attempted assassination of Captain General Arsenio Martínez Campos in 1893.[3] Then, on August 16, 1897 he unexpectedly came upon Crisanto Jorge, who, along with Julián García, had been sent to Ceuta to serve his sentence. As Blanco strolled beside one of the walls that provided security to the inhabitants of the town, he spotted Crisanto Jorge, who was tending the dusty plants of a small garden. Julián García was not with his brother-in-law. He had been sent to the Hacho fortress-prison located about one kilometer from the town and the Principal Barracks where Crisanto was confined. Blanco speculated that the two men were separated because of their deep-seated enmity. Although Crisanto Jorge was reluctant to talk, speaking only of his innocence and resignation at what had befallen him, Julián was eager to talk to the reporter when Blanco interviewed him later at the Hacho. Blanco believed that during his time in Ceuta experienced prisoners had coached the Chato on the advantages of publicity through newspaper coverage as he sought to appeal his sentence. According to Blanco, Julián wrote letters everyday to the prosecutor of the Supreme Court, to the judge at El Escorial, to the Civil Guard and to several newspapers demanding the right to an appeal on the grounds that extraordinary circumstances had not been taken into account during his trial. He also denounced certain people as the true authors of the crime.

Both before and during his trial, several reporters had stated that Julián was illiterate. Crisanto Jorge was described as the only one of the two who knew how to write; consequently, he signed the papers (the *acta del juicio*) required by the court every day. One reporter wrote that Julián had asked to be read to since he had never learned to read. When Julián wanted to mount an appeal after his conviction it was reported that he had to have someone else write for him since he could neither read or write. Domingo Blanco did not ask how Julián had procured the writing paper, pens and money needed to send letters every day to the Peninsula. Nor did he refer to the restrictions on the number of letters sent abroad and the censorship to which they were subjected.

Censorship was imposed in the penal colony by the Royal Decree of October 2, 1860. Prisoners were allowed to send a given number of letters each month depending on their placement in one of four categories of confinement. Many convicts sent and received their mail through family members or friends resident in Ceuta, thereby avoiding censorship. Moreover, good behavior increased the number of letters they were allowed.[4] Above all, despite his history of illiteracy detailed by reporters on the scene, Blanco did not ask how Julián had learned to write and, presumably, to read. He did ask why Julián had not spoken up at his trial about the circumstances he was currently citing. Julián responded that he had been assured that the trial would end in his favor, and that he had said something at the time that reporters refused to put in their dispatches. Domingo Blanco did not question him further about the latter allegation. Instead, the reporter expressed the opinion that prisoners who were advising Julián merely wanted an excuse to travel to El Escorial as witnesses in a new trial in order to flee en route.

If the prisoners in question entertained such a hope, it was not an idle fantasy. Official directives issued in 1885 aimed to deal with the rising number of escapes from train cell cars as prisoners were in transit, usually from one prison to another.[5] Blanco did not comment on escapes from prisons in Ceuta. It was a risky option since a bounty was paid to Moors who caught escaped convicts, although the captors might make an exception for escapees who had more than the amount of the bounty with them and who converted to Islam (Salvador, *Cabo de vara*, 70–71). The *cabo de vara* in Salvador's novel escaped and was returned by Moors to the Principal Barrack. Five years were added to his sentence as punishment. Pablo de la Concepcion included a chapter on "Fugas" ("Escapes") in his account of conditions in the Hacho from 1896-1898. He confirmed the bounty paid to Moors who turned in escapees, adding that before they were returned they were subjected to "repulsive acts of passion" ("asquerosos actos pasionales"). He also described the horrendous, nearly fatal beating suffered by a convict who was captured and returned to prison) *Prisioneros y deportados,* 369; 254-258).

Blanco informed his readers that Julián still looked like an orangutan. He also noted that he was significantly incapacitated by epilepsy. His seizures often led to his being excused from carrying water—a job performed by many convicts in Ceuta. Blanco believed that the authorities would soon be forced to send him to an insane asylum because of the extent to which his persecution complex governed his thoughts and actions. Julián described in detail to the reporter how people had manipulated him into an appearance of guilt by doing favors for him. Blanco noted that Julián would probably include him in the conspiracy he had fabricated because the reporter gave him five pesetas (equivalent at the time to $1.00) to buy a shirt, which he lacked, and broth because he was in visibly poor health.

Domingo Blanco's brief interviews with Crisanto Jorge and Julián García reinforced perceptions of the two men proffered by reporters during their trial. In addition to noting Crisanto Jorge's resignation to his fate as opposed to Julián's repeated attempts to appeal his sentence, Blanco observed that in Ceuta, Crisanto Jorge garnered more sympathy from people who knew him than did Julián, an assertion comparing the two men frequently made by reporters in their coverage of the crime. As townspeople and other observers had begun to suspect Julián after having initially disbelieved the charges against him, reporters sought to provide a contrast between the nature of the two men that would bolster their attempts to establish Julián's greater malevolence and crafty manipulation of his brother-in-law. Crisanto was represented, accordingly, as another victim of Julián. Crisanto's Christian resignation in Ceuta, as depicted by Domingo Blanco, fit in nicely with the narrative established earlier.

THE PENAL COLONY

The Royal Decree of December 26, 1888 declared Ceuta a "*colonia penitenciaria,*" thereby defining and fixing its primary status or identity, formerly understood as a military outpost and a prospective commercial center as well as the site of seven prisons. Alberto Baeza Herrazti explored the negative consequences of the decree, which in his view, blocked progress by ignoring commercial and political interests, turning Ceuta instead into "a jungle of convicts and a concentration camp" (*El presidio de Ceuta,* 149). In 1896 the Presidio of Ceuta was placed under civil authority, the Administration of Prisons, and answered to the Ministry of Justice. Fernando Cadalso pointed out that even so, delinquents sentenced by the military authority could be sent to Ceuta—an absurdity in his opinion.[6]

Penologists in Spain, France, England, the United States and elsewhere who were following the progress of prison reform in Europe and America took an interest in the prisons of Ceuta during the last two decades of the nineteenth and the beginning of the twentieth century. Travellers to Ceuta often included brief accounts of the town itself. In his *Céuta. Llave principal del Estrecho* (1897), Manuel Tello Amondareyn wished to dispel the erroneous ideas that many people held concerning Ceuta. He wrote:

> Although the town is stuck on its first step toward moral and material progress, incorrect, deplorable ideas about it are so widespread that it is astonishing to enter its harbor, to see the ravelin and the Marina, the paseo of San Amaro and the calle Real, the plazas of Ruiz, Africa and the Kings, and its small gardens and commerce; to observe its equable inhabitants—with the exception of its Hebrew colony which rules there with the crushing yoke of its repugnant greed—and to admire its walls studded by the mouths of cannon; its fortified areas, witnesses to one hundred contested battles; its powerful modern batteries that dominate the North and South bays, concealed behind brush and well-constructed parapets built along the line of forts that cover the frontier territory; those defenses, in sum, shaded as if under threat, by the shadows projected by the Heights of Sierra Bullones [beyond which lay Moorish territory]; for without that threat Ceuta would truly be unconquerable by land and sea. [7]

Nine years later Archibald R. Colquhoun was less impressed with the military post's fortifications, but he was struck by the novel spectacle of Ceuta's diverse population and the ubiquity of prisoners allowed to move freely about in the town,

> Besides the different tribes of Moors, Spanish merchants, Italians, Jews and a number of negroes (who are mostly brought as slaves from the Sudan), the streets of Ceuta are full of convicts, known by their round flat caps. These are allowed, after a certain time of their imprisonment is over, to work in the town, first in groups under supervision, and afterwards entirely at their own will, without any restrictions, earning whatever they can and returning at five o'clock to the barrack where they sleep. [8]

Tello Amondareyn's praise of the city and its fortifications did not prevent him from describing the deplorable condition of the prisoners whose work allowed them to circulate in the town:

> What really commands your attention is the sight of brigades of prisoners pulling small carts or extremely heavy cannons, or those who return free of cargo to the barracks of the Acho, the Principal Barracks and the Barcas, or to Jadú to take shelter, once their taxing work is done in the Port and in cleared terrain.
>
> Contemplation of this swarm of dirty, ragged, unkempt men, dressed haphazardly and without regard to the season, some with ravaged faces that reveal

> repugnant vices, most with animated visages that betray a certain Christian resignation, would lead anyone to think that this was not a military post, but rather a prison that has been flung open, not a modern city but rather a Moroccan encampment. And yet, nothing is further from reality than that assumption which is offensive to the city's inhabitants and contrary to reality.[9]

In his interviews with the convicted murderers of Pedro Bravo, Domingo Blanco referred to the work that Crisanto Jorge and Julián García performed: the former tended a garden and the latter carried water when he was not incapacitated by epileptic seizures. The total population of Ceuta was close to 12,000 in the period 1894–1896. The conditions set for work performed by the prisoners, who numbered approximately 2,649 in 1896, of whom about 2,300 were fit enough for labor, were reaffirmed by the Royal Decree of December 26, 1889. Baeza explained the conditions in the paraphrase that follows:

The progressive system in Ceuta was to unroll in four periods.

> The first period, lasting from six to twelve months, according to the request submitted by the penal authority, was to take place in isolation cells in the Hacho, which was impossible because there were no cells in the Hacho, nor were any built subsequently.
>
> During the second period the convict was to participate in collective work whether in Talleres, in other departments, or in military works.
>
> The third period was one of relative freedom—the convicts called it "from cannon blast to cannon blast"—during which they could work on their own account at various jobs or in domestic service, returning at nightfall to their prison.
>
> During the fourth period of free movement and conditional liberty,—"in conditions," as convict jargon termed it—they could establish their own dwellings, live there with their families, and await the completion of their sentences, reporting every two weeks or once a month to the authorities.[10]

In his own description of work conditions in Ceuta, Tello added several details to the above accounts. Tello noted that after six to twelve months of confinement, prisoners whose conduct was acceptable entered into the second period of their sentences and were able to work in shops or on the batteries under the special supervision of the notorious *cabos de vara,* as Tello put it, "genuine bravos who sold their mercies and permissions dearly and capitalized with interest on the most insignificant infractions of the rules" ("verdaderos bravacones que vendían carísimas sus mercedes y complacencias, y cobran con usura las mas insignificantes infracciones del reglamento" (*Céuta* 93). The *cabo*, meaning corporal, in line with the military nomenclature adopted by prison administrators, wielded a *vara* or stick. Gómez Bravo quoted Rafael Salillas on the *cabo de vara*. Salillas wrote that this figure was half-convict, subject to the discipline of the chain and the dormitory, and half-public functionary with epaulets and *vara*, which along with the *calabozo* (prison jail cell) and the irons were the most common means of punishment. *Cabos de vara* were paid 8, 12 and 16 *duros* [a *duro* equals five pesetas and five pesetas equaled one dollar] for their service (Gómez Bravo 146–147). In the Principal Barracks of Ceuta *cabos de vara* were assigned to keep the peace in each of the dormitories (Gómez Bravo 147). Tomas Salvador in his *Cabo de vara* (1958) presented a vivid picture of life in the prisons in Ceuta from 1883 to about 1888 including detailed accounts of the practices of the *cabos de vara.* Tello also noted that during the third period of relative freedom, which allowed the convict to work on his own at the job he chose or was qualified for, for example, as a domestic in private homes, the prisoner had to pay the State a monthly amount of 10 to 15 pesetas out of his earnings.

During the fourth period the convict could join his family in a private dwelling without any obligations other than those of paying the State the amount corresponding to his work, informing the Colony's principal authority of the location of his residence, and presenting himself for review every week or two (Tello 93–94).

Commentators on the Royal Decree of December 26, 1889, observed that it established by law what custom had imposed for many years regarding categories of convicts and their work. Fernando Cadalso noted that the prison regimen in effect in Ceuta entailed an infraction of article 107 of the 1870 *Penal Code,* which required convicts sentenced to *cadena perpetua* and *cadena temporal* to wear chains and to remain within the confines of their quarters. Nonetheless, the wearing of chains by such prisoners was seldom enforced in Ceuta nor were such prisoners confined to the precincts of their dormitory quarters except at night (*El Anarquismo* 39). Francisco Sánchez Montoya, in his "Independentistas cubanos en Ceuta (III parte)," quoted Pablo de la Concepción on the different treatment Cuban prisoners received initially. The insurrectionist leader described prisoners burdened by their chains pulling a cart filled with stones, sand or limestone up a hill, explaining that,

> When a prisoner entered Ceuta a thick, heavy chain was put on his foot with links of regulation size and weight corresponding to the years he was to serve, so that those sentenced to life wore chains that reached to the waist and were then doubled and placed around his shoulder. A regulation chain of this kind weighed from 40 to 50 kilos and with the chain around his body the convict had to perform forced labor until he completed a certain period of time with good conduct in accord with the latest approved regulation."[11]

As Pablo de la Concepción noted, the well-respected Cuban prisoner Juan Gualberto Gomez, through the influence of friends in high places, was able to get this onerous requirement lifted in 1896.

Fernando Cadalso repeated the observation that the Royal Decree of December 26, 1889 confirmed the four categories as listed above, which had long been in effect, but he noted that prisoners who fell into the first category and who were required by the Royal Decree to reside in cells during that period of time, did not since there were no cells in the prisons of Ceuta. Consequently, he wrote, the regimen in Ceuta displayed an ongoing infraction of the precepts of the Penal Code and the Royal Decree and therefore was much softer or much less severe than the regimen observed on the Peninsula, "So that's how we stand on prison issues!" ("Así andamos en cuestiones penitenciarias!" *El Anarquismo* 39–40).

When Domingo Blanco noted the varied types of work that prisoners performed in the city, he commented on their reliability and honesty—they didn't rob or steal despite opportunities to do so. He also quoted the remark of Dr. Salillas, that the city "is built on the backs of the convicts and whatever one might say, motivated by ridiculous scruples, the nerve center of Ceuta is its prisons" (Ceuta "está edificada sobre las espaldas de los forzados, y aunque otra casa se diga por escrúpulos ridículos, el nervio de Ceuta es el presidio" (Dispatch of September1, 1897 in *El Imparcial*).[12] Tomás Salvador noted a caveat in Salillas's thoughts on the system in Ceuta. He wrote that Salillas considered Ceuta's convict labor system an acceptable exception, "an economic function of the first order in the city" ("una función económica de primer orden dentro de la ciudad" (*Cabo de vara* 151–152). Gómez Bravo also commented on Ceuta's exceptional status insofar as convict labor was concerned, noting that in contrast to the economic benefits prized by the inhabitants of Ceuta, towns and cities on the Peninsula often opposed locating prisons nearby since convict labor deprived free labor of work (*Crimen y castigo,*149; 151–152). In contrast to Salillas's acquiescence in the city's reliance on convict labor, according to Blanco's quote, and Blanco's own apparent complacency in regard to the system, Alberto Baeza believed that the city's dependence on convict labor was nefarious. He wrote that for as long the prisons were in operation, "life in the city hardened, military authority was omnipresent, vigilance, intransigence, paperwork and prison rigor invaded everything, increasing discontent in the civil population. The prison expanded its atmosphere, its mode of living, stifling the internal development of Ceuta, its politics, its citizenry. The City was filled with prisoners and riffraff" (Op. cit., 64). He quoted Leonardo Caballero on the omnipresence of prisoners in the city, "there were convicts among the scribes in the jail, teachers in the schools. A prisoner headed the Municipal Library and now and then they even served as ministers at the altar. Prisoners cleaned the streets, transported coffins, cared for children, supplied water to the city's inhabitants, emptied cesspools; they were masons, carpenters or painters, collecting their daily wages" ("Y presos habia entre los escribientes del Juzgado, los maestros de las escuelas, preso el encargado de la biblioteca municipal, e incluso algún ministro del altar. Los presos limpiaban las calles, conducían los féretros, suministraban agua a domicilio, evacuaban los pozos negros, eran albañiles, carpinteros o pintores (cobrando algún jornal por su trabajo").[13]

Whatever else penologists or other observers wrote about Ceuta, they did not hesitate to deplore the miserable conditions in the Hacho and Principal Barracks where Julián and Crisanto were confined. Commentators concurred in condemning them for their overcrowding, unhygienic conditions, and lack of appropriate supervision. Tello Amondareyn, among others, noted the consequences of the absence of cells in these prisons, "there is nothing but a piling up of human beings, misery and rot. The human beast, delineated by Zola in his naturalist novels, has its most authentic and painful embodiment in the Colony of Ceuta" ("ni en todos ellos hay otra cosa que hacinamiento de seres, y miseria, y podredumbre. La bestia humana, que retrató Zola en sus novelas naturalistas, tiene en la Colonia ceutí su encarnación más auténtica y dolorosa" (*Céuta* 92). Hacho prison, where Julián was confined, was meant to hold 300 prisoners, but during the period in question it held 700 to 800 convicts. Pablo de la Concepción, one of about 400 Cuban insurgents imprisoned in the Hacho during Julian's time there, described the hole in the ground located in his gallery of more than 250 prisoners. He wrote that when a new Cuban prisoner came in, unless he had money for a bribe that would place him at some distance from it, he was made to lie on the ground next to the hole, where he was sickened by the odors emanating from it and splashed with urine, and stepped on by those who used it in the night (*Prisioneros y deportados cubanos 1895-1898*, 274-275).

On September 1, 1897 Domingo Blanco's dispatch in *El Imparcial* described what happened at night in the Hacho. It was futile, he wrote, to check on the prisoners locked in at night by looking through the small windows opening onto each gallery because only a limited part of the space the prisoners inhabited was visible. Left to themselves, prisoners engaged in the vices typical of confinement. Moreover, "Fights erupted, one, two or ten convicts fell bloodied to the ground and the door to the gallery was not opened so as not to disturb the governor of the prison, and the next day, those whose more or less serious wounds could have been taken care of if they had been treated in time, died from loss of blood" ("Surge la bronca, caen ensangrentados uno, dos o diez presos, y aquella puerta no se abre por no despertar al gobernador de la ciudadela, y al día siguiente, los que atendidos a tiempo pudieron ser heridos más o menos graves, han muerto de la hemorragia.")

The State spent 40 *centimos* on food per day per convict in 1895 according to Baeza (*El Presidio de Ceuta* 50). The food allotted to prisoners, most of whom worked at hard labor eight to ten hours a day, had improved somewhat in the opinion of Tello Amondareyn but rations were still insufficient. Prisoners received only six or seven spoonfuls of food in each of the two meals served every day, and sometimes not as much as that. Clean tin containers capable of holding twelve to twenty-four rations had replaced the disgusting, unsanitary wooden buckets in use formerly. Twice a week the prisoners were given tripe brought in from Gibraltar and fish caught in Ceuta. The bread, though better than before, could still be much improved. Convicts who had the money could buy a cup of coffee for ten *céntimos,* about one tenth the cost of a liter of milk on the Peninsula. After they finished their day's work, prisoners were summoned by cornet call, lined up for review, given their ration and five minutes to eat it before another cornet call signaled the return to their quarters. (Tello, *Céuta* 107–108)

Conditions in the Principal Barrack where Crisanto Jorge was confined were as miserable as those in the Hacho. Because of the poor ventilation the stench of the movable latrine located in each of the dormitories was overwhelming. Tomás Salvador bitterly observed that prisons were built to contain latrines given that they were cesspools of human misery (Prisons were constructed "para contener zambullos, siendo sentina de la miseria humana" (*Cabo de vara* 50). Salvador described prisoners wrapped in their filthy blankets who slept on the humid earthen floor, which had the singular advantage of providing them a place to conceal their weapons. Given these conditions, including the necessarily poor personal hygiene of the convicts, illness, especially tuberculosis, was a common cause of death. Salvador observed that tuberculosis was the natural cause of death in prisons (Ibid 70). Gómez Bravo provided statistics from 1883–1886 on causes of deaths in Spanish prisons, including tuberculosis (*Crimen y castigo* 201). By 1896 conditions in the Principal Barracks had improved somewhat according to M. Manzano in his communication to Henri Prudhomme (*Revue Penitencière* 590 and 593.) He wrote that masonry shelves or ledges were placed along two walls of each dormitory on which prisoners spread their mats to sleep. Manzano described the physical location and properties of the Principal Barrack in detail as well as how the inmates were supervised and by whom. As for how the prisoners experienced their confinement, he drew attention to overcrowding and poor ventilation, but did not comment on the misery the prisoners endured.

Seventeen years after Julián García and Crisanto Jorge were tried, convicted, sentenced and sent to Ceuta, the prisons in the Colony were shut down. By 1912 the 400 convicts who remained there were sent to prisons on the mainland. I have not been able to discover whether the two men from El Escorial died before then or survived to be transferred to another prison.

THE JURY IN SPAIN 1995

Despite the not uncommon perception in contemporary Spain that trial by the pure or popular jury has not been part of Spanish judicial tradition, it was first introduced in 1872 and has been instituted off and on since then. It was in effect from 1872–75; 1888–1923; 1933–1936, and 1995 to the present. From the outset it was intended to provide a pathway for active inclusion of Spanish citizens into a democratic society. Thus it was instituted following the Revolution of 1868 and suspended in 1875 with the Restoration. Liberal aspirations brought about its reinstitution in1888 while the dictatorship of Primo de Rivera put an end to it in 1923. The Second Republic reinstituted it in 1933, but in 1936 it was suspended by decree in the "national zone" controlled by the forces of General Francisco Franco. Following a long dormant period, it was revived again in 1995. Part VI, article 125 "Del poder judicial" of the Constitution of 1978 mandated or allowed for (depending on how individual jurists read article 125) the inclusion of the jury as an integral part of the judicial system.[14] The Ley *Orgánica* 5/1995 of May 22, 1995 reinstituted it.[15] The first two jury trials in Spain were celebrated in Palma de Majorca and Palencia on May 27, 1996 (*El Pais*, April 29, 1996).

The jury system was reinstituted in Russia in 2003.[16] That nation, like Spain, has persisted in rejecting the continental system of the *escabinato* in favor of the pure or popular jury. A mixed court of professional judges and lay assessors share responsibility in arriving at a verdict in the *escabinato* model while jurors alone, acting in accord with the provisions of the pure system, arrive at a determination of guilty or not guilty on the basis of evidence submitted to them, after which the magistrate president applies the law and imposes the penalty.[17]

Controversy surrounding the jury system, whether *escabinato* or pure, has typically revolved around its political import. Proponents have emphasized its future benefits as opposed to its present defects; opponents attack its contemporary deficiencies. In her 2012 article "Trial by Jury" (p. 4) Ekaterina Mishina concluded that

> Despite all these issues, and even despite their very limited jurisdiction, jury trials are still vitally important for Russia. As nineteenth-century political thinker Alexis de Toqueville put it: 'To look at jury trials as at any other judicial body means to limit its importance considerably. Jury trials affect court proceedings greatly and they affect the destiny of society even more, Jury trials teach people to think like judges, and that is the best way to prepare people for freedom."[18]

Mark Twain saw, above all, the defects of contemporary jury selection, "The jury system puts a ban upon intelligence and honesty, and a premium upon ignorance, stupidity, and perjury" (*Roughing It*, 321). He doubted that jury selection processes could be altered to remedy the effects he noted.

Mar Jimeno-Bulnes used Twain's quotation as the epigraph of her 2004 study on "Lay Participation in Spain: The Jury System," referred to above. At the end of her essay, she quoted George P. Fletcher, *Las victimas ante el Jurado,* 281, "Faith in a juridical system has a great deal to do with National Identity," adding that the jury system undoubtedly appears strange to Spanish people. At the end of her essay Jimeno-Bulnes speculated that in view of its strangeness it might be advisable for Spain to reconsider implementing the *escabinato*, thereby shifting the question away from the political significance of the promotion of democratic participation through the pure jury, in order to draw attention instead to its alleged cultural inappropriateness. In her article on "Jury Selection and Jury Trial in Spain" she listed "prestigious" supporters of the *escabinato*, including Stephen C. Thaman, who in "Spain Returns to Trial by Jury," 253, considered the mixed court as the best solution for Spain (Jimeno-Bulnes "Jury Selection," Note 2, p. 4). Criticism of the popular jury on similar grounds was common in Spain during the late nineteenth century, as was chronicled previously in Chapter Four.

During the jury trial of Julián García and Crisanto Jorge, the issues most commonly singled out for criticism were the reluctance of citizens to serve on a jury, the question of guilt beyond doubt, and the process of jury selection. The influence of the mass media was evident to everyone following the case, but it was seldom analyzed, except by jurists, as a truly troubling factor in jury decisions. Since then, media influence has become a major source of concern in connection with jury trials wherever they exist. The following pages discuss the continuities in criticism of the pure jury system in the 1894 decision on the Escorial case and criticism of the system at present with special attention to a 2013 case in Spain, which also involved child murder.

THE CASE OF JOSE BRETÓN

In her review of Marina Warner's *No Go the Bogeyman* (1998) in the *TLS* of November 27, 1998, Katy Emck wrote that Warner's study "shows that stories about crime against children are at the heart of Western culture, tracing a curvaceous line of descent from 'the founding myth of the Greek divine pantheon itself,' the tale of Kronos eating his offspring to prevent them from supplanting him, to the current 'bogeyman' of paedophilia" (25). Murder is the crime against children that elicits the greatest public outrage, especially when it is accompanied by sexual abuse, as was charged against Julián García. Instances of child murder pose the dramatic juxtaposition of innocence against unspeakable malice and cruelty and that combination guarantees widespread media coverage of the crime.

On October 8, 2011, José Bretón informed the police that he had lost track of his two children, six-year-old Ruth and two-year-old José, in a park in Córdoba. At the time, Bretón was in the midst of a separation from his wife, Ruth Ortiz, who resided in Huelva. In accord with the separation agreement, Ruth Ortiz had the children during the week and their father had them on weekends. One month after Bretón reported the children's disappearance, they had not been found. Public demonstrations in all the capitals of Andalusia expressed solidarity with the family of the children and their extended families. By November 26, 2011 half a million people marched in Madrid demanding the immediate recovery of the children. In the meantime, on October 21, 2011 Bretón, an ex-military man, who had served in Bosnia, was detained and jailed, accused of illegal detention (defined here as the disappearance of minors) and the simulation of a crime, i.e., his claim that the children might have been victims of a kidnapping when they disappeared in the park. The police investigation centered on an examination of the wells and sewers between the Guadalquivir River and the Parque Cruz Conde where the children had allegedly disappeared. Interpol began to investigate the case on December 20, 2011.

Since Bretón had been with his children at the *finca* (property) of his parents on the afternoon when he said that he took them to the park, on June of 2012 the investigation began to focus more closely on that house and its grounds, which were extensive enough to include an orange grove. On August 27, 2012, the Police and the *Unidad de Delincuencia Especializada y Violenta*, which took charge of the case, confirmed the discovery of the bones of two children in a bonfire Bretón had lit on the premises of the *finca* on the day of his children's disappearance. The bones were initially identified as those of animals, but ten months later, forensic anthropologists at the Universidad Complutense in Madrid, found that while they were much deteriorated, they were human bones. The reader may be reminded of the uncertainty regarding whether the hair found in the *desván* or loft of the García house belonged to Pedro Bravo or to a cat.

On September 19, 2012, Bretón's lawyer requested trial by a professional tribunal instead of a popular jury on the grounds that it would be difficult to find citizens who were "uncontaminated" by the publicity surrounding the case. Ruth Ortiz's lawyer also stated his preference for a trial by jurists. He stated that he was not in favor of the popular jury in this or any other case, "since our Law derives from Roman and not Anglo-Saxon Law and we are not accustomed to it" (*www.diariocordoba*, April 29, 2013). Neither Bretón's lawyer's request nor Ruth Ortiz's lawyer's request was granted since the Spanish Constitution requires that murder cases be tried by a popular jury. According to the modification of the *Ley Orgánica* 8/1995 of November 16, 1995, the jury decides cases against persons, crimes committed by public functionaries in the course of their duties, crimes against honor, crimes against liberty and security and arson. Relevant here is the *Codigo Penal's* categorization of crimes against persons, which includes assassination and homicide. [19] A later attempt by Bretón's lawyer on May 9, 2013 to have the case annulled was considered and opposed by the *Tribunal Superior de Justicia de Andalucia.*

On September 28, 2012, eleven experts ratified their finding that the bones discovered in the ashes of the bonfire were human and that they belonged to two children aged two and six. Shortly afterwards, on October 3, 2012, Ruth Ortiz addressed thousands of people who attended a mass in memory of her children in the Santa Iglesia Cathedral of Córdoba, averring that the "destiny" of Ruth and José was "to be children for a short time on Earth and angels for all eternity in Heaven" (Their "destino" was "ser niños durante poco tiempo en la Tierra y ángeles eternamente en el Cielo.")

On January 16, 2013 the State's attorney asked for 40 years imprisonment for Bretón for the alleged assassination of his two children, with the aggravating circumstance of parentage, plus an indemnization of 600,000 Euros for his ex-wife. On June 13, 2013 Interpol withdrew the photographs of the children from its website. Meanwhile, the *Audiencia Provisional* of Córdoba had set the date for Jose Bretón's trial for June 17, 2013. Despite the fact that the DNA of the bones had not been recoverable, on June 25, 2013, the police captain (*comisario)* who had headed the investigation expressed his belief that the missing children were dead and that the bones found in the bonfire belonged to the Bretón children "by logical deductions."[20] The verdict was handed down on July 22, 2013. Jose Bretón was sentenced to 40 years, twenty years for the assassination of each child with the aggravating circumstance of parentage.

THE POPULAR JURY IN 1894 AND AFTER ITS REINSTITUTION IN 1995

"Spikespike" commenting on an article in *El País,* "El caso Bretón toca a su fin," (July 8, 2013) wrote: "How shameful for Spanish justice, the guy's in jail and facing a trial for murder when it hasn't even been demonstrated that the children are dead" ("Qué vergüenza de justicia española, el tío en la cárcel y en juicio por asesinato cuando ni siquiera se puede demostrar que los niños estén muertos." Another commentator on an *El País* article "La fiscal: 'Ha sido acreditado que Bretón mató a sus hijos'" (July 8, 2013) wrote,

> If we were civilized, we would not have decided that he is guilty based on what the press and TV programs have said. Not a single medium has reproduced the defense's allegations, or the statements of its experts, or anything. Rather, it has incurred in the practice of relying solely on what has "supposedly" demonstrated his guilt. The only thing that is clear and notorious is that one

> wants him to be culpable, not that he is culpable. Or rather what is being asked for is that someone be hanged because one wants him to be culpable. Very civilized, to be sure. ("Si fuéramos civilizados no hubiéramos decidido que es culpable por lo que dice la prensa y los programas de TV. Ni un sólo medio ha reproducido el alegato de la defensa ni los informes de sus peritos, ni nada. Solamente se ha incidido en lo que "supuestamente" demostraba su culpabilidad. Lo único claro y notorio es que se quiere que sea culpable, no que sea culpable. O sea que lo que estás pidiendo es que se ahorque a alguien porque quiere que sea culpable. Muy civilizado, desde luego.").

A reporter for *El Nacional* had made a similar comment on the proceedings which led to the verdict at El Escorial in 1894, "We have been given a decision by the jury without proof of any kind" (Y hemos llegado al juicio por jurados sin prueba ninguna ni grande ni chica"). Moreover, "and the jury, when it delivered its verdict in the case against the Chato and his codefendants, did not overlook the proof because none was put forward by a *sumario* whose flimsiness subsequently weakened the verdict. But the jury did not strictly follow its own criteria. By condemning the Chato to *reclusión temporal*, it is astonishingly inconsistent, because the crime is so horrendous it admits of no intermediary punishment"). The reporter concluded, "And there are those who believe that they can explain the real reason for the legal inconsistency by observing that the sentence of *reclusión temporal* is not, in this case, a penalty, but rather a compromise the jury made between the extravagant demands of the public and their own consciences. They reconcile the two by sending the Chato to prison." (*Crime at El Escorial,* first edition, Chapter Four, Note 4).

The commentators quoted above voiced uncommon responses to the trials of Julián García and José Bretón. Much more common in the García case were reporters' assumptions of the defendants' guilt. Commentators on news reports, and the reporters themselves most often assumed José Bretón's guilt, although criticism of the *sumario,* the initial misidentification of the bones, suspicions regarding the breaking of the chain of custody in regard to the bones, the unavailability of DNA evidence, and concern over media influence did lead some reporters and readers to express caution.

THE *SUMARIO*

The *sumario* or the pre-trial investigation, which is to remain secret before trial except to the opposing parties, was presented to the Escorial jury in 1894. It is unavailable, as are all trial records in the case since they were destroyed during the Civil War. The Escorial *sumario* was criticized for its inadequacies primarily by jurists. Others criticized the fact that reporters were divulging information and misinformation obtained during the pre-trial investigation. The defense in the Bretón case in its request for an annulment of the case before the *Tribunal Superior de Justicia de Andalucia* in Granada—which was denied—argued that there was continual and "unjustified" secrecy imposed during the preliminary investigation when the *sumario* should have been available to the prosecution and defense. ("José Bretón se sentará en el banquillo el 17 de junio por el asesinato de sus hijos," www.elmundo.es, May 13, 2013.) Judges are, nonetheless, allowed in exceptional circumstances to order the *secreto del sumario* for a period of a month and to delay it again subsequently (www.Abogado.com/guia-legal/ante-la-justicia-penal/losprocedimientos-penales). On April 20, 2012 the secret of the *sumario* was lifted so that after five (ultimately seven) delays the lawyers on either side could see it (Google.es sumario caso Breton.)

In both the Escorial case and the Bretón case, reporters ferreted out information based on the pre-trial investigation. Their reporting was sensationalistic at times and, in the opinion of critics, contributed to creating bias in the jurors and in the public. From 1888 onwards, transparency and accessibility for all during the pre-trial investigation has remained a goal for some legal experts—in 1882 Alfonso Martínez characterized such advocates as belonging to "certain radical schools"—and a source of error for others (*Crime at El Escorial* first edition, Chapter Four, Note no. 19).

Once the questions regarding delays of the *sumario* and the imposition of secrecy were resolved, the issues at stake in the Bretón case revolved around that of evidence beyond doubt and media influence on jurors. Jury selection and the vulnerability of jurors underlay both issues in the minds of the public and of opponents and advocates of the popular jury.

JURY SELECTION

The 1888 *Ley del Jurado* listed the requirements for serving on a jury and may be reviewed by consulting note 10 in Chapter Four of this book. A fundamental change in jury selection was made in 1933 when women were allowed to serve on juries. Contemporary jury law has retained this change. The current qualifications for Spanish citizens to serve on juries, in accord with Article 8 of the Spanish Jury Law, stipulate that jurors must be over 18 years of age, possess the right to vote, be able to read and write, reside in any part of the province in which the offense was committed, and have no physical, mental or sensory disability that would prevent them from acting as jurors. Provisions are in place to disqualify potential jurors. Challenges for cause and, after jury selections have been made, peremptory challenges may also be advanced (Mar Jimeno-Bulnes, "Jury Selection and jury trial in Spain," 6–9). In 1894 it was generally assumed that local *caciques*, especially in rural areas, controlled the selection of jurors. Current jury law initiates a random selection of potential jurors from local electoral census ("Elegidos los 8,000 madrileños que formarán el jurado popular en 2013–2014," *El País*, September 18, 2012 explains this process for the public). A random selection process by computer selects 36 potential jurors when a trial is referred to a Provincial Court. Of these 36, eleven citizens (nine jurors and two alternates) are selected to serve with a magistrate/president chosen by lot from the list of judges serving in the Provincial Court. Jurors deliver a reasoned verdict, i.e., "a succinct rationale for their verdict, indicating the evidence upon which the verdict was based and the reasons for finding a particular proposition proved or not proved" (Thaman, "Europe's New Jury Systems," 254). They find the defendant guilty or not guilty according to their responses to questions based on the factual evidence presented to them. The presiding magistrate/president dictates a sentence based on the law as applied to the jury's responses.

Disagreements and reservations remain concerning certain elements of the Jury Law, including the issue of "hidden" conscientious objection, used by significant numbers of prospective jurors to evade jury duty (Mar Jimeno-Bulnes "Jury Selection" 5). Avoidance of jury duty persists as a serious problem in Spain. Individual control by *caciques* over jury lists, as was common in the past, has been eliminated, but questions regarding the quality of jurors who consent to serve and their vulnerability to media influence and to fear for their personal safety in politically charged trials such as the murder trial of Mikel Otegi, continue to fuel debate on the popular jury. Otegi, a Basque nationalist, had murdered two Basque policemen and was acquitted of the crime by a popular jury in 1997. On October 4, 2013 the Supreme Court upheld the 34-year sentence for murder imposed by the *Audiencia Nacional* in 2012 (www.lavozdegalicia October 4, 2013.) This article provides details on the crime as does Beatriz S. Rebollo ("Los jurados" 494–495 and 452) and Stephen C. Thaman, "Europe's new Jury Systems," 236–237; 251–252). "El jurado funciona, pero es mejorable" (*El País*, January 28, 2012) includes context for the jury's responses in the Otegi case.

BEYOND DOUBT

There were no eyewitnesses in the case of Julián García, just as there were none in the Bretón case. The individuals in the earlier case who initially accused Julian of kidnapping, sexually abusing and murdering Pedro Bravo all withdrew their accusations. The circumstantial evidence in the earlier case amounted to nothing more than the proximity of Julián's house to the house of Pedro's parents' house. The circumstantial evidence in the Bretón case was abundant, as the judge noted in the sentence he delivered on July 22, 2013. Yet, it was all circumstantial. The first and most obvious objection to the charge of murder in Bretón's case lay in the uncertainty regarding the whereabouts of the alleged victims' bodies and the controversy over the bones found in the bonfire. The modern case thus broached the issue once again of guilt beyond doubt. The question that Bretón's lawyer raised concerning the evidence against his client had to do with the initial misidentification of the bones and the alleged break in the chain of custody. The bones found in the bonfire were first identified as bones of animals and later as human bones belonging to a two-year-old and a six-year-old child. Two hundred bones were retrieved from the fire, but DNA was not recoverable. A rumor arose to the effect that the expert who initially identified the bones as those of animals, had shown them to the forensic expert, Francisco Etxebarría, in a bar where one of the bones was lost; "the bones had gone out for drinks" ("los huesos se habian ido de de copas") as a wag put it. At Bretón's trial, the expert in question denied that there had been a break in the chain of custody, although the loss of one of the fragments (three, according to Bretón's lawyer) was left unaccounted for.

The judge presiding over the Bretón trial addressed both questions in his sentencing document handed down on July 22, 2013. He granted that there was no DNA evidence to identify the remains (bones) as those of the two missing children nor had it been possible to establish the cause of death of the children whose bodies, living or dead, had not been found, but that, in view of everything known in the case, the judgment concerning the identity of the bones arrived at by the jury through inference was completely plausible and showed impeccable reasoning. We have said, he wrote, that judgment based on inference means choosing the most reasonable possibility, and we have defined the reasonableness of an inference as a "precise and direct link or connection according to the rules of human criteria" ("enlace preciso y directo según las reglas del criterio humano"). Indeed, he continued, if the question were reversed, the conclusion would be the same. If it is scientifically proven that the two children aged two and six were burned in the fire, whose bones were they if not those of Ruth and José?

Finally, the judge stated that the sentence he had handed down was open to appeal since neither the act of murder (*asesinato*) or the identity of the victims burned in the bonfire were proven, even though the jury and the magistrate/president expressed their moral (and juridical) certainty that the bones belonged to the two missing children. Moral certainty "in a criminal trial, [is] the reasonable belief (but falling short of absolute certainty) of the trier of the fact (jury or judge sitting without a jury) that the evidence shows the defendant is guilty. Moral certainty is another way of saying `beyond a reasonable doubt." Since there is no exact measure of certainty it is always somewhat subjective and based on 'reasonable' opinions of judge and jury" (http://dictionary.law.com.).[21] The case against José Bretón was built on a succession of inferences. The jury found that those inferences taken as a whole were plausible and reasonable and justified their conclusion of guilty.

It is unlikely that jurors sworn in under the Jury Law of 1995 would find Julián García and Crisanto Jorge guilty. The issue of guilt beyond doubt is not even relevant to their cases since there was no proof of guilt at all. In the Bretón case the issue is relevant so long as rational inference—even though it may be based on abundant circumstantial evidence—may be considered shaky grounds for conviction. In September 2013 José Bretón's lawyer filed an appeal for a new trial before the *Tribunal Superior de Justicia de Andalucía*. The question of the medications (Motivan and Orfidal) that Bretón allegedly gave the children before they were burned to death, the identity of the bones, the chain of custody, and media influence figured among the reasons advanced for a new trial ("El recurso de Bretón cuestiona la hipótesis de las pastillas y carga contra el 'juiciomediático'" (*ABC,* September 9, 2013). Bretón's lawyer emphasized the role of the media coverage that had led to his client's condemnation by the public, "Bretón has been put on display as if he were a monster at a fair and he has even been given the nickname of 'the monster of Las Quemadillas'" ("Bretón ha sido expuesto como un monstruo de feria, e incluso se le ha apodado como 'el monstruo de Las Quemadillas'"). On November 6, 2013 *El País* reported that the *Tribunal Superior de Justicia de Andalucía* rejected the appeal lodged by José Bretón's lawyer on all counts.

MEDIA COVERAGE

Reporters who covered the trial of Julián García and Crisanto Jorge in 1894 wrote extensively about the pretrial investigation and the trial itself, despite the fact that they were not admitted to the courtroom. The result was that considerable misinformation reached newspaper readers. Jurists and other observers at the time noted and criticized omissions and distortions in news reports. The coverage of the José Bretón case between October 2011 and July 2013 was far more extensive. The possibility that the media might bias the jurors became more urgent; the question was how to reconcile the rights of a free press with the rights of defendants to a fair trial uncontaminated by the "parallel trial" conducted by the media.

As had happened in some previous cases, there were appeals to limit media coverage. In May of 2013 the Minister of Justice in consideration of the possibility that a resolution adopted by a judge or popular jury might be swayed by prejudice formed by the media in public opinion during the pretrial investigation and instruction of the *sumario*, or in the course of the trial itself, proposed that judges should be allowed to require a media source to cease publication of information that might compromise the right to a fair trial or undermine the fundamental rights of those affected (*El País*, May 29, 2012). His proposal was withdrawn in view of the strong protests it elicited from the press in particular (Ibid). The *Ley de Enjuiciamento Criminal, Artículo* 301 establishes the secrecy of the *sumario* until the trial begins and *Artículo* 302 regulates the *secreto del sumario* in preventing all parties (with the exception of the state attorney) from knowledge of the investigation when the judge so orders. The law does not refer to media coverage nor does it envision any possibility of prohibiting the publication of information on cases declared secret.

Change of venue and sequestration of jurors have been used in some countries to defend jurors (and defendants) from bias. During the Bretón case, the President of the *Audiencia Provincial* in Madrid was questioned about the possibility of protecting the rights of another current defendant by trying his case in a different venue. She replied that changes in venue were permitted in other countries, but that a case like Bretón's, which was so "brutal" would affect citizens in the same way everywhere in Spain. Furthermore, she pointed out that change of venue is not permitted in Spain. Sequestration of jurors is permitted in Spain but in times of financial austerity the cost of sequestering jurors is a grave burden.[22]

Television and the press in Spain provided coverage of the Bretón case reminiscent of the all-encompassing coverage of notorious cases in the United States. The popularity of television shows that covered the Bretón trial led to a race for ratings, "The Bretón case feeds the morning ratings war between Ana Rosa Quintana and Susanna Griso" ("El 'caso Bretón' adelanta la Guerra por las mañanas entre Ana Rosa Quintana y Susanna Griso," August 28, 2012, www.vanitatis.com.). One of the assertions made in this article was that experts had identified the bones found in the bonfire as those of Bretón's children. In fact, experts stated only that the bones were those of two children aged two and six. This false assertion, identifying the bones as those of Bretón's children, appeared frequently in the Spanish press.

Two books on the Bretón case appeared before his trial in July 2013. The first was titled *Los pasadizos secretos de la mente: José Bretón no es un psicópata*. The author, Pedro Hernández-Guanir, is a psychotherapist and professor of Psychology and Clinical Psychology. His earlier book *Los moldes de la mente*, was read by Ramón Sampedro, a tetraplegic and the first Spaniard to demand the right to an assisted suicide (denied), and used by Alejandro Amenábar in his 2004 film about Sampedro, *Mar adentro*. The author's credentials did not prevent one reader, José Luis Mendez-Fernández, from commenting on the inappropriateness of the book on Hernández-Guanir's Amazon page, "how deplorable it is that there are people who buy books that shower their authors with money from super sales, authors who feed on social carrion, in this case at the expense of two unfortunate children" ("Qué lamentable que haya quienes compren libros que forren de dinero en superventas a los autores que se ceban con la carroña social, en este caso a costa de dos niños caidos en desgracia"). Deplorable as it may be, readers and television viewers everywhere do, in fact, enable the vultures when it comes to reading and viewing information about horrific crimes.

In another book published before the trial, *El secreto de Bretón* (2013), Vicente Garrido wrote about the crime from the point of view of a criminologist seeking to explain Bretón's motivations in the alleged killing of his children as well as the judicial procedures followed in the case. According to the reporter who described the book, Garrido "maintains that [Bretón] commits the double crime in order not to go crazy" (sostiene que [Bretón] comete el doble crimen para no volverse loco"). Garrido also commented on the question of trial by jury, opining that "it [the jury] almost always complies perfectly" with its mission. He added that "judges are people who are not free from pressures either and their own way of viewing the world" (*El País*, May 28, 2013).

Only days before Bretón's trial, the president of the *Audiencia Provincial* declared that it was barbaric that witnesses for the trial should have appeared on television. As others before him had done, he asked for limits to media coverage (www.diariocordoba.com July 2, 2013). The influence of biased, sensationalist and inaccurate media coverage is difficult to measure, but it is universally decried, except by the media, as real and problematical. Beatriz S. Rebollo considered the issue and concluded that there is no solution to the problem of media influence creating bias or to the problem of fear experienced by jurors in politically charged cases (*Los jurados en USA* 452; 444). Attempts to limit media coverage inevitably clash with the right of free speech and freedom from censorship. It follows, in her opinion, and in view of the history of such attempts, that there is no legal protection from media coverage available to defendants or for jurors. The situation has not changed in this respect since the trial of Julián García and Crisanto Jorge in 1894.

If Julián and Crisanto had been tried after the jury was reinstituted in 1995, would the jurors have found them "not guilty" for lack of evidence? There simply was no proof that either man was involved in the murder of Pedro Bravo, nor was there extensive and plausible circumstantial evidence indicating culpability in the earlier case as there was in the Bretón case. In cases where there is proof of culpability, jurors may still find the defendant not guilty. Since 1995 juries in Spain have delivered verdicts that contradict the findings of the *sumario,* judging, for example, that the accused was not guilty because of attenuating circumstances such as temporary insanity, "trastorno mental transitorio," as in the Mikel Otegi case, despite lack of evidence to that effect. In such cases, appeals to higher courts whether the Supreme Court of the province or the Supreme Court of Spain are available and have reversed the verdicts of juries, as happened in the Mikel Otegi case, "El Supremo confirma la condena de 34 años de cárcel a Mikel Otegi por matar a dos ertzainas" ("The Supreme Court upholds the sentence of 34 years imprisonment for Mikel Otegi for the murder of two Basque policemen," www.lavozdegalicia.es October 4, 2013).

Wherever the pure jury functions, jury selection is still questioned by critics who see those best qualified to serve evade jury duty, especially, in Spain, through the "hidden conscientious" exemption. The conduct of the pretrial investigation is subject to criticism, its findings, often publicized in a sensational manner by the media, lead potentially to the creation of bias in the public and the jurors. Verdicts based on an assessment of evidence as beyond doubt, insofar as they not absolutely definitive are still open to questioning. Nonetheless, the pure jury reinstituted in Spain and Russia in 1995 and 2003 respectively, has garnered support from jurists and the public as well, as has been noted above. Few observers continue to argue that professionals in the *escabinato* system are unfailingly fairer and unbiased, or that ordinary citizens are less capable of examining and judging evidence. Apart from a case such as that of Mikel Otegi, in which jurors were believed to have delivered a verdict of not guilty motivated by fear, or in cases where media influence has been thought to be instrumental in verdicts handed down, jurors are seen as generally fair and conscientious even though they may have been bombarded with media distortions and incorrect information. In a recent highly publicized and sensationalized case of alleged child murder by a parent in the United States, the jury found the defendant not guilty, although the public appears to have been convinced that Casey Anthony was guilty of murdering her child. If a jury committed to finding proof, handed a well-prepared *sumario* and resistant to outside pressure had been available to Julián and Crisanto, they might have been spared conviction and a hellish imprisonment in Ceuta.

NOTES

1. Domingo Blanco's article of August 20, 1897 for *El Imparcial*, entitled "Los Huéspedes de Ceuta" ("Ceuta's Guests") described his encounters with Crisanto Jorge and Julián García. According to M. Manzano in "Colonie penal de Ceuta," in the *Revue penitencière et de droit*, A. Chaux et cie (Paris: Librairie Marchal et Billard, 1897): 588–589, men sent to Ceuta were those sentenced to *cadena perpetua* (life imprisonment) from Cuba, as well as men from the Peninsula or adjacent islands sentenced to the same or to twenty years or less (*cadena temporal*). Also sent to Ceuta were those sentenced to confinement for life (*reclusión perpetua*) and confinement of twenty years or less (*reclusión temporal*), those sentenced to detention in a *presidio* and to *prisión mayor* whose confinement at hard labor varied from a minimum of six years and one day to a maximum of twelve. Men sentenced to *cadena perpetua* and *temporal* were to wear an iron chain from the waist to the foot during the whole of the first period of their time in Ceuta. But see below for the exception granted to the Cubans. See also the comments of Fernando Cadalso below on the general bending of this regulation in Ceuta. The four periods of confinement are discussed below.

2. Each one is described summarily by Alberto Baeza Herrazti, *El Presidio de Ceuta* (Ceuta: Grupo Aleo, 1987): 54–61; by M. Manzano, administrator of the prisons in Ceuta, as

communicated to Henri Prudhomme in his article, "Colonie penal de Ceuta," 588–596, and for a somewhat earlier period (1883—c1888) by Tomás Salvador in his historical novel, *Cabo de vara* (Barcelona: Ediciones Destino, 1958): 37–39 and throughout the work.

3. For an account of this event, see Temma Kaplan, *Red City, Blue Period* (Berkeley. Los Angeles, Oxford: University of California Press, 1992): 30–31.

4. For the above information, see the entry "El correo de España," an article by Eduardo Martínez Pérez published in number 12 of the magazine *El correo de España* in www.blogdeceuta.com.

5. Gutmaro Gómez Bravo, *Crimen y Castigo. Justicia y violencia en la España del siglo XIX* (Madrid: Los Libros de la Catarata, 2005):191.

6. *El anarquismo y los medios de represión* (Madrid: Romero, Impresor, 1896): 62. See also Gómez Bravo, *Crimen y Castigo*, 238.

7. "Aunque esa población se halle estancada en el primer grado de su progreso moral y material, resulta tan errónea y deplorable la idea que de ella existe, que no es maravilla sentir asombro al entrar en su bahía, ver el rebellín y la Marina y el paseo de San Amaro y la calle Real, y las plazas de Ruíz, de África y de los Reyes, y sus pequeños jardines y su naciente comercio; tartar [sic] a sus morigerados vecinos, excepción hecha de la colonia hebrea, que allí impera con el yugo abrumador de sus codicias repugnantes, y admirar ante todo aquellas murallas por las que asoman las bocas de los cañones; aquellos recintos fortificados, testigos de cien reñidos combates; aquellas ponderosas baterías modernas que dominan las bahías Norte y Sur, ocultas tras malezas y parapetos hábilmente construídas aquella línea de fuertes que cubre el campo fronterizo; aquellas defensas, en fin, sobre las cuales sólo caen, como una amenaza, las sombras que proyectan las Alturas de Sierra Bullones; que sin eso sería Céuta verdaderamente inexpugnable por mar y por tierra," *Céuta. Llave principal del Estrecho*. (Madrid: Imprenta de Fortanet, 1897): 14–15.

8. From his essay, "The African Gibralter." *Harper's Weekly* (June 9, 1906) Vol. 50, no. 2581): 13–814.

9. "Pero lo que realmente llama la atención, es ver algunas brigadas de penados que tiran de pequeñas carretas o de pesadísimos cañones, o que van de vacío a los cuarteles del Acho, el Principal y las Barcas, o a Jadú, a recluirse, concluída la ruda labor prestada en las baterías, en el Puerto y en los desmontes,

Al observer este enjambre de penados sucios, astrosos, vestidos sin uniformidad y en lucha con las estaciones; unos de caras macilentas que revelan vicios repugnantes, los más de rostros animados que delatan cierta Cristiana resignación, cualquiera pensaría que no se vive en una plaza militar, sino en un presidio suelto; no en una ciudad moderna, sino en un aduar marroquí. Y, sin embargo nada más lejos de la exactitud que aquel supuesto que ofende a los ceutíes, y que esa idea escontraria a toda realidad," *Céuta*, 39–41.

10. *El Presidio de Ceuta*, 39–41. See also M. Manzano's account of the four periods in Henri Prudhomme, "Colonie penal de Ceuta," 589–591.

11. "Cuando un preso ingresaba en Ceuta le ponían al pie una gruesa cadena reglamentaria, con eslabones de tamaño y peso reglamentario, en número relacionado con sus años de presidio, resultando que la cadena de los presidiarios condenados a *cadena perpetua*, llegaba del pie a la cintura, donde daban con ella una vuelta completa y el resto sobrante lo echaban por sobre el hombre, una cadena reglamentaria de tales dimensiones, pesaba de cuarenta a cincuenta kilos, y con ella unida a su cuerpo realizaba el confinado el trabajo forzado a que estaba obligado, hasta que cumplía cierto tiempo de su pena con buena conducta, de acuerdo con el último reglamento aprobado," www.verdadceuta.es. September 17, 2013, 1–2.

12. Rafael Salillas (1854–1923) was a medical doctor, anthropologist and criminologist who emphasized the importance of heredity, the environment and social pressures on delinquents. He authored *La vida penal en España* (1888) as well as many other studies on prisons and prison reform.

13. Leopoldo Caballero, *Ceuta en el recuerdo* (Ceuta: Publicaciones del Instituto Nacional de Enseñanza Media, 1965), 24.

14. *Constitución Española*. B.O.E. (Boletín Oficial del Estado) núm. 311 de 20 de diciembre de 1978): pp. 29313–29424. See Mar Jimeno-Bulnes for a brief discussion of whether the

Constitution mandates or simply permits the jury, "Lay Participation in Spain: The Jury System," *International Criminal Justice Review*, Vol. 14 (2004):169–170.

15. For essays on the new jury in Spain, see *La ley del jurado: jornadas para secretarios judiciales* (Madrid: Imprenta Nacional del Boletín Oficial del Estado, 1996); for an historical overview and description of the new law, see Mar Jimeno-Bulnes, "Lay Participation in Spain: The Jury System," 165–169.

16. See Stephen C. Thaman, "Europe's New Jury Systems: The cases of Spain and Russia," *Law and Contemporary Problems*, 62, No. 2 (Spring 1999): 233–259; Sergei Tokmakov, "Jury Trials in Modern Russia," The *ISCIP Analyst (Russian Federation) An Analytical Review*, Vol. XVI, Number 7 (January 28, 2010); Ekaterina Mishina, "Trial by Jury in Russia: Revival and Survival," *Institute of Modern Russia* (January 26, 2012).

17. For a discussion of the *escabinato*, see Beatriz S. Rebollo, *Los jurados en USA y en España: dos contenidos distintos de la misma expresión* (Madrid: Editorial Dykinson, 2004): 170; Stephen C. Thaman, " Spain returns to trial by jury," *Hastings International and Comparative Law Review*, Vol. 21, No. 2 (1998): 253.

18. See Alexis de Toqueville, *Democracy in America*. Translated by Arthur Goldhammer (New York; The Library of America, 2004): 311–338 for Toqueville's thoughts on the jury. For less sanguine views of the jury, see Jerome A. Cohen, " The jury's out," *South China Morning Post*, March 16, 2011 and Stephen C. Thaman, "The Nullification of the Russian Jury: Lessons for Jury-Inspired Reform in Eurasia and Beyond," *Cornell international law journal*, Vol. 40, No. 2 (2007): 355–428.

19. "Preguntas y respuestas sobre el Jurado Popular," www.rtv.es/noticias/20120127/preguntas-respuestas-sobre—jurado-popular/493098.shtml:2; See also Mar Jimeno-Bulnes, "a defendant in Spain cannot choose between trial by jury or a bench trial, at least in those cases in which the defendant is charged with a crime over which the Jury Court has sole competence in Spain," "Lay Participation," 73–74.

20. The information above is taken largely from "Los niños de Córdoba: cronología de la desaparición de los hermanos Ruth y José," www.20minutos.es/noticia/1212704.

21. See also Gianmarco Gometz. *La certeza juridical como previsibilidad* (Madrid: Marcial Pons, Ediciones Jurídicas y Sociales, 2012).

22. See Beatriz S. Rebollo, *Los jurados en USA*, 438-452 for her discussion of the sequestration of jurors. In effect, she concludes that there is no solution to the issues raised by media influence.

Bibliography

NEWSPAPERS

ABC.es (Madrid), 2013
El Correo (Madrid), 1894-1896
La Correspondencia de España (Madrid), 1893-1894
El Día (Madrid), 1893-1895
*Diariocordoba.es (*Córdoba), 2013
La Época (Madrid), 1894-1895
El Globo (Madrid), 1894, 1896
El Heraldo de Madrid (Madrid), 1893-1894
El Ideal (Madrid), 1894
La Ilustración Artística (Barcelona), 1889, 1894, 1897, 1903
La Ilustración Ibérica (Barcelona), 1893-1895
El Imparcial (Madrid), 1891, 1893-1895, 1897
El Liberal (Madrid), 1891-1895, 1892
Los Lunes de El Imparcial (Madrid), 1892, 1894, 1899
Madrid Cómico (Madrid), 1894
El Mundo.es (Madrid), 2013
El Nacional (Madrid), 1893-1895
The New York Herald Tribune (New York), 1893
El Nuevo Régimen (Madrid), 1892-1896
El País (Madrid), 1893, 1990, 1996, 2013
La Publicidad (Barcelona), 1894
El Pueblo (Valencia), 1894, 1898
El Socialista (Madrid), 1894, 1896-1897
La Vanguardia (Barcelona), 1896, 1903
Vanitatis.com (Madrid), 2012

Veinteminutos.es (Madrid), 2012
La Voz de Galicia.es (A Coruña), 2013

GENERAL

Aguirre, Manuel. *The Closed Space. Horror Literature and Western Symbolism*. Manchester: Manchester University Press, 1990.

Aldana, Juan de. "Memoria elevada al gobierno por el Fiscal del Tribunal Supremo Don Juan de Aldana," *Revista General de Legislación y Jurisprudencia* 85 (1894): 313–357; 572–584.

———. "La Memoria del Fiscal del Tribunal Supremo," *Revista de los Tribunales y de Legislación Universal* 28 (22 Septiembre 1894): 557–567; (29 Septiembre 1894): 573–581; (6 Octubre 1894): 592–598; (13 Octubre 1894): 615–619; (27 Octubre 1894): 646–677.

Alejandre, Juan Antonio. *La justicia popular en España. Análisis de una experiencia histórica: Los tribunales de jurados*. Madrid: Editorial de la Universidad Complutense, 1981.

Alvarez Junco, José. "Racionalismo, romanticismo y moralismo en la cultura política republicana de comienzos de siglo." In *Clases populares, cultura, educación. Siglos XIX–XX. Coloquio Hispano–Francés* (Casa de Velázquez, Madrid, 15–17 junio 1987). Madrid: Casa de Velázquez UNED, 1989: 355-375.

Alvarez–Uría, Fernando. *Miserables y locos. Medicina mental y orden social en la España del siglo XIX*. Barcelona: Tusquets Editores, 1983.

Amiel, Henri–Frédéric. *Journal intime*. Vol.1. Lausanne: Éditions l'Age d'Homme, 1976, 1:208.

Armengol y Cornet, Pedro. "Cuestiones relacionadas con la infancia y los menores," *Revista de los Tribunales y de Legislación Universal* 29 (8 Junio 1895): 410–412..

———. "Una gran deficiencia del Código civil," *Revista de los Tribunales y de Legislación Universal* 29 (22 Junio 1895): 398–400; 29 (29 Junio 1895): 410–412.

Aubert, Paul. "Culture et inculture dans l'Espagne de la Restauration: Un Nouveau discours sur l'école (1909–1923)." In *Clases populares, cultura, educación. Siglos XIX–XX. Coloquio Hispano–Francés*. Madrid: Casa de Velázquez UNED, 1989: 467-508.

Aubry, Paul. "De la influencia contagiosa de la publicidad de los hechos criminales," *Revista General de Legislación y Jurisprudencia* 83 (1893): 622–624.

Azaña, Manuel. *El jardín de los frailes*. Madrid: Alianza, 1982.

Baeza Herrazti, Alberto. *El Presidio de Ceuta*. Ceuta: Grupo Aleo, 1897.

Barcáiztegui y Orfila, Ventura. *Estudio teórico–práctico del concepto de la culpabilidad, medios probatorios y veredictos ante el Tribunal del jurado*. San Sebastián: Impr. de "La Voz de Guipúzcoa," 1894.

Bark, Ernesto. *El Internacionalismo*. Madrid: Biblioteca Germinal, 1900.

Barthes, Roland. "La Structure du fait divers." In *Essais critiques*. Paris: Seuil, 1964: 188-197.

Bartrina, Joaquín María. "La América precolombina." In *Obras en prosa y verso*. Ed. J. Sardá. Barcelona, Madrid: Texidó y Parera, 1881:127-168.

Barr, Martin W., M.D. "Mental Defectives: Their Classification and Training." In *Third International Congress For The Welfare And Protection of Children*. London: P.S. King and Son, 1902: 252-260.

Basdekis, Demetrios. "El populismo del primer Unamuno." In *La crisis de Fin de Siglo: Ideología y literatura*. Barcelona: Editorial Ariel, 1975: 242-251.

Behlmer, George K. *Child Abuse and Moral Reform in England. 1870– 1908*. Stanford: Stanford University Press, 1982.

Bellver de Oña, Antonio. *El juicio criminal. Manual teórico–práctico. Con el texto de las Leyes de Enjuiciamiento y del Jurado, formularios y doctrina de la Fiscalía del Tribunal Supremo*. Madrid: Ricardo Fé, 1899.

Benito y Alfaro, Alfonso. *La chula*. Zarzuela en un acto, original. Música del Maestro Teodoro San José. Madrid: R. Velasco, 1896.

Berenson, Edward. *The Trial of Madame Caillaux*. Berkeley: University of California Press, 1992.

Bernaldo de Quirós, Constancio. "Criminología de los delitos de sangre en España," *Boletín de la Institución Libre de Enseñanza* 30 (1906):115–120; 155–159.

———. *Las nuevas teorías de la criminalidad*. Madrid: Hijos de Reus, 1898.

———, and J.M. Llanas Aguilaniedo. *La mala vida en Madrid*. Madrid: B. Rodríguez Serra, 1901.

Black, Joel. *The Aesthetics of Murder. A Study in Romantic Literature and Contemporary Culture*. Baltimore: Johns Hopkins University Press, 1991.

Blasco Ruiz, Pilar. "Literatura popular en el Madrid decimonónico." In *Madrid en la sociedad del siglo XIX*. Eds. Luis E. Otero Carvajal and Angel Bahamonde. Vol.2. Madrid: Alfoz, 1986: 467-484.

Botrel, Jean–François. "Aspects de la littérature de colportage en Espagne sous la Restauration.," In *L'Infra-littérature en Espagne aux XIXe et XXe siècles*. Grenoble: Presses Universitaires de Grenoble, 1977: 103-123.

———. "La iglesia católica y los medios de comunicación impresos en España de 1847 a 1917: doctrinas y prácticas." Eds. Bernard Barrère et al. In *Metodología de la historia de la prensa española*. Eds. Bernard Barrère et al Madrid: Siglo XXI, 1982: 119-176.

———. "La Littérature du peuple dans L"Espagne contemporaine," *Clases populares, cultura, educación. Siglos XIX-XX*. Coloquio Hispano-Francés. Madrid: Casa de Velázquez UNED, 1989: 277-299.

———. "La novela por entregas: unidad de creación y consumo." In *Creación y público en la literatura española*. Eds. J.-F. Botrel and S. Salaün. Madrid: Castalia, 1974:111-155.

Boyle, Thomas. *Black Swine in the Sewers of Hampstead*. New York: Viking Penguin, 1989.

Brey, Gérard. "Ideología y acontecimiento en la poesía de un periódico obrero de Cadiz: `*El Proletario*' (1902–1903)." *Metodología de la historia de la prensa española*. Madrid: Siglo XXI, 1982: 43-57.

Bravo, Emilio. *Ley del jurado*. Madrid: P. Nuñez. 1888.

Brooks, Peter. *The Melodramatic Imagination. Balzac, Henry James, Melodrama, and the Mode of Excess*. New Haven: Yale University Press, 1976.

Burgos, Javier de. *Las mujeres*. Madrid: n. p. 1896.

Caballero, Leonardo. *Ceuta en el Recuerdo*. Ceuta: Publicaciones del Instituto Nacional de Enseñanza Media, 1965.

Cadalso, Fernando. "Memoria de la prisión celular de Madrid, presentada al Excmo. Señor Ministro de Gracia y Justicia por el Director de dicho establecimiento, Dr. Fernando Cadalso," *Revista de los Tribunales* 27 (1893): 70–143.

———. *E l Anarquismo y los Medios de Represión*. Madrid: Romero, Impresor, 1896.

Calvo Camina, Pedro. *La instancia única en lo civil y la organización de tribunales*. Pontevedra: José Eiras García, 1894.

Cambréal, André. *Le Jury criminel:comment se forme, délibère, et statue le jury de cours d'assises*. Paris: Rousseau & Cie., 1937.

Cansinos–Assens, Rafael. "Periodismo madrileño de principio de siglo," *Gaceta de la Prensa Española*," núm. 152 (Febrero 15, 1964): 43–45.

Carey, John. *The Intellectuals and the Masses: Pride and Prejudice Among the Literary Intelligentsia, 1880–1939*. London: Faber and Faber, 1992.

Castejón, Frederico. *Comentarios científicos–prácticos al Código Penal de 1870*. Vol.2. *Tratado de responsabilidad*. Madrid: Editorial Reus, 1926.

Celma Valero, María Pilar. *Literatura y periodismo en las revistas del fin de siglo. Estudio e índices (1888–1907)*. Madrid: Júcar, 1991.

Código penal de 1870: *Reformado y corregido con arreglo a la ley de 3 de enero de 1907*. Madrid: Casa Editorial Saturnino Calleja Fernández, 1913.

Cohen, Anthony. "Culture As Identity: An Anthropologist's View," *New Literary History* 24:1 (1993): 195–209.

Cohen, Jerome A. "The Jury's Out," *South China Morning Post*, March 16, 2011.

Colquhoun, Archibald R. "The African Gibralter." *Harper's Weekly*. June 9, 1906, Vol.50, no. 2581: 812–814.

Comparative Studies in Continental and Anglo–American Legal History. Eds. Helmut Coing and Knut Norr. Vol.4. Berlin: Duncker & Humblot, 1987.

Compère, Marie–Madeleine. Review of *Clases populares, cultura, educación. Siglos XIX y XX, Coloquio hispano–francés (Casa de Velázquez, Madrid 15–17 junio de 1987). Annales: Économies, sociétés, civilisations* 46/5 (septembre–octobre 1991):1171–1174.

Concepción y Hernández, Pablo de la. *Prisioneros y deportados cubanos 1895–1898 en la Guerra de Independencia*. Havana: Imprenta P. Fernández, 1932.

Constitución Española. B.O.E (Boletin Oficial del Estado) no. 311. December 29, 1978.

Costa, Joaquín. "Resumen de la Información," *In Oligarquía Y Caciquismo Como La Forma Actual De Gobierno En España. Urgencia Y Modo De Cambiarla.* Vol.1: Madrid: Ediciones de la Revista de Trabajo, 1975: 99-243.

"El Crimen de El Escorial," *Revista de los Tribunales y de Legislación Universal* 29 (7 Diciembre 1895): 769–773; 30 (18 Enero 1896): 33–39; 30 (25 Enero 1896): 49–54.

De Amicis, Edmondo. *Spain and the Spaniards*. Philadelphia: Henry T. Coates & Co., 1895.

Díaz Cobeña, Luis. "Notas biográficas." In *Colección de trabajos forenses y noticias biográficas de los más notables abogados de España y de las Repúblicas de la América Latina.* Madrid: Centro Editorial de Góngora, 1897: 83-117.

Díaz de Castro, Francisco J. and Isabel Moll Blanes. "Prensa conservadora a finales del siglo XIX: *El Ancora*, de Mallorca." In *Metodología de la historia de la prensa española.* Madrid: Siglo XXI, 1982: 58-80.

Donovan, James M. "Justice Unblind: The Juries and the Criminal Classes in France, 1825–1914," *Journal of Social History* 15 (1981–2): 89–107.

Dorado Montero, Pedro. "La criminalidad," *Nuestro Tiempo* (Mayo 1902): 815–833.

———. "A propósito de la causa de Varela," *La España Moderna* (Mayo 1894): 68–95.

———. "La psicología popular ante los crímenes llamativos," *La Lectura* (Febrero 1903):189–200.

Dwyer, Ellen. "Stories of Epilepsy, 1880–1930." In *Framing Disease: Studies in Cultural History. (Health and Medicine in American Society.)* Eds. Charles E. Rosenberg and Janet Golden. New Brunswick, N.J.: Rutgers University Press, 1992: 248-272.

Elorza, A. and M. Pérez Ledesma. *Prensa y sociedad en España (1820–1936)*. Madrid: Cuadernos para el diálogo, 1975.

Emck, Katy. "Look behind you." *TLS*, November 27, 1998: 24–25.

Esenwein, George Richard. *Anarchist Ideology and the Working–Class Movement in Spain, 1868–1898*. Berkeley: University of California Press, 1989.

Esmein, Adhémar. *A History of Continental Criminal Procedure with Special Reference to France*. Boston: Little, Brown and Company, 1913.

Espina García, Antonio. *El cuarto poder. Cien años de periodismo español*. Madrid: Aguilar, 1960.

Ferreras, Juan Ignacio. *La novela por entregas 1840–1900*. Madrid: Taurus, 1972.

———. *Los orígenes de la novela decimonónica 1800–1830*. Madrid: Taurus, 1973.

Field, Henry M. *Old Spain and New Spain*. New York: Scribner's Sons, 1888.

Fiestas Loza, Alicia. "Codificación procesal y estado de la Administración de justicia (1875–1915)." In *La España de la Restauración: política, economía, legislación y cultura.* Madrid: Siglo XXI, 1985: 413-433.

Fisher IV, Benjamin Franklin. *The Gothic's Gothic, Study Aids to the Tradition of the Tale of Terror*. New York: Garland Publishing Inc., 1988.

Fletcher, George P. *Las víctimas ante el jurado*,Valencia, Spain:Tirant lo Blanch, 1997.

Forsyth, William. *History of Trial by Jury*. 2nd ed. New York: Burt Franklin, 1971.

Foucault, Michel. *Moi, Pierre Rivière, ayant égorgé ma mère, ma soeur et mon frère: un cas de parricide au XIXe siècle*. Paris: Gallimard, 1973.

———. *Discipline and Punish*. Trans. Alan Sheridan. New York: Vintage, 1979.

Frank, Frederick S. *Guide to the Gothic. An Annotated Bibliography of Criticism*. Metuchen, N.J.: Scarecrow Press, 1984.

Furet, François, and Jacques Ozouf. *Lire et écrire. L'alphabétisation des Français de Calvin à Jules Ferry*. 2 vols. Paris: Les Éditions de Minuit, 1977.

García Sanz, S. "Botargas y enmascarados alcarreños (Notas de etnografía y folklore)," *Revista de Dialectología y Tradiciones Populares* 9 (1953): 467–492.

Garrido, Vicente and Patricia López. *El secreto de Bretón*. Madrid: Ariel, 2013.

Gissing, George. *New Grub Street*. Boston: Houghton Mifflin Company, 1962.

Gleisser, Marcus. *Juries and Justice*. South Brunswick: A.S. Barnes and Company, 1968.

Gometz, Gianmarco. *La certeza juridica como previsibilidad*. Madrid: Marcial Pons, Ediciones Jurídicas y Sociales, 2012.

Gómez Bravo, Gutmaro. *Crimen y Castigo.Cárceles, Justicia y Violencia en la España del Siglo XIX*. Madrid: Los Libros de la Catarata, 2005.

Gordon, Linda. *Heroes of Their Own Lives: The History and Politics of Family Violence 1880–1960*. New York: Penguin, 1988.

Gorham, Deborah. "The 'Maiden Tribute of Modern Babylon' Re-Examined: Child Prostitution and the Idea of Childhood in Late-Victorian England," *Victorian Studies* 21 (Spring 1978): 354–379.

Graff, Harvey J. *The Legacies of Literacy. Continuities and Contradictions in Western Culture and Society*. Bloomington: Indiana University Press, 1987.

———. *The Literacy Myth. Literacy and Social Structure in the Nineteenth–Century City*. New York: Academic Press, 1979.

Guarnieri, Patrizia. *A Case of Child Murder. Law and Science in Nineteenth–Century Tuscany*. Translated by Claudia Miéville. Cambridge, U.K.:Polity Press, 1993.

Guillais, Joëlle. *La Chair de l'autre. Le crime passionel au XIXe siècle*. Paris: Olivier Orban, 1986.

Hacking, Ian. "The Making and Molding of Child Abuse," *Critical Inquiry* 17 (Winter 1991): 253–288.

Hare, Augustus J.C. *Wanderings in Spain*. New York: G. Routledge & Sons, 1885.

Harris, Frank. *Presentation of Crime in Newspapers. A Study of Methods in Newspaper Research*. Hanover, N.H.: Sociological Press, 1932.

Harris, Ruth. *Murders and Madness. Medicine, Law, and Society in the "fin de siècle*." Oxford: Clarendon Press, 1989.

Harsin, Jill. "Gender, Class and Madness in Nineteenth–Century France," *French Historical Studies* 17/4 (1992): 1048–1070.

Hay, John. *Castilian Days*. London: William Heineman, 1903.

Hernández-Guanir, Pedro. *Los pasadizos secretos de la mente: Jose Bretón no es un psicópata*. Madrid: Cultivalibros, 2012.

Hudry–Menos, M. "La protección a la infancia,' *Boletín de la Institución Libre de Enseñanza* 22 (1898):194–198.

Hughes, Helen MacGill. *News and the Human Interest Story*. Chicago: University of Chicago Press, 1940.

Huret, Jules. *Enquête sur l'évolution littéraire*. Paris: Bibliothèque Charpentier, 1891.

Iglesias, Concepción. *Blasco Ibáñez. Un novelista para el mundo*. Spain: Silex, 1985.

Jimeno-Bulnes, Mar. "Jury Selection and Jury Trial in Spain." *Oñati socio–legal series*, Vol. 1 No. 9 (2011): 3–20.

———. "Lay Participation in Spain: The Jury System," *International Criminal Justice Review*, Vol. 14 (2004): 69–170.

Kalikoff, Beth. *Murder and Moral Decay in Victorian Popular Literature*. Ann Arbor, Michigan: UMI Research Press, 1986.

Kaplan, Temma. *Red City, Blue Period*. Berkeley. Los Angeles. Oxford: University of California Press, 1992.

Katz, Jack. *Seductions of Crime: Moral and Sensual Attractions in Doing Evil*. New York: Basic Books, 1988.

Kern, Robert W. *Liberals, Reformers and Caciques in Restoration Spain 1875–1909*. Albuquerque: University of New Mexico Press, 1974.

Langle Rubio, Emilio. *La mujer en el derecho penal*. Madrid: Hijos de Reus, 1911.

Lea, Henry C. *The History of Sacerdotal Celibacy in the Christian Church*. New York: Russell and Russell, 1957.

Ley de Enjuiciamiento Criminal de 14 de septiembre de 1882. Barcelona: José María Bosch, 1956.

La Ley del Jurado. Comm. D. Francisco de Asís Pacheco. Prol. Manuel Alonso Martínez. Madrid: *Revista General de Legislación y Jurisprudencia*, 1888.

La ley del Jurado: jornadas para secretarios judiciales. Madrid: Imprenta Nacional del Boletín Oficial del Estado, 1996.

Le Mahieu, D.L. *A Culture for Democracy. Mass Communication and the Cultivated Mind in Britain Between the Wars*. Oxford: Clarendon Press, 1988.

Litvak, Lily. *Musa libertaria. Arte, literatura y vida cultural del anarquismo español (1880–1913)*. Barcelona: Antoni Bosch, 1981.

Lois, Baldomero and E. Alonso y Orera. *Páginas de actualidad*. Vol.1. Madrid: Imprenta de Enrique F. de Rojas, 1895.

Lombroso, César. "Aplicaciones judiciales y médicas de la antropología criminal," *La España Moderna* (Mayo 1893):78–124.

M. L. "Juzgadores de Alforja," *Revista de los Tribunales* 26 (1 abril; 8 abril 1893): 97–108.

Maeztu, Ramiro de. *Hacia otra España*. Madrid: Rialp, 1967.

Mainer, José Carlos. *La edad de plata (1902–1939). Ensayo de interpretación de un proceso cultural*. Madrid: Cátedra, 1983.

———. "Literatura burguesa y pequeño–burguesa," In *Creación y público en la literatura española*. Eds. J.-F. Botrel and S. Salaün. Madrid: Castalia, 1974: 162-180.

———. "Notas sobre la lectura obrera en España (1890–1930)." In *Teoría y práctica del movimiento obrero en España (1900–1936)*. Valencia: Fernando Torres, ed., 1977: 173-239.

Maristany, Luis. *El gabinete del doctor Lombroso. Delincuencia y fin de siglo en España*. Barcelona: Anagrama, 1973.

Martin, Benjamin F. *Crime and Criminal Justice Under the Third Republic. The Shame of Marianne*. Baton Rouge and London: Louisiana State University Press, 1990.

Martín Perez, Eduardo "El correo de Ceuta," in "El correo de España" no.12. www.blogdeceuta.com.

Martínez Martín, Jesús A. *Lectura y lectores en el Madrid del siglo XIX*. Madrid: CSIC, 1991.

Martínez Ruiz, José (Azorín). *Anarquistas literarias*. Madrid: Librería de Fernando Fe, 1895.

Masson, Jeffrey Moussaieff. *The Assault on Truth. Freud's Suppression of the Seduction Theory*. New York: Harper Perennial, 1992.

Maza, Sarah. "Domestic Melodrama as Political Ideology: The Case of the Comte de Sanois," *American Historical Review* 94 (December 1989): 1249–1264.

Mishina, Ekaterina. "Trial by Jury in Russia: Revival and Survival," *Institute of Modern Russia,* January 26, 2012: 1–5.

Monroe, Will S. "Status of Child Study in Europe." In *The Pedagogical Seminary*. Vol. 6. Worcester, Mass.: J.H. Orpha, 1899: 372-381.

Montesinos, José F. *Introducción a la historia de la novela en el siglo XIX. Seguida del esbozo de una bibliografía española de traducciones de novelas (1800–1850)*. Valencia: Castalia, 1955.

Morales Muñoz, Manuel. "Asociaciones obreras de instrucción en Málaga (1892–1919)." In *Clases populares, cultura, educación. Siglos XIX–XX. Coloquio Hispano–Francés*. Madrid: Casa de Velázquez UNED, 1989: 403-437.

Nuñez de Cepeda, Hilario. *El jurado. Obra completa con el texto de la ley, capítulos interesantes sobre historia de la institución en España y nutrida jurisprudencia de importancia y necesidad*. La Coruña: n. p., 1933.

Nye, Robert A. "Crime in Modern Societies: Some Research Strategies for Historians," *Journal of Social History* 11 (1978): 491–507.

Ortega y Gasset, Manuel. *"El Imparcial." Biografía de un gran diario español*. Zaragoza: Librería general, 1956.

Ossorio y Gallardo, Angel. "Crónica de Tribunales," *Revista de los Tribunales y de Legislación Universal* 27 (22 Septiembre 1894: 661; 28 (3 Noviembre 1894): 661–665; 29 (23 Noviembre 1895): 744–751.

Ots y Esquerdo, V. "La locura ante los Tribunales," *Revista de los Tribunales y de Legislación Universal* 28 (21 Abril 1894): 213–221; (28 Abril 1894): 229–234; (5 Mayo 1894): 243–251; (19 Mayo 1894): 273–282; (2 Junio 1894): 304–309; (9 Junio 1894): 322–327; (23 Junio 1894): 351–357; (30 Junio 1894): 367–376.

Palacio, Eduardo del. "Juicio por jurados," *La Ilustración Artística* (14 Mayo 1894): 311–312.

Palacio Valdés, Armando. "El cuarto poder." In *Obras completas*. Vol.1. Madrid: Aguilar, 1959.

———. *La espuma*. 2 Vols. Barcelona: Imprenta de Henrich y Compañía en Comandita, 1890.

———. "El Maestrante." In *Obras completas*. Vol.2. Madrid: Aguilar, 1959.

———. "El origen del pensamiento." In *Obras completas*. Vol.2. Madrid: Aguilar, 1959.

Palmer, Thomas W. *Guide to the Law and Legal Literature of Spain*. Westport, Connecticut: Hyperion Press, 1979.

Papke, David Ray. *Framing the Criminal. Crime, Cultural Work, and the Loss of Critical Perspective, 1830–1900*. Hamden, CT.: Archon Books, 1987.

Pardo Bazán, Emilia. "Da. Emilia Pardo Bazán," In *Oligarquía Y Caciquismo Como La Forma Actual De Gobierno En España. Urgencia Y Modo De Cambiarla*. Vol. II. Madrid; Ediciones de la Revista de Trabajo, 1901: 289-298.

———. "La Tribuna." In *Obras completas*. Vol.2. Madrid: Aguilar, 1956.

Paris, Pierre. *L'Espagne de 1895 et 1897. Journal de voyage*. Paris: E. De Boccard, 1979.

Patey, Douglas Lane. Review of *"Beyond Reasonable Doubt" and "Probable Cause,"* by Barbara J. Shapiro. *Eighteenth–Century Studies* 26 (1992–93): 334–338.

The People's Law Dictionary. s v. "moral certainty." http://dictionary.law.com.

Pérez de Ayala, Ramón. *A.M.D.G.* Madrid: Biblioteca Renacimiento, 1911.

———. *A.M.D.G.* Ed. Andrés Amorós. Madrid: Cátedra, 1983.

Pérez Galdós, Benito. "Halma." In *Obras Completas*. Vol. 5. Madrid: Aguilar, 1951.

Perrot, Michelle. "Fait divers et histoire au XIXe siècle," *Annales: Économies, sociétés, civilisations* 38 (juillet–août 1983): 911–919.

Pessina, Enrique. *Elementos de derecho penal*. Madrid: Hijos de Reus, Editores, 1913.

Pick, Daniel. *Faces of Degeneration. A European Disorder, c. 1848–c. 1918*. Cambridge: Cambridge University Press, 1989.

Piqueras Arenas, José A. "Educación popular y proceso revolucionario español." In *Clases populares, cultura, educación. Siglos XIX-XX*. Coloquio Hispano-Francés. Madrid: Casa de Velázquez UNED, 1989: 77-95.

Prudhomme, Henri. "Colonie penal de Ceuta, "*Revue Penitencière et droit*. A. Chauxet cie. Paris: Librairie Marchal et Billard, 1897: 588–596.

Przybos, Julie. *L'Entreprise mélodramatique*. Paris: Librairie José Corti, 1987.

Punter, David. *Literature of Terror: A History of Gothic Fictions from 1765 to the Present Day*. London: Longman, 1980.

Quadrado, José María and Vicente de la Fuente. *Castilla la Nueva*. Barcelona: Daniel Cortezo y Cia., 1885.

La Question de la "bourgeoisie" dans le monde hispanique au XIXe siècle. Bordeaux: Éditions Bière, 1973.

Rebollo, Beatriz S. *Los jurados en USA y en España: dos contenidos distintos de la misma expresión*. Madrid: Editorial Dykinson, 2004.

Reynolds, Oliver. "Melon Cocktail." Review of *The Man in the Bowler Hat*, by Fred Miller Robinson. *The Times Literary Supplement*, 28 May 1993: 8.

Riding, Alan. "For Some Newspapers, Spain Proves to be a Trap," *The New York Times*, 23 March 1992.

Rivera, D. Marcelino. "Piedrahita." In *Reformas sociales. Información oral y escrita publicada de 1889-1893*. Vol. 4. Ed. Santiago Castillo. Madrid: Ministerio de Trabajo y Seguridad, 1895: 308-309.

Roca León, J.L. *Vicente Blasco Ibáñez*. Valencia: Ediciones Prometeo, 1967

Romances horrorosos. Selección de romances de ciego que dan cuenta de crímenes verídicos, atrocidades y otras miserias humanas. Ed. Isabel Segura. Barcelona: Editorial Alta Fulla, 1984.

Romero Tobar, Leonardo. *La novela popular española del siglo XIX*. Madrid: Ariel, 1976.

Rubio Jiménez, J. *Ideología y teatro en España: 1890–1900*. Zaragoza: Pórtico, 1982.

Rush, Florence. *The Best-Kept Secret. Sexual Abuse of Children*. Intro. Susan Brownmiller. Englewood Cliffs, New Jersey: Prentice–Hall, Inc., 1980.

Salaün, Serge. "El género ínfimo: Mini-culture et culture des masses." In *Clases populares, cultura, educación. Siglos XIX–XX. Coloquio Hispano–Francés*. Madrid: Casa de Velázquez UNED, 1989: 337-353.

———. "Problematique de l'infra–culture." In *Les productions populaires en Espagne, 1850–1920*. Paris: Éditions de Centre National de la Recherche Scientifique, 1986. 353-368.

Salvador, Tomás. *Cabo de vara*. Barcelona: Ediciones Destino. 1958.

Sánchez Montoya, Francisco. "Independentistas cubanos en Ceuta (111parte)," April 5, 2013. 3. www.verdadceuta.es .

Sánchez Sanz, María Elisa. "La censura popular en Aragón." In *Les productions populaires en Espagne 1850–1920*. Paris: Éditions du Centre National de la Recherche Scientifique, 1986: 77-97.

Schneider, Frank. "E.T.A. Hoffmann en España: apuntes bibliográficos e históricos." In *Estudios eruditos in memoriam de Adolfo Bonilla y San Martín (1875–1926)*. Vol. I. Madrid: Jaime Bates, 1921: 279-287.

Scott, Sir Walter. *Waverley*. London: J.M. Dent and Co. Ltd., 1915.

Seven Gothic Dramas 1789–1825. Ed. Jeffrey N. Cox. Athens: Ohio University Press, 1992.

Shapiro, Barbara J. *"Beyond Reasonable Doubt" and "Probable Cause."* Berkeley: University of California Press, 1991.

Shubert, Adrian. *A Social History of Modern Spain*. London: Unwin Hyman, 1990.

Silvela, L. "El derecho penal y los sistemas fatalistas y deterministas de la antropología criminal," *La España Moderna* (Febrero 1898):116–145.

Solá, Pere. "Acerca del modelo asociativo de culturización popular." In *Clases populares, cultura, educación. Siglos XIX–XX. Coloquio Hispano–Francés*. Madrid: Casa de Velázquez UNED, 1989: 393-402.

Stokes, John. *In the Nineties*. Chicago: University of Chicago Press, 1989.

"Sumario." www.Abogado.com/guía-legal/antelajusticia-penal/los procedimientos-penales.

"Sumario": Google.es. Sumariocaso Bretón.

Taboada, Luis. "De todo un poco," *Madrid Cómico* 15 Mayo 1894.

Taylor, John. "Pursued by the Plastic People." Review of *Vendetta. American Express and the Smearing of Edmond Safra* by Bryan Burroughs. *The New York Times*, 21 June 1992, Book Review section.

Taylor, Katherine Fischer. *In the Theater of Criminal Justice. The Palais de Justice in Second Empire Paris*. Princeton, N. J.: Princeton University Press, 1993.

Tello Amondareyn, Manuel. *Céuta. Llave principal del Estrecho*. Madrid: Imprenta de Fortanet, 1897.

Thaman, Stephen C. "Europe's New Jury Systems: the Cases of Spain and Russia," *Law and Contemporary Problems*, 62, No. 2 (Spring 1999): 233–259.

———. "The Nullification of the Russian Jury: Lessons for Jury–Inspired Reform in Eurasia and Beyond." *Cornell international law journal*. Vol. 40, No. 2 (2007): 355–428.

———. "Spain returns to trial by jury." Hastings international and comparative law review, Vol. 21, No. 2 (1998): 241–537.

Tobio Fernández, Jesús. *Las ideas sociales de Concepción Arenal*. Madrid: CSIS, 1954.

Tokmakov, Sergei. "Jury Trials in Modern Russia," *The ISCIP Analyst (Russian Federation) An Analytical Review*. Volume XIV, Number 7, January 28, 2010.

Tomkins, J.M.S. *The Popular Novel in England, 1770–1800*. London: Constable & Co. Ltd., 1932.

Toqueville, Alexis de. *Democracy in America*. Translated by Arthur Goldhammer. New York: The Library of America, 2004.

Torres Balbás, L. "La vivienda popular en España." In *Folklore y Costumbres de España*. Vol. 3. Barcelona: Casa Editorial Alberto Martín, 1946: 139-502.

Tracy, Ann B. *The Gothic Novel, 1790–1830; Plot Summaries and Index to Motifs*. Lexington: University Presses of Kentucky, 1981.

Trial Jury in England, France, Germany. 1700–1900. Ed. Antonio Padoa Schioppa. Berlin: Duncker & Humblot, 1987.

Trinidad Fernández, Pedro. *La defensa de la sociedad. Cárcel y delincuencia en España (siglos XVIII–XX)*. Madrid: Alianza, 1981.

Twain, Mark. *Roughing It*. Berkeley, Los Angeles, London: University of California Press, 1993.

Unamuno, Miguel de. *En torno al casticismo*. Buenos Aires: Espasa Calpe, 1952.

Valera, Juan. "El periodismo en la literatura (Contestación al discurso de recepción de don Isidro Fernández Flórez en la Real Academia Española el 13 de noviembre de 1898)." In *Obras Completas*. Vol. 3. Madrid: Aguilar, 1947: 1179-1186.

Valero de Tornos, Juan. *España de fin de siglo*. Madrid: "Sucesores de Rivadeneyra," 1894.

Valls, Josep–Francesc. *Prensa y burguesía en el XIX Español*. Barcelona: Antropos, 1988.

Villacorta Baños, Francisco. *El Ateneo científico, literario y artístico de Madrid (1885–1912)*. Madrid: CSIC, Centro de Estudios Históricos, 1985.

Villegas, F.F. "La Prensa Periódica," *La España Moderna* 49 (1893): 200–207.

Vincent, David. *Literacy and Popular Culture/England 1750-1914*. Cambridge: Cambridge University Press. 1989.

Viñao Frago, Antonio. "A la cultura por la lectura. Las bibliotecas populares, (1869–1885)." In *Clases populares, cultura, educación. Siglos XIX–XX. Coloquio Hispano–Francés*. Madrid: Casa de Velázquez UNED, 1989: 301-335.

———. "History of Literacy in Spain: Evolution, Traits, and Questions," *History of Education Quarterly* 30 (1990): 573–599.

Vipegón (Vicente Pérez González). *Guía de los jurados*. Madrid: Librería de Fernando Fé, 1901.

Walkowitz, Judith R. *City of Dreadful Delight. Narratives of Sexual Danger in Late–Victorian London*. Chicago: University of Chicago Press, 1992.

Welsh, Alexander. *Strong Representations: Narrative and Circumstantial Evidence in England*. Baltimore: Johns Hopkins University Press, 1992.

Williams, Raymond. *Keywords: A Vocabulary of Culture and Society*. London: Fontana, 1976.

Wolff, Larry. *Postcards from the End of the World. Child Abuse in Freud's Vienna*. New York: Atheneum, 1988.

Zavala, Iris. *Fin de siglo: modernismo, 98 y bohemio*. Madrid: Ed. Cuadernos para el diálogo, 1974.

Zehr, Howard. *Crime and the Development of Modern Society; Patterns of Criminality in Nineteenth–Century Germany and France*. Totowa, N.J.: Rowman & Littlefield, 1977.

Index